SOCIAL WORK AND SOCIETY

Political and Ideological Perspectives

Edited by
Sarah Pollock, Kate Parkinson and Ian Cummins

P

First published in Great Britain in 2020 by

Policy Press
University of Bristol
1-9 Old Park Hill
Bristol
BS2 8BB
UK
t: +44 (0)117 954 5940
pp-info@bristol.ac.uk
www.policypress.co.uk

North America office:
Policy Press
c/o The University of Chicago Press
1427 East 60th Street
Chicago, IL 60637, USA
t: +1 773 702 7700
f: +1 773-702-9756
sales@press.uchicago.edu
www.press.uchicago.edu

© Policy Press 2019

British Library Cataloguing in Publication Data
A catalogue record for this book is available from the British Library

Library of Congress Cataloging-in-Publication Data
A catalog record for this book has been requested

978-1-4473-4470-4 paperback
978-1-4473-4473-5 ePdf
978-1-4473-4471-1 ePub
978-1-4473-4472-8 Mobi

Cover design by Andrew Corbett
Front cover image: Stuart Case (stucase@hotmail.co.uk)
Printed and bound in Great Britain by CMP, Poole
Policy Press uses environmentally responsible print partners

Contents

Contents

List of case studies

Editor biographies

Sarah Pollock is a senior lecturer in Social Work at Manchester Metropolitan University, UK. She is a qualified and registered social worker and her practice experience includes working with adults in both community and hospital settings in North West England. Sarah has recently completed her PhD, which explores the under-representation of minority ethnic older women in health and social care services by analysing narratives about their interactions with state welfare systems. Her research interests include social justice, the impact of poverty and adult safeguarding. Sarah has published on the use of family group conferences in safeguarding adult procedures and the rise in food poverty in the UK. She teaches units on adult assessment and intervention, safeguarding and social work practice with adults.

Kate Parkinson is a lecturer in Social Work at the University of Salford, UK. Prior to commencing her role at the University of Salford she worked for several years in the field of children and families social work, including managing family group conference and children's centre services. Kate's research interests are family group conferences and other restorative approaches to practice. She has co-edited and written a book on the use of family group conferences in social care and is currently undertaking a PhD in this area. Kate is programme leader of the MA in Social Work at the University of Salford and teaches on the MA, BA and Step Up to Social Work programmes. She is a passionate advocate for the social work profession and enjoys teaching and inspiring future social work practitioners.

Ian Cummins is a senior lecturer in Social Work at the University of Salford, UK. Prior to taking up academic posts he worked as a probation officer and mental health social worker. His research interests reflect these practice experiences, with a focus on mental health issues in the criminal justice system and the history of community mental health services. Ian has published widely on the subject of mental health; his most recent publication, *Mental Health Reimagined*, was published with Policy Press in 2019.

Author biographies

Philip Brown currently holds a chair of Social Change in the School of Health and Society at the University of Salford, UK, and is Director of the Sustainable Housing and Urban Studies Unit. He has broad experience and interests, working in fields as diverse as social inclusion, migration, homelessness, fuel poverty, energy efficiency and regeneration. Prior to joining academia, Philip worked for the Asylum and Refugee Resettlement Projects in Leeds, UK, from 1999 to 2004.

Scott Massie qualified as a social worker in 2000 and has worked for local authority social services departments since this time, initially working with adults with learning disabilities before moving into the mental health field in 2004. Scott has been an Approved Mental Health Professional since 2005 and continues to practise in this role. He was social work practice manager in a multidisciplinary community mental health team prior to joining Liverpool Hope University, UK, as Senior Professional Tutor in Social Work in 2016. Scott is currently studying for an education doctorate, undertaking research focusing on student mental health. Scott has particular interests in mental health and adult social work, issues in human rights and civil liberties, anti-oppressive practice, and gender and sexuality.

Lucy Mort completed a PhD at Manchester Metropolitan University, UK, in the Department of Social Care and Social Work in 2017, with a thesis exploring migrants', refugees' and service providers' experiences of austerity. She is a qualified social worker and her practice experience is primarily in the voluntary sector with migrant and refugee organisations and in women's domestic violence refuges. Lucy is committed to women's rights and is a passionate trustee of Safety4Sisters, a grassroots organisation in Manchester that supports migrant women with no recourse to public funds who have experienced gender-based violence. She is working on publications from her thesis and has recently joined the Institute of Public Policy Research as a research fellow.

Rich Moth is a senior lecturer in Social Work in the School of Social Sciences, Liverpool Hope University, UK. Before moving into his current role in social work education, he worked for 15 years in the social care field in a variety of roles in both statutory and voluntary sectors, including as a mental health social worker. Rich has been involved in a number of mental health, welfare and anti-austerity campaigns and is a long-standing member of the national steering committee of the Social Work Action Network.

Donna Peach is a lecturer in Social Work at the University of Salford, UK. She has 30 years' practice experience in working with children and families where there have been concerns about the safety of children. Since 2014 her academic and consultancy roles have included research and developmental projects working with voluntary and statutory health, local government and police services to better understand the phenomenon of the sexual abuse and exploitation of children and our responses to it.

Ben Williams is a tutor in Politics at the University of Salford, UK. He completed his PhD at the University of Liverpool between 2009 and 2013 and has written for a range of books, magazines, blogs and journals covering British politics. His most recent publications are *The Evolution of Conservative Party Social Policy* (2015) and *John Major: An Unsuccessful Prime Minister?* (co-edited with Kevin Hickson, 2017).

Alex Withers is a teaching consultant at Manchester Metropolitan University, UK. He is a qualified and registered social worker whose main area of practice is adults with substance misuse issues. Alex teaches across a range of modules, including Global Inequalities and Substance Misuse.

Chris Yianni is a senior lecturer at Manchester Metropolitan University, UK, where he heads and delivers modules on Addictions, Sociology and Social Policy. His research interests include sports sociology and he has written and delivered work exploring motivations for drug use in sport.

Acknowledgements

The idea for this book came from our combined teaching experience in university social work departments in the UK, where we have witnessed at first hand how some students entering social work programmes can struggle to engage with politics and ideology. Although some are well prepared for the political context within which the social work and care professions operate, others haven't previously been exposed to these ideas and are challenged by the relationship between the two. It is hoped that this text will support students to connect politics and ideology to the everyday practices of social work and its allied professions.

Social work is inherently political; the very nature of supporting others to live fulfilled lives and to participate and achieve in society, and how 'participating' and 'achieving' are defined, are shaped by political ideology. We believe that recognising this is fundamental to the future of both the social work profession and those who interact with it, hence the idea for this book was developed to explore the interconnectedness of social work and politics.

As an editing team we would like to offer our sincere thanks to all the contributing authors, without whose hard work, commitment and knowledge this book would never have been realised. We would also like to thank Catherine Gray, Shannon Kneis and the team at Policy Press for being so supportive of this project from the beginning and for allowing us the freedom to make it our own.

From Sarah Pollock: Thank you to Arran for your patience and support, and for constantly ensuring that I don't take myself too seriously. This book is for Toby for inspiring me to be a better person every day, and for my parents, Pam and Andy.

From Kate Parkinson: Thank you to Stuart for all of your support and for fabulous photography! This book is for my mum and, as usual, for Ruby, Sam and Scarlett.

From Ian Cummins: I would like to thank my family and friends for all their support. I am also very grateful to my fellow editors, who have done all the hard work.

All of the editors would like to thank Stuart Case for the cover photograph.

List of abbreviations

AMHP	Approved Mental Health Professional
BAME, BME	Black (Asian) and Minority Ethnic
CA	Care Act [2014]
CJS	criminal justice system
CMHT	Community Mental Health Team
CSA	child sexual abuse
CSE	child sexual exploitation
CTO	community treatment order
DPs	Direct Payments
DWP	Department for Work and Pensions
EU	European Union
FTT	fixed term tenancy
HRA	Human Rights Act [1998]
HVN	Hearing Voices Network
IAPT	Improved Access to Psychological Therapies
IEA	Institute of Economic Affairs
IFSW	International Federation of Social Workers
LGBT	lesbian, gay, bisexual and transgender
MCA	Mental Capacity Act [2005]
MHA	Mental Health Act [1983 or 2007]
NHS	National Health Service
NHSCCA	National Health Service and Community Care Act [1990]
NI	Northern Ireland
NPM	New Public Management
Ofsted	Office for Standards in Education
PAP	Poverty Aware Paradigm
RISC	Rational Informed Stable Choice
SCT	Supervised Community Treatment
SPD	Social Democratic Party (Germany)
SWAN	Social Work Action Network
UN	United Nations
UNCRC	United Nations Convention on the Rights of the Child
UNHCR	United Nations High Commissioner for Refugees

Introduction

Sarah Pollock

Social work and ideology

The role of the contemporary social worker is broad and varied. Practitioners work with a whole spectrum of different people including adults, children and their families, people with mental or physical health issues and those with learning disabilities, to name just a few. Many people may have a complex combination of different issues impacting on their lives. Social workers also support people at times of crisis, for example following life-changing injuries, bereavement or when arriving in the UK to seek asylum. Alongside their varied roles, social workers and their colleagues in the social care field are employed by a range of different organisations. Most people may think about social workers as working for a local authority, carrying out statutory tasks (those required by law), but increasingly, practitioners have been positioned in charitable or voluntary organisations, working with an even wider section of society. This book explores the relationship between social work, in its broadest sense, and the ideological shifts within society. Social work practice does not occur in a vacuum, it is influenced by the context, both political and social, and, simultaneously, social work can influence this context too.

Heywood describes an ideology as 'a perspective, or "lens", through which the world is understood and explained' (Heywood, 2012, p 1). Although simple, this definition allows us to understand that our experience of the world can be seen not as an objective reality, with us as passive observers, but as filtered through a series of perspectives. This approach to understanding the world is referred to as social construction. Social constructionists believe that there is little external, objective 'reality', and that all aspects of our lives are constructed through our interactions. Burr (2003, pp 3–5) identifies four central features of social construction:

1. 'A critical stance towards taken for granted knowledge'; here Burr encourages us to think about the divisions in society, for example, the stereotypes and expectations we have of certain individuals or groups, and to reflect on where these have come from and why we believe them to be true.
2. 'Historical and cultural specificity'; if something is recognised as true only in certain places or at certain times, Burr suggests that this means it is socially constructed. For example, the age of consent to have sexual intercourse, or to marry, or even to drink alcohol or gamble money is different in many countries across the world and has been altered over time within the same country.

3. 'Knowledge is sustained by social processes'; processes such as the introduction of policy and the role of the media enable and facilitate the continuation of socially constructed beliefs. An example of this is the abundance of 'poverty porn' television shows and the disproportionate impact of government-introduced austerity measures on those in the lowest socioeconomic groups, which sustain a negative perception of those living in poverty.

4. 'Knowledge and social action go together'; once we have accepted socially constructed ideas as truths, this influences the way we act towards certain groups. For example, the historic assumption that able-bodied people are 'normal' has led to the exclusion of people with physical disabilities; buildings have been planned without appropriate access routes or toileting facilities. Only relatively recently have rights campaigns triggered legal duties to ensure equality.

Foucault defined socially constructed sets of ideas as 'discourses', developed about certain groups by those in positions of power as a system to enable maintenance of their positions and to ensure that those with less power did not recognise their oppression. For those working in social work and social care, whose roles include empowerment (supporting individuals to recognise their own strengths in order to take control of their lives), understanding how discourse and ideological perspectives influence our understanding is essential (Mills, 2003). The contributors to this volume explore the influence of such ideologies and how the developed discourses impact on the diverse spectrum of work that social work and care professionals undertake, each deconstructing their specific area of practice expertise.

Scope and remit of the book

The editors have selected topics that we believe are of interest to current social work students and those studying related disciplines and that reflect the current curriculum requirements in the UK, thus endeavouring for the book to be both useful and engaging. There are, of course, an endless number of different chapters that could have been included; for example, radical social work, green social work, social work responses to crises and natural disasters, social work with LGBTQ+ people, 'race' and ethnicity and so on. Unfortunately, there is not space within one volume to encompass every issue and therefore difficult but practical decisions have been made on what to include. We hope that the variety of subjects covered within this text will inspire readers to engage critically with all aspects of social welfare provision, and we encourage you to seek out such critical explorations of practice issues that you are passionate about.

Our contributors

The contributors to this volume include authors with a wealth of experience in diverse areas of practice; they are academics, social workers and volunteers. This means that each chapter is unique and can be read alone to support learning about a specific issue; alternatively, the whole volume can be used as an aid to accompany a modular curriculum. Using experts in their fields to contribute to a book like this does mean that there may be elements of several chapters that feel similar. Essentially, many fields of social work and social care practice have similar underpinning principles. While some repetition is necessary to support the stand-alone nature of the chapters, this also supports the consolidation of learning for those who choose to read the whole text.

Social work as political

Social work has always been political and the global definition from the International Federation of Social Workers (IFSW) recognises this in its understanding that social work is more than working with individuals on a case-work basis, acknowledging that the profession has a broader responsibility towards social justice and challenging oppression and discrimination.

> Social work is a practice-based profession and an academic discipline that promotes social change and development, social cohesion, and the empowerment and liberation of people. Principles of social justice, human rights, collective responsibility and respect for diversities are central to social work. Underpinned by theories of social work, social sciences, humanities and indigenous knowledge, social work engages people and structures to address life challenges and enhance wellbeing. The above definition may be amplified at national and/or regional levels. (IFSW, 2014)

In 2010 the Coalition government in the UK took the decision to implement austerity measures in response to the 2008 global financial crisis. This has had a significant and disproportionate effect on the wellbeing of those requiring support from the welfare state (Garthwaite, 2016; Jordan and Drakeford, 2012). Social workers have an ethical responsibility to oppose such discrimination, and Gray and Webb (2013) propose that critical social work possesses the attributes necessary to provide such opposition.

The near-decade of austerity measures since 2010 has seen services close, budgets for remaining provision cut and increasing workloads for professionals. In the face of this practice reality, it is increasingly important that new social workers, and those in allied professions, qualify with the recognition that they have an ethical responsibility to challenge discrimination at global and societal levels, not just in their daily practice. It is hoped that this collective work includes the necessary information to prepare those entering the social work and care fields with the knowledge required to contribute to this new era of socially just practice.

Devolution

Devolution refers to a process whereby central government can delegate some of its powers to its constituent nations' respective governing bodies. In the UK this means that England, Wales, Scotland and Northern Ireland have the power to manage certain aspects of their legal and ruling systems differently. In all four countries, social work is a registered profession, but each nation has its own regulatory body.

The impact of devolution on social work practice is not clear cut. Some areas of practice are maintained across country borders and others are not. England and Wales currently have the most similarities in their legal processes. For example, the Children Act 1989 applies to England and Wales, with Scotland implementing the Children (Scotland) Act 1995 and Northern Ireland following the Children (Northern Ireland) Order 1995. In comparison, the Human Rights Act 1998 maintains across the UK as a whole, with all four nations upholding its duties.

Throughout this volume, where the impact of devolution is relevant, individual authors will outline the different legal systems and will identify in which countries the laws they explore are enacted.

Organisation of the book

This book is divided into three parts. Across all three parts, each chapter ends with critical questions for the reader. These questions are set in order to challenge the reader to engage with the content of the chapter in a critical way, encouraging analysis of the information presented and reflection on their own experiences. The inclusion of further reading for each chapter points students in the direction of more specific information about the content; this includes textbooks, monographs and journal articles with a varied level of complexity, so that readers can choose how to continue their learning.

Part I: The first part of the book explores the historical and contemporary context of political ideologies. The chapters in this part explore the relationship between political parties and ideological perspectives, considering the influence that these perspectives have on the provision of social welfare generally. Topics covered include socialism, liberalism, neoliberalism, conservativism and feminism. Although feminism is not a specific political ideological perspective, it is described as 'cross cutting' (Heywood, 2012) in its reach. This means that each political ideology will be influenced by its perspective on gender and on feminism. The feminist perspective has such reach that it is necessary to explore it independently here. Each chapter in this part includes a section titled 'Comparative perspectives', where authors discuss key international issues related to their subject, and following the 'Conclusion', there is a boxed 'Key features' section which summarises the ideological position.

Part II: Once readers have a basic understanding of the belief systems included in each of the political ideologies, the second part of this book explores how these perspectives have influenced the arena of social work. Each chapter in this part considers a different area of practice as it has traditionally been divided, including work with adults, child protection, mental health and criminal justice. The chapters track the historical development of the profession and include challenges for contemporary practice, allowing readers to connect ideological perspectives to the policies and practice that guide their work. The chapters include practice examples to enable the establishment of clear links between political ideology and practice, alongside the critical questions and further reading.

Part III: The final part of the book considers the influence of political ideology on more diverse areas of practice, where social work may not always have occupied a position. The chapters explore emerging practice or the provision of support that has evolved away from the traditional divisions of local authority-provided services. Chapters in this part include insecurity, migration and asylum, abuse and exploitation, addiction and, finally, radicalisation.

References

Burr, V. (2003) *Social Constructionism*, London: Routledge.

Garthwaite, K. (2016) *Hunger Pains: Life inside Foodbank Britain*, Bristol: Policy Press.

Gray, M. and Webb, S. (2013) *The New Politics of Social Work*, Basingstoke: Palgrave Macmillan.

Heywood, A. (2012) *Political Ideologies: An Introduction*, London: Palgrave.

IFSW (International Federation of Social Workers) (2014) *Global Definition of Social Work*, https://www.ifsw.org/what-is-social-work/global-definition-of-social-work/ [accessed 11 October 2018].

Jordan, B. and Drakeford, M. (2012) *Social Work and Social Policy under Austerity*, Basingstoke: Palgrave Macmillan.

Mills, S. (2003) *Michel Foucault*, London: Routledge.

PART I

Political ideologies in context

Introduction to Part I

Sarah Pollock

The first part of this book explores five different ideological perspectives or 'lenses' and analyses how these influence practice through both government policy and other mechanisms (such as the media). Throughout this volume, the authors refer to political ideology, and this refers to the perspectives or sets of beliefs that have developed into a specific political perspective. This political ideological position then filters the way that people who subscribe to it perceive the world. In relation to social work and social care, this includes opinions on all aspects of society, for example the role of welfare, education, government, employment and the criminal justice system.

Confusion can arise when discussing political ideology in terms of the mainstream political parties both internationally and in the UK, particularly in England and Wales, as the names of the main parties, for example *Conservative* and *Liberal* Democrat can indicate an affinity with a specific political ideology. Often, these links are very loose, and/or historic in nature. For example, the current Conservative Party can be seen to have beliefs that align closely with a neoliberal, rather than traditional conservative, ideological perspective. This can lead to divisions between members of political parties. For this book, it is important to be aware that capital letters denote reference to political parties throughout, whereas lower case indicates the ideological perspective.

Social work and political ideology

Social work is an inherently political profession (Fook, 2016); practitioners are often employed by local authorities and other organisations that are funded by government and required to ensure the safety of those who are deemed to be vulnerable or 'at risk'. In fields such as child protection (discussed in Chapter 7) and mental health (discussed in Chapter 8), this tension is explicitly played out via the legal duty to act as a protector to those the practitioner works with, often having to implement interventions against the will of the individuals and families they support. Simultaneously, social workers are driven by, and committed to, a set of values that include but are not limited to social justice, empowerment, honesty, integrity and respect (BASW, 2014). This disconnect between the expectation to operate on behalf of the state and also to value and respect the rights of individuals is often referred to as 'care versus control'.

Different political ideologies have different expectations of how this balance between care and control is enacted by social work and related disciplines, with some ideological perspectives valuing individual rights and others privileging public safety or universality. Social work values are often, but not unequivocally, situated on the socialist ideological spectrum and therefore, throughout this volume, the authors are likely to present arguments that reflect these ideological positions. This text is not meant to be politically neutral; rather, it hopes to explore the influence that changing political ideologies have had over the different fields of practice, acknowledging the challenges and opportunities of each perspective.

This first part of the book explores the impact that specific ideological perspectives have had on the field of social welfare. They explore socialism, liberalism, conservativism, neoliberalism and feminism. Although feminism is a 'cross-cutting' ideology (Heywood, 2012), its influence is such that it is fundamental to the development of social work and care professions, and therefore is represented in this part.

References

BASW (British Association of Social Workers) (2014) *Code of Ethics for Social Work*, www.basw.co.uk/about-basw/code-ethics [accessed 11 October 2018].

Fook, J. (2016) *Social Work: A Critical Approach to Practice*, 3rd edn, London: Sage.

Heywood, A. (2012) *Political Ideologies: An Introduction*, London: Palgrave.

1

Socialism

Rich Moth

Introduction

We live in a world of characterised by immense inequalities. Figures from 2018 show that the 42 richest individuals globally own the same wealth as the poorest half of the world's population (3.7 billion people). What's more, these unequal trends are accelerating. In the decade since 2008 the wealth of billionaires has risen on average by 13% per year, six times faster than the wages of ordinary workers (Alejo Vázquez Pimentel et al, 2018). These global patterns are reflected in the UK, where the proportion of wealth owned by the 1,000 richest people is already more than that of the poorest 40% of households put together, and the gap is growing (Equality Trust, 2018). Alongside inequality, high levels of poverty are also visible, with over one fifth of the UK population (14 million people) officially classified as poor (JRF, 2017). Furthermore, 1.5 million people in Britain, including 365,000 children, were destitute at some point in 2017, meaning they were unable to access basics like heating, housing or food (Fitzpatrick et al, 2018).

That inequality, poverty and destitution on this scale should exist in the midst of an economy the size of Britain's, the fifth largest in the world (IMF, 2018), invites interrogation about the causes of these phenomena. From a socialist perspective, poverty and inequality are not inevitable features of the world, nor do they arise solely due to the greed of a certain layer of wealthy people within society or because the rich work harder. Rather, the cause is located in the functioning of our current socioeconomic system – capitalism. The core ideas of socialism represent a comprehensive critique of this market system, exposing the ways in which capitalism creates inequality and fundamentally undermines wellbeing. However, socialism involves not only critique but also a political practice that aims to transform capitalism into an alternative form of society based on the promotion of human welfare.

The chapter is organised in five sections through which these two dimensions of socialism, theory and practice, will be examined. The first section provides an overview of the various strands of socialist thought, focusing on two that have exerted significant influence: revolutionary and reformist socialism. The following section shows how the theorisation of oppression is integral to and incorporated within a socialist framework. The chapter then goes on to outline a socialist perspective on the welfare state. In the fourth section implications for social work are discussed, beginning with the theory of alienation and its implications for social work, moving on to a socialist analysis of the tensions between care and control in practice and then an outline of the influence of socialist ideas on the development of radical social work in the UK. The chapter concludes with a comparative perspective that notes the influence of socialist ideas on welfare policy and grassroots practices in particular national contexts.

Historical development of socialist thought

While the roots of socialist thinking can arguably be traced back as far as the ancient world, contemporary socialism emerged in the late 18th and 19th centuries as a set of political and economic ideas that excoriated industrial capitalism for the iniquitous social effects it generated (Dean, 2008). Its foremost exponent was Karl Marx (1818–83), who developed a 'materialist conception of history'. In this approach, the distribution of ownership of the natural, technological and economic resources required to meet humans' 'material' needs for food, shelter, clothing and so on fundamentally shapes how society is organised. Historically, struggles emerged between the dominant classes who owned and controlled such resources and those without access. Such conflicts are, for Marx, the engine of historical change.

The current stage of development, capitalism, is characterised by an increase in the productive forces through technological advances, meaning that for the first time in human history the needs of all could potentially be met. And yet, Marx argued, the working class (or proletariat) do not have access to the resources necessary for subsistence – they have become *alienated* from the means to meet their own needs. Consequently, they have to sell their capacity to work to the capitalist class (or bourgeoisie), the social layer who own the tools, machinery or technology (what Marx calls the means of production) required to manufacture goods and services. Moreover, workers are *exploited* by the capitalist class when they sell their capacity to work, as they do not receive the full monetary equivalent of the value of their labour – the bourgeoisie take a portion of the value created as profit. In this way two significant divisions are visible. The first is between the owners of capital and workers, who are in a mutually dependent but antagonistic relationship. Workers and capitalists have fundamentally opposed interests, with workers seeking to enhance their pay and conditions while capitalists try to reduce these in order to increase their levels of profit. The other division is between the various owners of capital. While capitalists have a wider shared interest both in maintaining this economic structure and in the exploitation of workers, they are part of a competitive system of firms (or units of capital) engaged in an existential struggle for market share and profit maximisation.

Following from this Marx demonstrates how these unjust social divisions represent politically significant points of weakness for capitalism. The instability created by the competition between capitals renders it unstable and prone to cycles of boom and slump. At the same time, opposing class interests lead to class conflict. These economic and political contradictions and inequalities represent fault lines out of which emerge the possibility for the working class to be both gravedigger of capitalism and agent of egalitarian social transformation. As the most numerous[1] and at the same time exploited social class, workers have both the rationale and the potential to engage in the political struggles needed to usher in a different way of organising work and society. Moreover, the experience of workers in production processes both engenders a shared interest in collective solidarity and resistance and foreshadows the kinds of alternative and more equal social organisation that would emerge from such struggles, in particular common ownership and democratic control of the means of production. As the logic of competition under capitalism becomes redundant, Marx argued, new social arrangements based on cooperation could be foregrounded. These recognise humanity's mutual interdependence and enact collective relations of reciprocity and solidarity across society. Central to this would be a comprehensive redistribution of resources to realise the fundamental goal of social equality (Callinicos, 2010; Heywood, 2012).

However, while they share these broad principles, historical differences have emerged between socialists concerning the most effective means for realising social change. These are reflected in the divergent strands of thought that have developed since the 19th century, from libertarian and autonomist versions of socialism[2] to Stalinism.[3] While there is not space to summarise the full range of such perspectives here, the chapter will focus on two of the most prominent traditions, reformist (or gradualist) and revolutionary socialism.

Reformist socialism

It was the revolutionary Marxist Rosa Luxemburg who first theorised the emergence of the division between revolutionary and reformist socialism at the end of the 19th century. She was a member of the German Social Democratic Party (SPD), at that time the largest socialist party in Europe. She argued that, while formally committed to revolution, the SPD's strategy was in practice one of gradualist transition to socialism. The party's stance had been influenced by the work of leading SPD member Eduard Bernstein, who developed a theory of evolutionary socialism following contact with the Fabian wing of the Labour Party in England (Luxemburg, 1989). By the early 20th century the reformist strategy had achieved widespread dominance across Europe both in the SPD and in the influential social democratic parties of Scandinavia as well as many other socialist organisations, including the UK Labour Party (Dean, 2008).

According to this gradualist or reformist approach[4] the revolutionary overthrow of capitalism was no longer considered necessary. This period had seen working-class interests gain powerful institutional representation through the trade union movement and political parties, with social and industrial struggles leading to an expansion of working-class suffrage and rights. As a consequence, a parliamentary route to control of the state was now deemed feasible and the transition to socialism was regarded as possible through the election of a progressive government tasked with implementing an incremental programme of social reforms.

While such reformist policy agendas often maintained a rhetorical commitment to common ownership of the means of production, this was often as much informed by analysis of the waste and inefficiency of unfettered competition under capitalism as by values of social justice (Lund, 2006). Moreover, by the middle of the 20th century the goals of reformist parties had become more modest, oriented to humanising rather than overthrowing capitalism (Page, 2008). In practice, this involved the creation and extension of a mixed economy, retaining the market in some sectors but utilising state intervention or public ownership to ameliorate its worst effects in others. An exemplar of this approach is the post-war 1945 Labour government in Britain that used nationalisation of some industrial sectors and welfare services as the primary policy lever to realise social justice. The creation of the National Health Service (NHS) represents perhaps the crowning achievement of that government and the wider reformist approach. However, as the political scope for public ownership reduced, Labour administrations from the 1960s retreated from nationalisation, instead utilising progressive taxation to redistribute wealth and income and increase social spending as its major form of intervention (Lund, 2006).

However, while theorists within the reformist tradition from the SPD's Bernstein in the 19th century to New Labour's Gordon Brown in the late 20th century have claimed that it is possible to manage or even overcome capitalism's boom/bust cycle, this aim has proved elusive in practice (Lavalette, 2006). Moreover, by the early 21st century reformist administrations such as New Labour had effectively accommodated to capitalism, offering relatively minimal intervention in markets (Dean, 2008).

Revolutionary socialism

There is, however, another strand, revolutionary socialism, which has sought to maintain the core of and also extend and develop Marx's theory. This 'classical' Marxist tradition (Anderson, 1976) has three principal dimensions. The first is the need to understand capitalism as a differentiated but interconnected whole; the second is that the struggle for social reforms is an integral part of wider revolutionary change; and the third is the centrality of working-class self-emancipation.

The starting point for a revolutionary socialist approach is to view capitalism, in its totality, as a dynamic and internally differentiated *system*. This means that the various aspects of the contemporary world such as the economy, the state, structures of welfare provision, poverty and employment should be treated not as separate and discrete entities but as interacting parts of a wider whole (Ferguson et al, 2002). As a consequence of these interrelationships, changes in one part of the system have an impact on others. For instance, market-oriented economic reforms since the 1980s have tended both to negatively impact on security of employment and push down rates of pay in many sectors and simultaneously to lead towards increased retrenchment and conditionality within welfare systems. For those in the revolutionary tradition, such interconnectedness underpins the relative resilience of the institutions of capitalism in spite of gradualist and targeted political and economic policy changes that have been introduced by reformist governments.

In view of this, revolutionary theorists have argued that simply to ameliorate the most harmful impacts of capitalism is insufficient and, following Marx, that deeper social transformation is necessary to end exploitation and the social divisions that arise from it. However, while the aim is fundamental change to realise a democratically controlled and planned social system oriented to meeting human need, this does not mean that revolution is counterposed to social reforms. Rather, it is argued that campaigning for immediate improvements in people's lives by prioritising human need over the market forms an integral part of the wider struggle against capitalism. The contrast with reformism is that, for revolutionary socialists, such agitation does not represent the limit of such resistance (Ferguson et al, 2002).

The third dimension of the revolutionary orientation is the necessity for the working class[5] to be active agents of social transformation, in contrast to the tendency under reformism for enlightened leaders to use the state to implement top-down reforms on their behalf (Callinicos, 2010). At the heart of this is the proposition that to realise a socialist society requires the *self-emancipation* of the working class. This is because it is only from the lived experience of wresting control of powerful institutions and the state from the capitalist class and the assertion of radical democratic control to serve the needs and interests of the vast majority that genuine 'socialism from below' can emerge (Draper, 2001).

While the revolutionary orientation has always been a minority strand within the socialist movement, instances of revolutionary change led by the working class have erupted at regular intervals and continue to do so, from the Paris Commune of 1871, through the Russian Revolution of 1917,[6] to the Arab Spring of 2010/11. While revolutionary and reformist movements have continued to challenge the iniquities of capitalism throughout this period, there has recently been an upturn in the profile and wider resonance of socialist ideas, and it is to this that we turn next.

Socialism in the current political context

The widening chasm of wealth and income inequality that has opened up during the current neoliberal stage of capitalism was noted in the introduction. A comprehensive body of evidence has demonstrated how worsening inequalities are linked to a variety of phenomena, including increased levels of mental distress in society, shortening life expectancy, rising infant mortality and a host of other challenges (Wilkinson and Pickett, 2010, 2018). Following the global financial crisis of 2008 wealth and income inequality continued to grow in countries such as Britain, and at an even faster rate than before. However, this state of affairs has drawn intensifying criticism and challenge since the financial crisis, with levels of protest against economic injustice increasing rapidly (Dorling, 2014). Perhaps the most visible of these was the Occupy movement of 2011, which coined the slogan 'We are the 99%' to highlight escalating inequalities between the richest 1% and the rest of society. Occupy encampments sprang up in New York, London and countless other cities around the world, including many parts of the global South, providing an organising centre for diverse coalitions of activists from a number of political traditions including anarchists, socialists and social justice campaigners. Socialists played an important role in building the movement by strengthening links between Occupy activists and wider labour and trade union networks (Roesch, 2012). Though Occupy itself proved relatively short lived, arguably its legacy is visible in the greater prominence for redistributive politics in the UK and the US (Yagci, 2016, 2017). In particular, the relative success of two politicians from the Left reformist tradition – Jeremy Corbyn, whose election as leader of the UK Labour Party in 2015 confounded mainstream expectations, and Bernie Sanders, narrowly defeated as 2016 US presidential nominee for the Democratic Party – has contributed to rehabilitating the ideas of socialism and moving debates around inequality, social insecurity and class into the political mainstream (Trudell, 2016).

Class, identity and oppression

While class analysis is central to socialist critiques of capitalism and strategies for its transformation, this does not mean that other forms of oppression are not integral to this framework. This section will contest the view of socialism as class reductionist by illustrating its analyses of various forms of oppression.

Critics of socialism frequently refer to the changing class structure, in particular the relative decline of the manual working class employed in factories in countries such as the UK, to argue that socialism is no longer relevant in the 21st century. However, as the discussion above suggests, forms of class inequality have not disappeared but, rather, class composition is subject to change as capitalism develops. For instance, the workforce in Britain has undergone a transformation, so it is now more diverse in terms of gender and ethnicity. This changing working class is now primarily based in the white-collar and service sectors, as well as including professional groups experiencing 'proletarianisation' such as social workers (Harris, 2003). Moreover, the latter face the same kind of work intensification and exploitation as their colleagues in factories or call centres (Ferguson, 2011). In view of this, the core socialist insight that there is a fundamental divide between those who need to sell their labour power in order to survive (whether in manual, clerical or service sectors) and those who own and control significant amounts of capital remains salient (Dean, 2008).

However, some suggest that, in spite of the enduring relevance of class analysis, the growth of a politics of identity and the emergence of new social movements has displaced a focus on class politics. Such newer movements, including those of feminism, anti-racism, lesbian, gay, bisexual and transgender (LGBT) and disabled people, are regarded as addressing issues of recognition rather than the distribution of material resources. However, socialist thinkers have developed resources for integrating recognition with redistributive concerns (Fraser, 2000). In contrast to the common conception of socialist thought as 'class reductionist', the analysis of oppressions has long formed a significant theme within it. In particular, socialists have identified how an economic system based on exploitation creates divisions within society and the working class. In general terms, under capitalism, workers are compelled to compete with each other for jobs, housing and other resources. These processes reinforce social cleavages that may then manifest as types of oppression. However, the nature of the capitalist system as a differentiated whole means that there are particular and distinct material processes shaping the operation of each of the various forms of oppression. For the purpose of illustrating these causal dynamics two examples will be briefly outlined: women's oppression and racism.

A socialist analysis indicates how women's oppression is underpinned by a dual requirement for women to participate in production and social reproduction. This means that there is pressure on women to engage in paid employment and also to take on a significant role in domestic reproductive labour via tasks within the family such as providing sustenance for its members, caring for relatives and replenishing the supply of future workers for capitalism through child rearing. It is out of the interaction between these contradictory dynamics under capitalism that women's oppression primarily emerges, though how this contradiction is experienced also depends on class position, with middle-class women more able than those from the working class to purchase domestic support in the market (Bhattacharya, 2017; German, 2018). An extensive body of theory also underpins socialist analyses of racism. This approach identifies the central role of New World slavery in the birth of capitalism, with the ideology of racism emerging as a justificatory framework for this dehumanising endeavour (Blackburn, 1997). However, this ideology has endured into the present because of capitalism's demand for migrant labour in a wider context of competition for employment between workers. Here racism functions to undermine consciousness of the shared interests between diverse groups of workers in challenging their common experience of exploitation. Instead it offers to workers from the dominant group the compensatory 'psychological wage' of an imagined shared community with their exploiters, while in actuality maintaining racial divisions that undermine the potential collective power of a united multi-racial working class (Callinicos, 1993).

Socialist perspectives on oppression identify the bases of these various forms of inequality within class society itself and illustrate the role of capitalism in exacerbating social divisions. In doing so, their aim is to create the conditions for collective resistance and alliance building across difference to challenge these manifestations and the system that generates them (Fraser, 2000; Dean, 2008).

The welfare state: a socialist analysis

We will now turn to discussion of the socialist contribution to both the creation and theorisations of the welfare state.

The reformist socialist perspective was significant in the emergence of the welfare state in the post-war period, though the work of two liberal theorists, Keynes and Beveridge, played an important role within this. The programme of the 1945 Labour government was informed both by economist John Maynard Keynes' theoretical rationale for state intervention in the economy to boost demand at a time of recession and by William Beveridge's proposals for a more universal and broad-based system of social insurance and public provision of health, housing and care services to ameliorate poverty and social inequalities. However, while noting the progressive dimensions of these developments, revolutionary critics drew attention to the top-down nature of this reform programme and its failure to reflect on and incorporate the perspectives of service users (Beresford, 2016). Moreover, its gender bias (in the 'male breadwinner' model) and discriminatory policies towards migrant workers, underpinned by racist assumptions, were among the many grievances that led to resistance and challenges by welfare movements 'from below', particularly from the 1960s onwards (Barker and Lavalette, 2015).

A radical socialist analytical framework for understanding the welfare state sheds light on these contradictions. Ferguson et al (2002) draw on Saville (1983) to highlight the importance of a range of economic, historical, political and social factors in shaping welfare settlements under capitalism. They argue that three strands are of particular significance. The first strand is *the economic and social requirements of capitalist society*, for instance the need to ensure a healthy and educated workforce, and care for non-workers such as children and older people. The second is *the political calculations of the ruling class*, which refers to policies promoted by particular sectional interests within the capitalist class, for example current divisions relating to the European Union (EU) and its social legislation agendas. The third is *pressure from the mass of the population*, which is articulated either through reformist electoral or labour movement mechanisms or collective action from below, an example being the mobilisations that underpinned the success of the movement to repeal abortion restrictions in Ireland (Kennedy and Orr, 2018). These strands overlap in practice, but this framework highlights the deeply political nature of welfare and the central role of class struggle and economic and social contradictions in shaping welfare developments.

Alienation, control and resistance in social work

Having set out socialist perspectives on welfare in general, the next three sections of the chapter will consider social work in particular. The first part utilises the theory of alienation to explore the experiences of social workers, the second examines the tensions between care and control in social work practice, while the third section provides an analysis of activism and resistance in social work.

Alienation in the social work labour process

We briefly noted earlier Marx's use of the term *alienation* to describe how, under capitalism, workers are separated from the means to meet their needs through lack of access to the resources and tools necessary to produce for themselves. For this reason they are forced to sell their capacity to work in order to survive. As a result workers have neither control over the process of producing, which is determined for them by the work setting (e.g. the production line of the factory or call centre), nor the product made (e.g. the smartphone or car) which is owned by the employer. Marx contrasts these two forms of alienation, 'in process' and 'from product', with pre-capitalist societies where people had more control both over the 'craft' of how they made what they needed and how they used or sold these products. Marx went on to identify two further dimensions of alienation. The first is alienation from other people, which can manifest in two ways. As noted above workers are exploited and this alienates them from their employers who have the capacity to assert control over them in the workplace. The other is from their fellow workers with whom they are forced to compete to survive in the jobs market. This, as noted above, has the potential to exacerbate social divisions leading to racism, sexism and other forms of oppression. Finally, we are alienated from our human nature, which is to express and develop our creative, physical and intellectual capacities through labour. However, under capitalism, this creative human potential is degraded by the labour process, which leads us to experience work as a burden to be shunned whenever possible (Lavalette and Ferguson, 2018).

In welfare services that have been reshaped by neoliberalism, the socialist analysis of alienation helps us understand the impact on social workers of factors such as increasing and intensified workloads, decreasing levels of discretion and control over the conduct and outcomes of assessments, and the constraints placed on relationship-based practice with service users by the need to meet targets and performance indicators (Lavalette and Ferguson, 2018). Moreover, while such chronic negative working conditions characterised by high demands and low control are extremely stressful for social workers, risk-averse practice environments that impede opportunities for practice based on social work values further compound these challenges leading to 'ethical stress' (Fenton, 2015; Ravalier, 2018).

Care and control in social work practice

Social work is a contested field and the profession has long embodied a number of contradictions and ambiguities. In this section we will examine one in particular, the tension between care and control. Historically, mainstream social work has tended to understand the challenges faced by service users as arising at the individual or familial level with a consonant requirement for intervention via a casework model. As a result social work input has tended to balance the support offered ('care') with close monitoring and supervision to ensure the individual adapts and conforms to dominant social and behavioural expectations within capitalist society ('control'). However, for socialists, this mainstream model fails to recognise that the difficulties faced by service users are underpinned by the unequal structures of capitalist society that generate poverty, alienation and discrimination. Moreover, the controlling elements of social work practice arise predominantly from the contradictory functions of and forces shaping the welfare state that were noted in the previous section, with pressures from above (the requirements of capitalism and the state) coming into conflict with demands from below (social needs articulated through the struggles of workers and oppressed groups). Consequently, for socialists, such tensions and contradictions can only be resolved and transcended through fundamental reform and transformation of capitalism itself. In the next section we will examine the role of socialist and radical social workers in conceiving a form of practice which embodies these socially transformative aims.

Socialism and resistance: radical social work in the UK

While socialist theory can assist our understanding of the impact of neoliberal reform and the tensions between care and control in social work, socialist ideas have also played an important role in informing activism and resistance to oppressive processes in practice and inspired struggles for a more egalitarian and liberatory social work. In this final section the influence of socialism on what has been called social work's 'radical kernel' will be outlined. This focuses on two particularly important historical moments: the political ferment in the early 20th century and the radicalism of the 1970s. It then goes on to consider contemporary pull and push factors towards a renewed radical social work in the 21st century.

The roots of state social work in Britain have been linked with the formation of the Charity Organisation Society (COS) in 1869. While the pathologisation of the 'undeserving poor' by COS prompted more humane welfare responses such as the Settlement movement in the late 19th century, there is also a hidden history of more agitational orientations within social work (defined in its broad sense). This 'radical kernel' was deeply influenced by the emerging socialist movement during the late 19th and early 20th century in the context of intensified trade union struggles and unrest (Ferguson and Lavalette, 2007). Forms of community-based welfare work and political campaigning were commonly combined in the early 20th century by figures such as socialist and suffragette activist Sylvia Pankhurst (Lavalette, 2017) and future Labour Prime Minister Clement Attlee. The latter's stance is illustrated by the title he gave to one chapter of his 1920 book: 'The social worker as agitator' (Ferguson and Woodward, 2009). The radical tradition reasserted itself with, arguably, greater influence on social work during the 1970s. The reasons for its emergence at this time include on the one hand the return of economic crisis in the early 1970s and growing class struggle, and on the other the legacy of the 1960s movements for racial, gender and sexual equality. Though this radical orientation was, even then, a minority strand within social work the influence of both revolutionary and reformist socialism was prominent within the movement.[7] The revolutionary approach was visible among those linked to the radical rank and file social work activist magazine *Case Con* (Weinstein, 2011; Feldon et al, 2018), while the reformist strand oriented around defence of the welfare state through trade union and Labour Party activism (Langan and Lee, 1989).

Though this movement declined under the wider assault of the 'New Right' and neoliberalism during the 1980s, contemporary social work is subject to both push and pull factors towards a renewal of radical approaches. Neoliberal retrenchment and reform has undermined community, collective and relationship-based approaches to social work practice, creating discontent that has constituted a push factor for professional networks and individual practitioners towards a more critical and political stance (Lavalette, 2011). Activist groups such as the Social Work Action Network (SWAN) have emerged to challenge this agenda. Socialist ideas have been influential within SWAN and have informed its orientation towards cross-sectional campaigning alliances both between social work organisations (around issues such as austerity cuts to services and neoliberal reforms to social work education) and joint practitioner-service user campaigns (Moth and Lavalette, 2019). Meanwhile, the pull of social movements is also exerting an influence. 'New welfare movements', for instance disability and service user movements (themselves in part influenced by socialist theory), have reshaped social work practice by promoting new and valued understandings of lived experience and demands for less paternal and more participatory forms of provision (Oliver, 1990). The more recent re-emergence of a radical strand within the disabled people's and survivor movements in the face of the onslaught of austerity (Slorach, 2016) has both inspired social work activism and seen the formation of new practitioner-service user alliances (Moth and Lavalette, 2019). Moreover, in the same way that the social movements of the 1960s played an influential role in the renewal of radical social work in the 1970s, the influence of wider contemporary struggles against inequality such as the anti-capitalist and more recent Occupy movements has shaped radical social work in the present. As a result of the confluence of these factors a contemporary model of radical social work practice informed by socialist ideas has recently re-emerged. This has a triple emphasis on: (i) liberatory forms of individual relationship-based casework based on solidarity, challenging oppression and 'conscientisation';[8] (ii) engagement in community work and development; and (iii) involvement in collective political action, alongside and in coalition with service users, trade unions and social movements to demand social reform but with the overarching aim of wider societal transformation (Ferguson et al, 2018).

Comparative perspectives

In this final section of the chapter we will briefly consider welfare policy applications of socialism from a comparative perspective.

The Nordic welfare model in Scandinavia is usually regarded as an exemplar of the implementation of reformist socialist ideals. In Sweden this approach historically involved universal and comprehensive state welfare services which were decommodified (that is, enabling their existence outside of market relations), with a minimal role for private provision (Esping-Andersen, 1990). Consonant with these wider values, in the social work field social problems tended to be viewed through the lens of structural rather than individual causes, with a preventive approach to practice being adopted (Blomberg et al, 2015). However, since Sweden's economic crisis of the 1990s there have been significant market reforms of welfare and social services (Blomqvist, 2004). As a consequence, the Swedish welfare system is regarded as having abandoned core reformist socialist tenets under the pressures to adapt to neoliberal orthodoxy (Page, 2008). Here we can detect parallels with the transition noted above from the post-war Keynesian welfare state to market-oriented reforms in the UK.

Since Russia in 1917, there have been a number of 'revolutionary rehearsals', with uprisings in countries as diverse as France, Poland and Egypt during the 20th and 21st centuries (Barker, 2008; Naguib, 2011). However, eventual experiences of defeat or counter-revolution in those contexts mean that it is not possible to identify specific examples of national-level welfare policy implementation from a revolutionary socialist perspective. Nonetheless, resistance to capitalism continually re-emerges. Until recently, one dimension of socialist and anti-capitalist activism that was under-recognised was a tendency towards what has been called 'popular social work' or the organisation by activists within social movements of small-scale welfare initiatives. One example is the mutual aid hurricane relief efforts in the US in 2012, known as Occupy Sandy,[9] in response to the hurricane of the same name. This initiative filled the gaps left as a result of failures in response by formal disaster management agencies due to cuts and neoliberal reform (Lavalette and Ioakimidis, 2011; Jones and Lavalette, 2013). Another example is the 'solidarity clinics' that were set up in Greece in response to the 2009 economic crisis and the imposition of harsh austerity measures and swingeing public sector cuts to health and social care. These grassroots clinics were run by social workers and health professionals, frequently in an unpaid or low-paid capacity, and provided vital services and support to poor and marginalised communities in the absence of government healthcare provision (Teloni and Adam, 2018).

Conclusion

The chapter began by presenting a critique of capitalism as a fundamentally unequal way of organising society and then outlined the potential for new forms of social organisation informed by socialist ideals to transcend damaging aspects of capitalism, such as alienation and oppression. However, there have been different orientations to the achievement of such aims within the socialist movement, and the chapter sketched the main features of two major traditions, reformist and revolutionary, highlighting similarities and divergences between these perspectives. The chapter then presented a socialist analysis of the welfare state and implications for social work. It was argued that socialist theory can assist our understanding of a variety of pressures and contradictions experienced by social workers in their day-to-day practice. The chapter also identified the role of socialist ideas in informing resistance and radical social work alternatives to current forms of practice, before ending with examples of socialist welfare policies and practices in particular national contexts. In a world of stark and increasing inequalities, renewing an orientation to radical practice informed by socialist ideas is an urgent necessity. Moreover, doing so offers the potential not only to improve the everyday experiences of service users and social workers but also to contribute to the progressive transformation of welfare futures and the wider society.

Key features of socialism

- For socialists, the way in which the capitalist economic system is organised creates inequality and undermines human wellbeing.

- Inequality under capitalism is a product of the exploitative relationship between classes; that is, the capitalist class, which owns the means to produce services and goods, is able to extract profit from the labour of working-class people. Moreover, competition under capitalism tends to exacerbate social cleavages, thereby reinforcing divisions that may manifest as types of oppression.

- Exploitative pressures under capitalism create a tendency towards collective struggle by working-class people in order to achieve greater economic equality. This offers a basis upon which capitalism can be transformed into an alternative form of society based on more fundamental equality and the promotion of human welfare.

- Socialist theory enables an understanding of the contradictions of the welfare state and welfare professions such as social work under capitalism. It does so by identifying how welfare systems and professions operate at the interface between the economic and social requirements of capitalism, the political calculations of dominant classes and pressure from the mass of the population.

- Socialist ideas have been an important resource for the radical social work movement, informing activism and resistance to oppressive processes in practice (through theories of coalition building) and through the development of models for egalitarian and liberatory social work (for example, conscientisation).

Critical questions

1 Why does wealth and income inequality matter, and what are its effects?

2 What should be the role of the welfare state and professions like social work in addressing inequality and poverty?

3 Should we regard welfare professionals such as social workers as part of the working class?

4 How can ideas like exploitation and alienation help us to understand the experiences of social workers and service users?

Further reading

• Callinicos, A. (2010) *The Revolutionary Ideas of Karl Marx*, London: Bookmarks.
This text combines a sophisticated account of Marx's key ideas with an accessible style and thereby provides an excellent basic introduction to this thinker's work.

• Ferguson, I. (2008) *Reclaiming Social Work: Challenging Neoliberalism and Promoting Social Justice*, London: Sage.
A socialist analysis of the deleterious impact of neoliberalism on contemporary social work which also offers proposals for a more socially just approach to practice.

• Ferguson, I. and Woodward, R. (2009) *Radical Social Work in Practice: Making a Difference*, Bristol: Policy Press.
Building on *Reclaiming Social Work*, this text has a greater focus on how socialist ideas and values might be introduced into social work practice, offering numerous practical proposals and case studies.

• Lavalette, M. (ed) (2011) *Radical Social Work Today*, Bristol: Policy Press.
This edited collection begins with a look back at the legacy of radical social work in the 1970s and brings the discussion up to date via contemporary analyses of class, gender, race and LGBT liberation (among other topics) by leading figures within the current radical social work movement.

References

Alejo Vázquez Pimentel, D., Macias Aymar, I. and Lawson, M. (2018) *Reward Work Not Wealth*, Oxfam Briefing Paper, Oxford: Oxfam International.

Anderson, P. (1976) *Considerations on Western Marxism*, London: New Left Books.

Barker, C. (2008) *Revolutionary Rehearsals*, Chicago: Haymarket Books.

Barker, C. and Lavalette, M. (2015) 'Welfare changes and social movements', in D. della Porta and M. Diani (eds), *The Oxford Handbook of Social Movements*, Oxford: Oxford University Press, pp 711–28.

Beresford, P. (2016) *All Our Welfare: Towards Participatory Social Policy*, Bristol: Policy Press.

Bhattacharya, T. (2017) *Social Reproduction Theory: Remapping Class, Recentering Oppression*, London: Pluto.

Blackburn, R. (1997) *The Making of New World Slavery: From the Baroque to the Modern, 1492–1800*, London: Verso.

Blomberg, H., Kallio, J., Kroll, C. and Saarinen, A. (2015) 'Job stress among social workers: determinants and attitude effects in the Nordic countries', *British Journal of Social Work*, vol 45, no 7, pp 2089–105.

Blomqvist, P. (2004) 'The choice revolution: privatization of Swedish welfare services in the 1990s', *Social Policy and Administration*, vol 38, no 2, pp 139–55.

Callinicos, A. (1993) *Race and Class*, London: Bookmarks.

Callinicos, A. (2010) *The Revolutionary Ideas of Karl Marx*, London: Bookmarks.

Dean, H. (2008) 'The socialist perspective', in P. Alcock, M. May, and K. Rowlingson (eds), *The Student's Companion to Social Policy* (3rd edn), Oxford: Blackwell, pp 84–90.

Dorling, D. (2014) *Inequality and the 1%*, London: Verso.

Draper, H. (2001 [1966]) *Socialism from Below*, Alameda, CA: Center for Socialist History.

Equality Trust (2018) 'UK rich increase their wealth by £274 billion over five years', Equality Trust (13 May), www.equalitytrust.org.uk/wealth-tracker-18.

Esping-Andersen, G. (1990) *The Three Worlds of Welfare Capitalism*, Cambridge: Polity Press.

Feldon, P., de Chenu, L. and Weinstein, J. (2018) 'The Case Con generation, 1970–75', *Critical and Radical Social Work*, vol 6, no 1, pp 107–14.

Fenton, J. (2015) 'An analysis of "ethical stress" in criminal justice social work in Scotland: the place of values', *British Journal of Social Work*, vol 45, no 5, pp 1415–32.

Ferguson, I. (2011) 'Why class (still) matters', in M. Lavalette (ed), *Radical Social Work Today: Social Work at the Crossroads*, Bristol: Policy Press, pp 115–34.

Ferguson, I. and Lavalette, M. (2007) 'The social worker as agitator: the radical kernel of British social work', in M. Lavalette and I. Ferguson (eds), *International Social Work and the Radical Tradition*, London: Venture Press, pp 11–32.

Ferguson, I. and Woodward, R. (2009) *Radical Social Work in Practice: Making a Difference*, Bristol: Policy Press.

Ferguson, I., Ioakimidis, V. and Lavalette, M. (2018) *Global Social Work in a Political Context: Radical Perspectives*, Bristol: Policy Press.

Ferguson, I., Lavalette, M. and Mooney, G. (2002) *Rethinking Welfare: A Critical Perspective*, London: Sage.

Fitzpatrick, S., Bramley, G., Sosenko, F. et al (2018) *Destitution in the UK 2018*, York: Joseph Rowntree Foundation.

Fraser, N. (2000) 'Rethinking recognition: overcoming displacement and reification in cultural politics', *New Left Review*, vol 3 (May/June): 107–20.

German, L. (2018) 'Marxism, class and women's oppression', *Critical and Radical Social Work*, vol 6, no 2, pp 141–57.

Harris, J. (2003) *The Social Work Business*, London: Routledge.

Heywood, A. (2012) *Political Ideologies: An Introduction* (5th edn), Houndmills: Palgrave Macmillan.

IMF (International Monetary Fund) (2018) *World Economic Outlook: Cyclical Upswing, Structural Change*, Washington, DC: IMF.

Jones, C. and Lavalette, M. (2013) 'The two souls of social work: exploring the roots of "popular social work"', *Critical and Radical Social Work*, vol 1, no 2, pp 147–65.

JRF (Joseph Rowntree Foundation) (2017) *UK Poverty 2017: A Comprehensive Analysis of Poverty Trends and Figures*, York: Joseph Rowntree Foundation.

Kennedy, S. and Orr, J. (2018) 'Repeal: a victory for women everywhere', *Socialist Review*, no 436, http://socialistreview.org.uk/436/repeal-victory-women-everywhere.

Langan, M. and Lee, P. (1989) 'Whatever happened to radical social work?', in M. Langan and P. Lee (eds), *Radical Social Work Today*, London: Unwin Hyman.

Lavalette, M. (2006) 'Marxism and welfarism', in M. Lavalette and A. Pratt (eds), *Social Policy: Theories, Concepts and Issues* (3rd edn), London: Sage, pp 46–65.

Lavalette, M. (ed) (2011) *Radical Social Work Today: Social Work at the Crossroads*, Bristol: Policy Press.

Lavalette, M. (2017) 'Sylvia Pankhurst: suffragette, socialist, anti-imperialist... and social worker?', *Critical and Radical Social Work*, vol 5, no 3, pp 369–82.

Lavalette, M. and Ioakimidis, V. (2011) *Social Work in Extremis*, Bristol: Policy Press.

Lavalette, M. and Ferguson, I. (2018) 'Marx: alienation, commodity fetishism and the world of contemporary social work', *Critical and Radical Social Work*, vol 6, no 2, pp 197–213.

Lund, B. (2006) Distributive justice and social policy', in M. Lavalette and A. Pratt (eds), *Social Policy: Theories, Concepts and Issues* (3rd edn), London: Sage, pp 107–23.

Luxemburg, R. (1989 [1898]) *Reform or Revolution*, London: Bookmarks.

Molyneux, J. (2003) *What is the Real Marxist Tradition?*, Chicago: Haymarket.

Molyneux, J. (2012) *Anarchism: A Marxist Criticism*, London: Bookmarks.

Moth, R. and Lavalette, M. (2019) 'Social policy and welfare movements "from below": the Social Work Action Network (SWAN) in the UK', in U. Klammer, S. Leiber and S. Leitner (eds), *Social Work and the Making of Social Policy*, Bristol: Policy Press.

Naguib, S. (2011) *The Egyptian Revolution: A Political Analysis and Eyewitness Account*, London: Bookmarks.

Oliver, M. (1990) *The Politics of Disablement*, Basingstoke: Macmillan and St Martins Press.

Page, R. (2008) 'Social democracy', in P. Alcock, M. May and K. Rowlingson (eds), *The Student's Companion to Social Policy* (3rd edn), Oxford: Blackwell, pp 77–83.

Ravalier, J.M. (2018) 'Psycho-social working conditions and stress in UK social workers', *British Journal of Social Work*, online first, https://doi.org/10.1093/bjsw/bcy023

Roesch, J. (2012) 'The life and times of Occupy Wall Street', *International Socialism*, vol 2, no 135, http://isj.org.uk/the-life-and-times-of-occupy-wall-street/#135roesch_2

Saville, J. (1983) 'The origins of the welfare state', in M. Loney, D. Boswell and J. Clarke (eds), *Social Policy and Social Welfare*, Milton Keynes: Open University Press.

Slorach, R. (2016) *A Very Capitalist Condition: A History and Politics of Disability*, London: Bookmarks.

Teloni, D. and Adam, S. (2018) 'Solidarity clinics and social work in the era of crisis in Greece', *International Social Work*, vol 61, no 6, pp 794–808.

Trudell, M. (2016) 'Sanders, Trump and the US working class', *International Socialism*, vol 2, no 150, http://isj.org.uk/sanders-trump-and-the-us-working-class/

Vickers, T. (2015) 'Marxist approaches to social work', in *International Encyclopedia of the Social and Behavioral Sciences*, London: Elsevier, pp 663–9.

Weinstein, J. (2011) 'Case Con and radical social work in the 1970s: the impatient revolutionaries', in M. Lavalette (ed), *Radical Social Work Today: Social Work at the Crossroads*, Bristol: Policy Press, pp 11–26.

Wilkinson, R. and Pickett, K. (2010) *The Spirit Level: Why Equality is Better for Everyone*, London: Penguin.

Wilkinson, R. and Pickett, K. (2018) *The Inner Level: How More Equal Societies Reduce Stress and Improve Wellbeing*, London: Allen Lane.

Yagci, A. (2016) 'How the Occupy movement may have facilitated political change', LSE Blogs: British Politics and Policy (27 April), http://blogs.lse.ac.uk/politicsandpolicy/impact-of-occupy-movement/

Yagci, A. (2017) 'The Great Recession, inequality and Occupy protests around the world', *Government and Opposition*, vol 52, no 4, pp 640–70.

2

Liberalism

Ian Cummins

Introduction

As with other political philosophies, liberalism should be seen as an umbrella term that covers a range of views, approaches and positions. Neoliberalism, for example, is clearly a form or branch of liberalism. Liberalism has evolved over a period of time. Modern liberalism, for example, would be more suspicious than its forebears of claims of the supremacy of the market. A further complication in examining liberalism is that the term can be applied in both the economic and social spheres. The two spheres are not necessarily compatible. David Cameron was both an economic and a social liberal. The austerity policies that his government followed were partly based on a classic liberal belief in a smaller state. At the same time, he was a social liberal, the introduction of gay marriage being an example of liberal social legislation. Gay marriage does not square with traditional Tory values and policies. This chapter will explore the roots and subsequent development of liberalism, which has been one of the key political ideologies of the last 300 years.

The roots of liberalism can be traced back to the late 16th or early 17th century. It became a clear philosophical school during the Age of Enlightenment. Its emergence as an intellectual tradition is associated with the writings of key figures such as Locke, Rousseau and Kant. Early liberals were opposed to the dominant political forces of feudal capitalism of the period: the established church, absolutist monarchs and the landed gentry. They were committed to an alternative group of ideas, which included freedom of religion, constitutional rule, individual property and free trade.

The influence of liberalism was extended as a result of the American and the French Revolutions. Thereafter the liberal tradition was instrumental in what Huntington (1991) refers to as the 'three waves of democratization'. The first wave saw the election of liberal governments and the introduction of social welfare provision in Europe and the Americas in the 19th and early 20th centuries. The second wave occurred after the Second World War. This period saw the establishment of democratic regimes to replace authoritarian regimes in, for example, Germany and Italy. The post-war period also saw a period of decolonisation where, for example, former colonies of the British Empire became independent nations. Huntingdon's third wave is the period after 1974, which saw the overthrow of military dictatorships in Spain and Portugal as well as those in Latin America. It should be noted that this is not a linear process – the coup in Chile in 1973, which saw the overthrow of the socialist Allende government and the establishment of a military dictatorship, ran counter to this. The third wave also includes the post-1989 collapse of the communist regimes of the Eastern Bloc. There is a danger that these huge changes are presented as inevitable.

Liberty

Cranston (1967) saw liberty as the prime political value of liberalism: 'By definition a liberal is a man who believes in liberty'. This is in contrast to other political values or aims such as equality. This is a modern statement of the values that can be found in the works of Locke and Mill. Locke outlined a state of perfect freedom in which human beings would act in ways that they saw fit. They would not need the permission or authority of others to do so. Mill argued that if society wanted to restrict the freedom of individuals, then the burden of proof lay with the authorities, however they might be constituted, to demonstrate why the restriction was justified.

Social contract theories of the development of political institutions developed from these basic premises. These are concerned with attempts to provide a justification for the existence of the modern state. There are fundamental issues to be addressed here such as: on what basis does the authority of the state exist? When might it be right to overthrow a state? Hobbes, Locke and Rousseau argued that the social contract is the means by which modern civic society, including government, develops. Before the existence of the social contract there was a condition of stateless anarchy, sometimes referred to as a 'state of nature'. The state of nature is not an ideal state; it allows for chaos and there is no rule of law. As society and social relations become more complex, each person agrees to surrender some (or all) of his or her original rights and freedoms to a central authority – a form of government. They do so on the condition that all other members of the society do the same and that any breaches of laws will be punished by the central authority. The motivation for surrendering some individual rights in this way is that each member will enjoy certain benefits – particularly domestic peace – that a central authority can provide.

Negative and positive liberty

Berlin (2016) identified two categories or forms of liberty – *negative* and *positive*. Liberty is conceived as the absence of coercion. One is then able to make choices. Negative liberty can be viewed as an opportunity concept; it is freedom from constraint – from legal or social sanctions – to act on one's free will. Mill argued that the only justification for the restriction of liberty would be if the action resulted in harm to another individual. Adults are free to make poor choices – and they have to live with the consequences. In its most extreme libertarian form, this argument would support the removal of legal sanctions against drug use or other behaviour which does not harm others. It also underpins the thinking of those groups who criticise the so-called 'nanny state', which they regard as patronising and hectoring in the advice that it offers across a range of life-style and health issues. Taylor (1979) argued that negative liberty sees freedom as a matter of what options are available to us, whether we choose to exercise them or not.

Positive liberty is viewed as the capacity to act of one's free will. A person is free only if they are self-directed and autonomous. The classical notion of liberty has its roots in Roman society – a *liber* was a free person, the opposite was a *servus*, a slave. From this, the republican notion of liberty develops which sees the role of government as being to ensure that no body or agency, including its own, has arbitrary power over any citizen. These various conceptions of the fundamental notion of liberty are an area where the liberal political theory splinters.

Private property and human rights

The trends of economic and social liberalism are two key elements of this political tradition. Two key concerns of liberalism are the question of private property and the issues of human rights. Classic economic liberals of the 19th century saw private property and liberty as inextricably linked. Private property represents the foundation of an economic system that will provide individual liberty. Alternative economic systems that challenge these fundamentals of private property will inevitably lead to restrictions on liberty. In its purest form, a market system based on private property and where individuals are free to make contracts and sell their labour is regarded the purest form of liberty. In addition, the dispersion of power that private property represents is seen as providing protection to the liberty of subjects.

Liberalism seeks to guarantee a series of fundamental rights. This includes freedom of assembly and worship, freedom from arbitrary arrest and a range of civic and political rights. These fundamentals are incorporated in the UK Human Rights Act 1998 (HRA). The various articles of the HRA seek to establish a balance between the individual and the state. Liberalism is concerned with the overdue exercise of state power; the HRA places limits on state power but also provides the individual with potential legal remedies. Other features of a liberal democracy are a strong civil society – a free press, rights for workers and limits on monopolies and other powerful forces.

The role of the state

One of the key concerns of liberalism is the role of the state. Liberalism is naturally wary of the potential power that state agencies can have. Liberals would be opposed to state surveillance and monitoring of citizens unless this was justified on security grounds. A liberal approach seeks to ensure that the scope for state intervention in the lives of citizens is restricted. It recognises that the state should be able to intervene, but there must be a clear process and individuals must have legal representation to be able to challenge. In the same way, liberals are concerned with the way that commercial monopolies are able to exploit their position to the detriment of consumers.

Despite being temperamentally wary of the state or any expansion of its power, liberals have had a key role in the creation of the modern welfare state. The liberal concern with inequality and the individual underpins the concern with the excesses of the free market. Beveridge, a liberal, was one of the key architects of the modern welfare state that was established in the UK following the Second World War. The role of government planning in the war, the recognition of the huge suffering that the nation had endured and a realisation of the need to avoid an economic slump similar to that of the 1930s all contributed to a shift in attitudes. In all of Beveridge's proposals there was an attempt to strike a balance between the individual and the state. There was also a concern that benefits should not be seen as too generous.

The post-war liberal democracy

Commitment to full employment and Keynesian management of the economy meant that Beveridge viewed unemployment benefits as a temporary support while workers were looking for new jobs. Liberalism is thus concerned with providing a state safety net for the most vulnerable individuals in society. However, it is also concerned at the same time with maintaining a balance between the individual, the family and state agency. This is combined with a commitment to localism and voluntary organisations. State agencies can be seen as the intervention of last resort.

Social mobility

Social mobility and creating an environment where individuals are provided with the support to make the most of their skills is a recurring theme in modern liberal democratic societies. As noted above, the original thinkers whose ideas underpin liberalism were opposed to the established forces of absolutist monarchy, the church and related institutions. There are echoes of this in modern politics. Conservative Prime Minister Theresa May stated that she would seek to 'fight against the burning injustices' of poverty, race, class and health, and give people back 'control' of their lives (Swinford, 2016). She also stated that her administration would not 'entrench the advantages of the privileged few'.

Littler (2013) highlights the fact that the rhetoric of meritocracy is universal, and notes that the overwhelming majority of those who use the term assume that it has a positive, progressive and anti-elitist meaning. All politicians seem to be committed to the creation of a meritocratic society. Young (2004) coined the term as a warning, however. It was a satirical comment on a society in which elites were publicly committed to a more egalitarian society but actually followed policies that entrenched their position. Littler (2016) argues that they thus use the idea of meritocracy to actively extend their own interests and power.

The development of the post-war international political framework is based on fundamental liberal principles. This period saw the establishment of a series of international and national institutions which are grounded in fundamental liberal principles. These include liberty and the equal rights of all, political freedom, economic opportunity, social emancipation and equality before the law (Gray, 2004). The end of the Cold War and the tearing down of the Berlin Wall were represented as a great triumph of liberal political values. Fukuyama (1989) famously declared that this political triumph marked the 'end of history'. By this he meant that debates about the relative merits of political systems had been settled and liberal democracy had won. Even if one accepts the basic premises in his arguments, political events in the 2010s – the re-emergence of neo-fascist, anti-immigrant and anti-welfare parties across Europe, Brexit, the election of President Trump in the US and President Putin's ongoing control of the Russian political system – have raised serious doubts about the security of liberalism's triumph. Fukuyama (2018) himself has somewhat backtracked on the claims of his 1989 article, the influence of which was, in part, that it provided an intellectual support to the argument of neoliberals that free markets were inevitably linked to political freedoms.

Human rights

After the military defeat of Nazism in 1945 there were international efforts to ensure that the cataclysms of the Holocaust and Second World War were never repeated. Nazism fundamentally denies that all people should be afforded the same rights. The legal framework that was established sought to ensure that citizens would be afforded a basic minimum set of rights that would balance the potential arbitrary exercise of state power (Habermas, 2010). The UN Declaration of Human Rights states in Article 1 that 'All human beings are born free and equal in dignity and rights' (United Nations General Assembly, 1948). A common set of moral values that recognise the equal dignity of all humans underpins this discourse, which is not restricted to the legal sphere; it is also a key component in broader ethical discussions that overlap with the law – bio-ethics and end-of-life care being two clear examples. This modern notion is a recasting of Kant's (1996) categorical imperative that every person should be viewed as an 'end in themselves'. In *A Theory of Justice*, Rawls argued that a concept of justice must be based on the rights of individuals, as 'each person possesses an inviolability founded on justice that even the welfare of society as a whole cannot override' (Rawls, 1971, p 3). Communitarians argue that this conception of liberal individualism overlooks the fact that individuals live in communities.

The post-Second World War discourse of human rights has moved these notions into much wider areas than the liberal rights of freedom of association and religion, protections against arbitrary arrest and so on (Habermas, 2010). These so-called democratic rights of participation or classical civil rights were a buffer to prevent the intrusion of the state into the private sphere. Despite their egalitarian and universal rhetoric, they were not enjoyed by all – women and minorities being two obvious examples of excluded groups. Rawls (1971) argued that the classical civil rights of political liberalism acquire equal value for citizens only when they are accompanied by social and cultural rights. Fraser (1995; 2010) sees dignity as the fundamental basis for the equal respect of citizens, arguing that, for it to have value, the claim for equal treatment on the basis of identity must have within it a simultaneous claim for redistribution. Dworkin (1995) notes that dignity is both a powerful concept and a vague one. This is part of its attraction, but also, perhaps, part of its weakness. Dworkin also adds that any notion of human rights has to accept that dignity will be at its core.

There are two broad objections to the notion of human dignity and the discourse of human rights as outlined above. The first echoes Dworkin (1995) in claiming that dignity is a vague concept (Pinker, 2008). The second challenge to the notion of the human rights discourse sees it as a liberal fraud, in that these rights are available only to those living under regimes that accept Western concepts of human rights and social values (Badiou, 2015).

Popper on intolerance

In the age of social media and 24-hour rolling news, one of the recurring debates revolves around the nature of what should be seen as acceptable in public political debate. One of the most often repeated claims by commentators on the political Right is that political correctness means that there are certain issues, particularly in the fields of race and gender politics, that are not debated. The argument here is that individuals will be characterised as racist, sexist or homophobic for even raising concerns. There is a certain irony in that this point is made, most forcefully, by white heterosexual men such as Rod Liddle, Jeremy Clarkson and Richard Littlejohn who are handsomely rewarded by national newspapers for writing weekly columns that claim they are denied freedom of expression. These debates have been given increased significance since the 2016 Brexit referendum.

As noted above, liberalism identifies freedom of expression as a key component of civil society which acts as a balance against powerful government or commercial interests. This leads to the difficult question as to what limits, if any, can be placed on freedom of expression. The First Amendment to the US Constitution states: 'Congress shall make no law respecting an establishment of religion, or prohibiting the free exercise thereof; or abridging the freedom of speech, or of the press; or the right of the people peaceably to assemble, and to petition the Government for a redress of grievances.' This is perhaps the purest statement of the right to freedom of expression. Colin Kaepernick, a quarter-back for the San Francisco 49ers in the National Football League, has been one of the most prominent campaigners against police brutality in the US. Supporters of his 'taking the knee' protest argue that he is exercising his First Amendment rights to free speech. In contrast, since 1945 symbols of Nazism such as the Hitler salute and the swastika have been banned in Germany. Libertarians would argue that the banning of any symbols or the expression of views, however objectionable they might be, is an unacceptable restriction on the liberty of individuals.

The paradox of tolerance

Popper's *The Open Society and Its Enemies* (2012), written in the shadow of Stalinism and Nazism and published in 1945, is often viewed as a classic liberal argument against totalitarianism. Popper was committed to the maintenance of liberal political values, which he saw as a bulwark against the emergence of authoritarian forms of government. He also confronted the paradox that liberal democracy creates. How should liberal political systems respond to political parties and movements that are fundamentally opposed to liberalism's key tenets and would deny citizenship to religious, racial and sexual minorities? He termed this the 'paradox of tolerance'.

Unlimited tolerance must lead to the disappearance of tolerance. If we extend unlimited tolerance even to those who are intolerant, if we are not prepared to defend a tolerant society against the onslaught of the intolerant, then the tolerant will be destroyed, and tolerance with them. In this formulation, this does not imply, for instance, that we should always suppress the utterance of intolerant philosophies – so long as we can counter them by rational argument and keep them in check by public opinion, suppression would certainly be unwise. But we should claim the right to suppress them if necessary, even by force; for it may easily turn out that the proponents of intolerant philosophies are not prepared to meet us on the level of rational argument, but begin by denouncing all argument. They may forbid their followers to listen to rational argument because it is deceptive, and teach them to answer arguments by the use of fists or pistols. We should therefore claim, in the name of tolerance, the right not to tolerate the intolerant. We should claim that any movement preaching intolerance places itself outside the law, and we should consider incitement to intolerance and persecution as criminal, in the same way as we should consider incitement to murder, or to kidnapping, or to the revival of the slave trade, as criminal.

Popper's argument has been criticised for being in favour of unjustified restrictions on freedom of speech and assembly. The notion of tolerance can be viewed as problematic in itself. Civic and political freedoms should be based on tolerance – which implies a form of polite or passive acceptance – but inherent rights that should be afforded to all citizens.

Critical approaches

There are two main critical approaches to liberal ideas and their focus on equality and individual rights. From the political Right, liberalism's focus on equality is naive and hopelessly optimistic, as it fails to acknowledge that society is unequal. This is because skills and knowledge are not spread equally across society. Any attempt to alter this will lead to a restriction on the freedom of some individuals. From the political Left, liberalism's commitment to civil rights ignores economic conditions. The argument here is that more economically powerful individuals have greater access to resources – for example, legal advice – which enable them to exercise these rights. In capitalist societies there is a disconnect between the theoretical commitment to civil rights and the reality.

The fall of the Berlin Wall and the collapse of the Soviet bloc were meant to usher in a new, triumphant phase of liberalism and liberal democracy. This has proved to be wildly optimistic. If we regard a liberal democracy as one in which all adult citizens, men and women, have the vote and can exercise it freely, then it is a relatively new and limited phenomenon. For example, the US, a self-proclaimed haven of democracy, effectively denied African-American citizens the vote until the civil rights movement led to the signing of the Voting Rights Act in 1965. This Act was designed to ensure that African-Americans living in the South could register and vote. The post 9/11 world has seen the key institutions and beliefs of liberalism come under increasing pressure. Terrorist attacks have seen calls for the suspension of the rights of suspects, the use of torture and the increased surveillance of individuals and communities (see Chapter 14, 'Radicalisation', for further discussion). The argument against these increased powers for the state is that their use undermines the very liberal freedoms upon which democracies are based.

Elitism and populism

The critics of liberalism – from both the Left and the Right – often elide liberalism with elitism. 'Liberal elite' has become a pejorative term used to described affluent, middle-class, metropolitan, well-educated, left-of-centre voters who claim to represent the interests of the working class. The term liberal elite is used by populist politicians in an attempt to distance themselves from what they claim to be a self-serving and corrupt group.

Populism is based on the notion that there are two groups in society: 'the people' and 'the corrupt elite'. The populist leader claims that he or she represents the 'will of the people'. This places the leader in opposition to an enemy. The 'enemy' is a grouping of those who represent the current system, which is seen to operate against the interests of 'the people'; Trump and his claim that he would 'drain the swamp' is an excellent example of this. This leads to situations in which politicians who are clearly members of the elite seek to deny that they are part of it. British prime ministers Major, Blair, Brown and Cameron, in an attempt to establish their 'regular guy' credentials, all tried fairly unconvincingly to claim that they had a lifelong interest in football. The Brexit referendum is another example. The leaders of the Brexit campaign presented themselves as leading a campaign to 'Get our country back'. The most prominent Brexit campaigners – Nigel Farage (then leader of UKIP) and the Conservative cabinet members Boris Johnson and Michael Gove – were all privately educated. Farage was a stockbroker and Johnson and Gove had both been journalists for leading Tory-supporting newspapers. Populist parties exist across the political spectrum. Part of the populist claim is to go over the heads of academics, experts and other members of the liberal elite directly to the wider public. Alongside this, populists claim that media stories are distorted, and so on – Trump's so-called 'fake news'. This adds to claims that the liberal elite is also a conspiracy against 'the people'.

Snyder argues that the rise of Trump and populist parties poses an existential threat to the basic premises of liberalism: 'The mistake is to assume that rulers who came to power through institutions cannot change or destroy those very institutions – even when that is exactly what they have announced that they will do' (Snyder, 2017, p 10).

His book is a restatement of liberal values and a call for re-engagement in public and civic processes. His 20 lessons include the following:

- Do not obey in advance.
- Defend institutions.
- Believe in truth.
- Investigate.
- Listen for dangerous words.

Snyder suggests that the disconnection between electorates and politicians has created an opportunity that populists exploit.

Comparative perspectives

Esping-Andersen (1990) included *liberal* as one of his three models of welfare. A liberal welfare regime was outlined as one that had limited state intervention. This means that there are limited welfare benefits. In a liberal model of welfare, large areas of provision such as education and health are based in the private sector. There is limited public provision. The use of public services is stigmatised. In this model, individuals have to take out private insurance as protection against ill-health or unemployment. Esping-Andersen included the US and Australia as examples of liberal welfare states. This liberal model is contrasted with the social democratic models of the Scandinavian systems, where higher personal and corporate taxes are used to fund public services. In the social democratic model, the investment in and the quality of public services mean that these are not regarded as inferior. The other important area for social work is liberalism's concern with the dangers of state interference in private and family life. There is a concern that social workers have too much power, particularly in children and families work. A liberal perspective would see state intervention as unjustified unless there is a clear risk of physical danger or abuse and neglect. This dilemma over when and how it is appropriate for the state to intervene is at the heart of many contemporary social work practice concerns.

Conclusion

Liberalism is one of the most influential political ideologies of the modern period. It has splintered into a number of different variants. There are some tensions between economic and social liberals. However, in all its forms there are some consistent features. These are the focus on political and civil rights, the market and a commitment to a legal framework that balances the rights of the community and individuals. The institutions of civil society – a free press, trade unions, voluntary and community associations, churches and so on – act as a brake on a possible over-mighty state. Modern liberal political thought is concerned with the increase in inequality that has resulted from the rolling back of social protection and welfare systems.

Key features of liberalism

- There is a focus on the importance of individual freedom and choice.
- Liberalism is wary of the concentration of power, for example in the hands of corporations or state agencies.
- Society needs to be tolerant of and accept the expression of a range of views.
- There is a focus on individual civic rights such as freedom of expression and freedom of association, and freedom to follow religious faith.
- Individual citizens' rights have to be protected.

Critical questions

1 What are the rights that all individuals should have in liberal democratic societies?

2 How do we balance the rights of individuals against the rights of the wider community?

3 How should liberal democratic societies respond to individuals and groups who express extremist views?

4 What should the limits be on the powers of social workers and other professionals to intervene in family life?

Further reading

- Freeden, M. (2015) *Liberalism: A Very Short Introduction*, Oxford: Oxford University Press.
  An excellent introduction to this area.

- Habermas, J. (2010) 'The concept of human dignity and the realistic utopia of human rights', *Metaphilosophy*, vol 41, no 4, pp 468–80.
  This article examines the notion of human rights as a cornerstone of modern liberal thinking.

- Snyder, T. (2017) *On Tyranny: Twenty Lessons from the Twentieth Century*, New York: Tim Duggan Books.
  This short book is a defence of some of the key institutions in liberal societies – for example, the free press. It shows the way that they are challenged by authoritarian politics.

References

Badiou, A. (2015) *Theoretical Writings* (Bloomsbury Revelations), London: Bloomsbury.

Berlin, I. (2016) 'Two concepts of liberty', in D. Miller (ed) *Liberty Reader*, Abingdon: Routledge, pp 33–57.

Cranston, M.W. (1967) *Freedom*, Longmans.

Dworkin, R. (1995) *Life's Dominion*, London: HarperCollins.

Esping-Andersen, G. (1990) *The Three Worlds of Welfare Capitalism*, Cambridge: Polity Press.

Fraser, N. (1995) 'From redistribution to recognition? Dilemmas of justice in a "post-socialist" age', *New Left Review*, vol 212, pp 68–146.

Fraser, N. (2010) 'Who counts? Dilemmas of justice in a postWestphalian world', *Antipode*, vol 41, pp 281–97.

Fukuyama, F. (1989) 'The end of history?', *The National Interest*, vol 16, pp 3–18, www.newyorker.com/magazine/2018/09/03/francis-fukuyama-postpones-the-end-of-history

Fukuyama, F. (2018) *Identity: The Demand for Dignity and the Politics of Resentment*, New York: Farrar, Straus and Giroux.

Gray, J. (2004) *Heresies*, London: Granta Books.

Habermas, J. (2010) 'The concept of human dignity and the realistic utopia of human rights', *Metaphilosophy*, vol 41, no 4, pp 468–80.

Huntington, S.P. (1991) 'Democracy's third wave', *Journal of Democracy*, vol 2, no 2, pp 12–34.

Kant, I. (1996) *The Metaphysics of Morals* (edited and translated by Mary J. Gregor), Cambridge: Cambridge University Press.

Littler, J. (2013) 'Meritocracy as plutocracy: the marketing of "equality" under neoliberalism', *New Formations*, nos 80–81, pp 52–72, doi: 10.3898/NewF.80/81.03.2013.

Littler, J. (2016) 'Mayritocracy: neoliberalism with new borders', Lawrence and Wishart blog (22 November), www.lwbooks.co.uk/blog/mayritocracy-neoliberalism-with-new-borders

Pinker, S. (2008) 'The stupidity of dignity', *The New Republic*, vol 238, no 9, pp 28–31.

Popper, K. (2012) *The Open Society and Its Enemies*, Abingdon: Routledge.

Rawls, J. (1971) *A Theory of Justice*, Cambridge, MA: Harvard University Press.

Snyder, T. (2017) *On Tyranny: Twenty Lessons From The Twentieth Century*, New York: Tim Duggan Books.

Swinford, S. (2016) 'Theresa May pledges to fight injustice and make Britain "a country that works for everyone" in her first speech as Prime Minister', *The Telegraph*, www.telegraph.co.uk/news/2016/07/13/theresa-mays-pledges-to-fight-injustice-and-make-britain-a-count/

Taylor, C. (1979) 'What's wrong with negative liberty', in A. Ryan (ed), *The Idea of Freedom*, Oxford: Oxford University Press, pp 211–29.

United Nations General Assembly (1948) *Universal Declaration of Human Rights*, UN General Assembly, 302(2).

Young, M. (2004) *The Rise of the Meritocracy* (2nd revised edn), London: Transaction Books.

3

Conservatism

Ben Williams

Introduction

When focusing on the subject matter of ideology, conservatism is generally viewed as being one of the older and most established types, along with liberalism and socialism. However, on a very fundamental level there has been some significant academic debate and disagreement as to whether conservatism constitutes an ideology or not. This is because, unlike other core ideologies, many of its leading figures and advocates over the years have rejected the influence of 'abstract' theories and idealistic principles and have instead sought to base their political arguments on experiences and aspects of everyday life (often referred to as 'empiricism'). Within this more empirical context, therefore, for most of its history since the early 19th century, the UK Conservative Party has largely rejected explicit ideological principles and instead been influenced by often vague concepts such as tradition, instinct and pragmatism as its main guiding objectives when developing and making key policies.

Prominent historical examples of this non–ideological form of conservatism have been the 20th-century prime ministers Stanley Baldwin and Harold Macmillan, and the philosopher Michael Oakeshott. Indeed, Oakeshott's post-war writings have referred to the existence of a 'natural order' within society, favouring slow and cautious change, and argue that conservatism essentially represents an 'instinctive' mood or a natural 'feeling'. This perspective echoes the views of another key theorist, Edmund Burke (in the late 18th century), who specifically highlighted the dangers of sudden revolution and radical change when observing the events in revolutionary France in 1789. Yet, such conservative theoretical influences have often appeared to represent nothing more than a pragmatic desire to 'conserve' and to react against other ideologies by resisting major social change, as opposed to offering a distinct identity or a coherent alternative position. This in itself has sometimes created problems when it has come to conservatism having a clear identity of its own or devising coherent policy making.

Nevertheless, it was during the final decades of the 20th century from the mid-1970s that conservatism became a more explicitly ideological entity. This reflected broader global economic and social trends, as well as the breakdown and failure of the post-war political consensus in the UK in particular. This subsequently saw the emergence of the agenda of the New Right and its associated ideas and more specific policy framework. Influenced by key international academics and theorists such as F.A. Hayek and Milton Friedman and bolstered by UK-based think-thanks such as the Institute of Economic Affairs (IEA), this more ideological type of conservatism generated two high-profile figures in the form of UK Prime Minister Margaret Thatcher and US President Ronald Reagan. As leaders of mainstream Western political parties associated with conservatism, both leaders consequently sought to develop and articulate practical policies that stemmed from theoretical ideas and coherent ideological principles and offered a clearer, longer-term political vision. This reflected an evident historical transformation of the ideology of conservatism, and how this change has impacted on the evolution of social policy making within a British and, indeed, global context will now be explored in fuller detail.

Origins and history of conservatism

Within a British context, conservatism is fundamentally associated with the Conservative Party. As a political organisation it has a long and illustrious history, with some historians claiming that its alternative name of the 'Tories' was first noted and observed during the 17th century, under the reigns both of Charles I before the English Civil War of the 1640s, and then of his son Charles II during the Restoration period in the latter half of the century. The party's modern form dates from approximately 1834 within the more organised system of democracy and party politics following the Great Reform Act of 1832. On this specifically British historical basis, therefore, the ideas and policies of conservatism can be dated back over several centuries and linked to one of the country's oldest political parties.

As already highlighted by its very name, the Conservative Party has traditionally resisted change and generally sought to 'conserve' what it feels are traditions and values worth conserving. On this premise, conservatism broadly acknowledges that significant social or political change should ideally be cautiously managed and gradually implemented, as advocated in the 18th century by Edmund Burke. The Burkean perspective declares that society should be viewed as a living organism that requires careful nurturing and cultivation, and on this basis it is therefore incorrect to say that conservatism opposes 'change' completely. Rather, it is often suspicious of it, and consequently aspires to manage and control it in a cautious manner so as to maintain society's 'natural order' or hierarchy. Another historic influence on how conservatism evolved was Thomas Hobbes, whose key text, *Leviathan* (1651), was written during the English Civil War and highlighted the importance of maintaining social order and stability, along with the need for authoritative rule by government. The Hobbesian view also provided a negative interpretation of human nature, and primarily saw humans as brutish and aggressive. Both Burke and Hobbes infused conservatism with the realities of experiences drawn from everyday life, and it was these influential contexts that provided general conservative values and guidelines from its earliest stages of development as a political creed.

With democracy steadily extending and society rapidly changing as the 19th century progressed, British conservatism faced a number of significant social policy challenges throughout the period commonly known as the Victorian era (1837–1901). Victorian Britain was a harshly divided society, with extreme wealth existing alongside absolute poverty. Presiding over the largest and most powerful empire in the world had generated financial and economic success for some British citizens primarily engaged in business and trade, but others fell by the wayside into severe social hardship and destitution. At this point in history, there was no welfare safety net to catch and support such unfortunate individuals and families. This fairly desperate and unequal environment was often depicted in the contemporary Victorian tales of Charles Dickens such as *Oliver Twist*, where reliance on charity and the bleak workhouse beckoned for those who had nowhere else to go. Begging, pickpocketing, urban violence and various other forms of crime were rife in the densely populated cities, which on one level could be linked to the negative conservative analysis of human nature. However, such poverty and human brutality could, alternatively, be interpreted as a symptom of deep-rooted poverty to which most of the mainstream political parties and ideologies, conservatism included, had by this point offered limited and inadequate solutions.

Early conservative social policies

By the late 19th century it was evidently apparent that there were some serious socioeconomic tensions within British society, most notably within the urbanised areas, and which could be linked to the legacy of the Industrial Revolution, the associated poor living conditions and the consequent high concentrations of poverty. A similar environment existed across much of capitalist-aligned Western Europe; France had experienced a revolution in 1789 due to such conditions and sustained social unrest. This led to recurring fears among the British establishment that Britain could potentially follow the same destabilising route if something drastic was not done in terms of producing effective and popular policies to address such issues. Yet, how to deal with these deep-rooted problems was not obvious among the political classes, and Victorian conservatism had an initial tendency to be reactionary, namely, to suppress and control simmering social unrest in a repressive manner that focused on keeping order, rather than to propose clear and positive solutions. In addition to this, leading Conservative politicians were often seen as representing privilege, wealth and vested interests and were firm supporters of the economic system of capitalism which was the basis of British society both then and now. Overall, the prevailing political mood and approach of the ruling elite was 'laissez-faire' (leave alone) – which in terms of broader policy making offered a model of limited government that didn't seek to interfere with the free market of the capitalist economy, and which therefore had little or no inclination towards significant state intervention in individual and personal socioeconomic affairs.

However, a key figure in offering new 'conservative' solutions to this scenario was the emerging politician Benjamin Disraeli, who served as Conservative Prime Minister on two separate occasions in the latter part of the 19th century. Disraeli was also a writer of novels, and in some of his books he wrote about the appalling and desperate social conditions that existed within the country. In doing so he indicated that he had a paternalistic social conscience for the condition of the country's poorest communities. Disraeli had described this situation as being akin to the existence of two distinct nations within a single country. Indeed, in his novel *Sybil (or The Two Nations)*, published in 1845, he described contemporary Britain as: 'Two nations between whom there is no intercourse and no sympathy; who are as ignorant of each other's habits, thoughts, and feelings, as if they were dwellers in different zones, or inhabitants of different planets ... The rich and the poor.'

A few years later, in 1848, Disraeli again made the valid connection between social disharmony and potential revolution when he declared in a public speech that 'The palace is not safe, when the cottage is not happy'. Such comments formed the basis of Disraeli's argument that capitalism was not serving the entire population well, that the ruling class were detached and disconnected from the masses of the wider public and that this sense of separation put their long-standing position of power and privilege in jeopardy. Therefore, in order to address the country's significant poverty and long-term social problems, for British politicians of the late 19th century like Disraeli, a more interventionist approach was evidently required, in particular when it came to social policy making. The motive for this could be seen as a combination of selfish political gain and pursuit of the wider social good. This was certainly the case within the environment of an increasingly democratic society, specifically if politicians wished to remain in power and achieve political goals. This democratic element became even more significant when further Reform Acts in 1867 and 1884 increased the electorate's size to approximately 60% of all men aged over 21, before full-blown adult suffrage was established for all adults of both sexes by 1928. Yet, adopting this reformist and proactive approach challenged the traditional instincts of conservativism to maintain the status quo, to conserve the social equilibrium and to 'leave alone'. However, Disraeli concluded that leaving alone was no longer a feasible option and that directing and controlling socioeconomic change was preferable to losing political control amid social unrest, and possibly even revolution.

This outlook led to a notable amount of social legislation from the 1860s onwards which entailed greater intervention by the state in ordinary people's lives. This newer approach became known as 'One Nation Conservatism', which had the principal aim of creating a more stable and unified society that would reduce tensions between the different social classes, specifically in terms of improving the prospects of the very poor, and their living conditions in particular, while at the same time securing the 'natural order' of the ruling class in power. As a further means of instilling greater national unity, the Disraelian approach to government also cultivated the patriotism and nationalism that has become associated with conservatism, promoting the country and, particularly, the British Empire as a source of national pride and social unity. Echoes of this nationalist tendency can be seen in British Conservative Euroscepticism towards the EU from the 1970s onwards.

During his most sustained period as prime minister, between 1874 and 1880, Disraeli introduced a range of social legislation that was considered fairly radical and progressive for the time, and which some historians have remarked represents one of the earliest notable phases of social reform in the UK. These new laws included the Factory Act 1874, aimed at improving conditions in the workplace; the Artisans Dwelling Act 1875, which sought to improve public housing conditions; the Public Health Act 1875, which aspired to improve the broader living and working environment; and the Chimney Sweepers Act 1875, which focused on tackling the exploitative issue of child labour. There was also legislation that improved workers' rights in general by granting additional legal powers to trade unions. This period of government therefore indicated that conservatism could embrace social reform, oversee managed change and instigate significant legislation to improve the lives of ordinary working people, although it was not as radical as many socialists and trade unionists of the period demanded. However, such policies never sought to create a more equal society but, rather, to narrow the gap between the most extreme cases of rich and poor, for, while conservatism preaches equality of opportunity, it fundamentally believes that socioeconomic inequality is a natural feature of everyday life linked to people's differing talents and abilities. Nevertheless, as the 19th century moved into the 20th, the ideology of conservatism was evolving and adapting to meet the demands of a changing society.

Early 20th-century conservatism and management of the welfare state

As the 20th century commenced, British society came to embrace an extended and growing system of welfare, which was increasingly provided by the state as opposed to charities and arbitrary, localised bodies and institutions. This was a logical reaction against the demoralising poverty of the 19th century, and much of this welfare growth was driven by rival ideologies, in the first instance by liberalism prior to the First World War, and after 1945 by a combination of liberal and socialist influences which some historians have referred to as representing 'Keynesian social democracy'. The New Liberal government of 1906–14 and the Labour government of 1945–51 thus established the UK welfare state as we now know it, with the first administration establishing a framework of welfare services and the second enlarging and 'universalising' many of them. However, Stanley Baldwin's Conservative governments of the 1920s and 1930s also offered some modest social reforms relating to pensions, housing and unemployment benefit.

The harsh workhouses were gradually abolished from the late 1920s. Following the 'hungry 1930s' and the economic depression of that decade, public demand for a more generous welfare model was high, leading to the popular Beveridge Report of 1942 which set out the blueprint for the post-war welfare state.

In practical terms, the post-war settlement entailed a whole range of financial and social benefits for the neediest members of society, to be provided by the state. These included old-age pensions, family allowances, unemployment benefit and, the most ambitious of all, the National Health Service, which came into existence in 1948. By the end of the 1940s the use of such welfare services was not linked to any prior financial contribution by the individual – which went against many conservative beliefs linked to the values of self-reliance and self-sufficiency. Indeed, the ideology of conservatism had some specific concerns about the pace of such changes and the potentially negative 'moral' impact of the state's giving citizens 'something for nothing'. Consequently, Conservative MPs opposed implementing the Beveridge Report in full and voted against the foundation of the NHS in the proposed form in which it was originally established. However, once such major social reforms were firmly in place and proved to be popular with the general public, any initial opposition subsided and Conservative politicians came to pragmatically accept them. This was consistent with the writings of Michael Oakeshott, in particular, who argued in texts published during this post-war period that it was the natural instinct of conservatism to react and respond in line with the broader public mood.

Thus, despite such initial difficulties in coming to terms with the often-demanding political needs of a democratised and socially divided country, for much of the 19th and 20th centuries the ideology of conservatism seemed to pragmatically adapt, survive and flourish. As a result, the Conservative Party came to establish itself as the 'natural party of government', such was its political success and dominance of British politics. It governed either alone or in coalition for approximately two-thirds of the 20th century, and this meant that it had an important role in wielding the political power by which to shape and implement key policies, both social and economic. It has, consequently, managed key institutions like the NHS and the broader welfare network for longer than any other UK political party. As its ideology gradually evolved and developed, much of the Conservative Party's electoral success in the democratic era can ultimately be linked to conservatism's pragmatic ability to align itself with and reflect the mood and instinct of mainstream public opinion, which (as earlier highlighted) stems from its inclination to reject political radicalism and abstract theoretical arguments.

Post-war conservatism (1945–75)

Having flexibly adapted to the era of the British welfare state, conservatism sought to stamp its own mark on it after 1945. Consequently, during the 1950s and early 1960s senior Conservative politicians such as Harold Macmillan, 'Rab'

Butler and Iain Macleod pursued a largely Disraelian 'One Nation' political agenda. Indeed, Macmillan had specifically articulated such ideals during the depression-hit 1930s in his book *The Middle Way*, which concluded that the lack of state support for the poor during this period was not acceptable in the future. This post-war variant of conservatism therefore involved supporting further generous investment in the NHS, a significant house-building programme (many homes were 'council houses' for social rent) and broader, 'interventionist' support for funding and maintaining the welfare framework established by the Labour government of 1945–51. This degree of general support for 'welfarism' within the Conservative Party's leadership led to various historians declaring that an era of 'consensus' had now been visibly established between the two main political parties of the UK. This again reflected the pragmatism of conservatism as an often loose and adaptable ideology, yet internal party tensions regarding this new political structure remained. For example, various Conservative MPs had concerns about the financial cost of the new welfare settlement, as well as the power and 'control' of the growing state and how it impacted on individual freedom and personal choice. This viewpoint had been initially evident in a landmark book, *The Road to Serfdom* by the conservative-inclined Austrian economist F.A. Hayek (1944), which argued that increasing state powers in the form of expanded welfare services would ultimately lead to excessive and even repressive control by government bureaucracy over the individual citizen, who would effectively be reduced to 'serfdom' (poverty under state control) in the process.

From the perspective of the ideology of conservatism, evidence of the long-term expense of the UK's welfare state could be identified from its earliest stages of development. The most obvious example of this was when the Labour government that established the NHS in the 1940s had, by the early 1950s, imposed financial charges for dental and optical services, such services being deemed unaffordable if they were provided on a 'universal' basis. In the years that followed, a notable number of Conservative politicians continued to voice concern at such broad welfare costs, and in 1955 the influential think-tank the IEA was formed. This body served to reflect such anxieties about the scale and cost of an expanding state and enlarged welfare provision and would often cite the US system as a preferable model of a free-market, capitalist-orientated society. By the late 1960s the deep-rooted individualistic tradition that has always existed within the ideology of conservatism feared that its original concerns about an expanding state welfare structure were being realised, as the high levels of government spending associated with it appeared to be spiralling out of control. Such trends were subsequently said to have suppressed the dynamics of the capitalist free market and hampered the performance of the UK economy. Particular symptoms of this were increases in taxation, inflation and industrial unrest (strikes) during the 1960s and 1970s, which adversely impacted on an individual's freedom of economic choice – a core priority of conservatism. Matters came to a head when the UK plunged into economic crisis in the 1970s, culminating in the Labour government of the time seeking a financial loan from the International Monetary Fund in 1976. With the UK facing potential bankruptcy and financial humiliation, the cost of the country's generous welfare state appeared to have reached breaking point, and this event represented a catalyst in the ideological development of conservatism and steered it in a markedly new direction.

Conservatism and the New Right in the 1980s

The 1970s were thus a turning point for the ideology of conservatism, and similar trends emerging on both sides of the Atlantic gave its evolution a more global significance. In 1975 the UK Conservative Party selected Margaret Thatcher as its new leader. She was a politician who embraced the New Right ideological agenda that was linked to identifiable ideas, specific theoretical principles and much clearer political goals or outcomes. This was a contrast to the more pragmatic image of conservatism during the earlier 20th century and, on being elected to power in 1979, Thatcher was given the opportunity by the British people to put her solidified ideology into practical action. The impact of this political development was magnified by parallel events taking place in the US, where in 1980 the conservative Republican politician Ronald Reagan was elected to the presidency. As enthusiastic advocates of New Right conservatism, both Thatcher and Reagan had much in common in terms of how they viewed the world, and each identified with a similar type of conservative ideology and offered similar solutions to long-standing social and economic problems in their respective countries. Such ideological solutions could be linked to key 20th-century academic theorists such as Hayek and Friedman in particular, both of whom generally argued for a low-tax, smaller state with controlled and limited welfare provision.

Both the UK and the US experienced economic turbulence during the 1970s, which, according to the New Right's analysis, could be broadly linked to the excessive growth of the state's powers that interfered in the capitalist free market. Within a primarily British context, a symptom of this could arguably be seen in stagnant economic growth and rising inflation, resulting in a phenomenon which some contemporary observers described as 'stagflation'. Thatcher therefore boldly declared that in relation to economic and social policy making she would overturn the high-spending post-war consensus and 'roll back the frontiers of the state'. One academic observer has described this approach as seeking to secure a 'free economy and a strong state' (Gamble, 1988), which suggested that the broader political system would be strengthened by an economic model that was liberalised and freed from the tentacles of state control. However, this approach was viewed by some as not being traditionally associated with conservatism but being rather more in tune with the free market-based liberalism of the 19th century. Consequently, Thatcher and Reagan were often referred to as 'neoliberals' rather than conservatives, and debate has since ensued to whether the New Right's fairly radical views were actually consistent with the political heritage of conservatism at all. However, the New Right did endorse some traditional aspects of conservatism, namely its moralistic support (often linked to Christian influences) for social standards such as traditional marriage and the conventional family unit, as well as the social value of religion. Some have referred to this attitude as seeking a return to the 'Victorian values' of a bygone era and, as a result, the New Right agenda expressed a degree of 'neoconservative' suspicion towards new social trends, such as rising divorce and abortion rates, alternative and non-orthodox life-styles, as well as more public displays of homosexuality – patterns of social behaviour that had grown in prominence since the more socially liberal period of the 1960s. It could therefore be argued that the predominant form of conservatism that appeared in the 1980s across parts of Western Europe and the US was a combination of neoliberalism in economic terms, and neo-conservatism in social terms.

Conservatism's usual links with maintaining the political status quo mean that it is not usually described as a radical ideology. However, as a further curious feature of this historical period, because the UK's post-war political settlement was based on a left-wing (social democratic) agenda, a radical model of conservatism had the opportunity to function and flourish at that point in time. The New Right's emergence was an expression of this trend, and evidence of such radicalism could be seen by the early 1980s, when the broader levels of UK government spending had been markedly cut and many formerly state-run industries had been privatised. This in turn curbed inflation and trade union power and was later followed by significant cuts in taxation. Privatisation was perhaps the most radical policy of this period, resulting in significant socioeconomic change and being driven by clear ideological goals. However, this conservative radicalism had a negative social impact in terms of the extent of cuts being made to core public services, leading to a reduced welfare state and rising unemployment. The social impact of such New Right policies has subsequently been the subject of much political and academic debate, namely as to whether the challenging social implications created by such economic reforms were properly addressed. What is perhaps most negative is that in both the UK and the US, two countries where the New Right political experiment was pursued in its fullest form, the gap between rich and poor grew considerably wider as the 1980s progressed. 'Thatcherism' in the UK and 'Reaganomics' in the US were thus often accused of prioritising economic policy over social policy, and their respective societies experienced various divisions and hardships during this decade. Thatcher's personal views on the concept of 'society' were also somewhat controversial, and in a 1987 interview with *Woman's Own* magazine she remarked:

> "And, you know, there is no such thing as society. There are individual men and women, and there are families. And no government can do anything except through people, and people must look to themselves first. It's our duty to look after ourselves and then, also, to look after our neighbour."

Although some conservatives have said this quote was taken out of context, to critics of Thatcherism this appeared to indicate that this revamped form of conservatism represented selfish individualism. The tone seemed to lack empathy and concern for the social consequences of its neoliberal economic policies, particularly given the rising inequality and unemployment of the time.

Beyond the New Right

The New Right's ultimate legacy was the creation of a more individualistic (yet unequal) society attached to a smaller state, with less emphasis on social community and a less generous welfare model. However, a negative consequence was that, despite a general focus while in power on reducing welfare benefits, the New Right's policies ultimately led to higher unemployment and more long-term benefit recipients, which created a further financial cost to the state. This resulted in a significant growth in the 'dependency culture', as opposed to the prevalence of greater personal independence as had been the ultimate ideological goal. Thatcher's immediate successor as Conservative prime minister, John Major (1990–97), sought to address this by imposing more 'conditionality' on the receipt of welfare payments, with policies such as Jobseekers' Allowance and Incapacity Benefit introduced in the mid-1990s as part of this new approach. However, following Margaret Thatcher's departure as prime minister in 1990, shortly after the end of Reagan's political tenure in 1989, conservatism went through something of an identity crisis in both Britain and other Western democracies. John Major prioritised 'rebalancing social policy' (Major, 1999) and revived aspects of the 'One Nation' tradition in order to address the perception that conservatism had become harsher and inflexible in its ideological tone, and too economic in its political narrative. Other conservative figures from this period endorsed Major's analysis and argued for the development of 'civic conservatism' and greater focus on an innovative and attractive social policy agenda (Willetts, 1994).

However, by the end of the 1990s conservatism needed to further revise its image and identity, having lost popular support and being out of national office in the US from 1992 for the rest of the decade, and in the UK from 1997 for the next 13 years. The poor condition of public services that had worsened under the Conservative Party's rule was seen as a significant reason for the scale of its heavy electoral defeat in the UK in 1997. By the end of the 1990s in the US, Republican presidential candidate George W. Bush was preaching about 'Compassionate Conservatism' as a further reflection of the revised approach, and similar political trends were evident in other countries. Such developments reflected the fact that the New Right's disruptive socioeconomic agenda, which peaked in the 1980s, appeared to have undermined the longer-term popular appeal of this ideology, destabilising society as well as the traditional pragmatic equilibrium of conservatism in the process.

In 2010 the Conservative Party returned to power in the UK after 13 years in opposition, albeit at the head of a coalition supported by the Liberal Democrats.

Incoming Prime Minister David Cameron made it clear that he wished to widen the party's popular appeal and he offered a 'modernised' version of conservatism that would support and invest in key public services like the NHS, which he hoped would override past criticisms of his party's underfunding of such services. However, part of his modernising approach was to restructure state provision of welfare/social support in pursuit of greater financial efficiency and value for money for the taxpayer. This was a priority in the context of the rising national deficit and the ongoing significant cost of 'welfarism', which by then absorbed approximately 7.5% of the UK's gross domestic product (almost £200 billion a year). While this economic angle was important, Cameron also instilled a more social emphasis into his policy making, pursuing his flagship agenda of the 'Big Society' while in opposition from 2009 onwards, and then in power after 2010. This entailed less focus on the 'big state' to provide solutions to everyday socioeconomic problems. He instead placed greater emphasis on charities, communities and individuals on a localised and often voluntarist level to fix what he called the 'broken society'. Cameron also distanced himself from New Right rhetoric, encouraged a more communitarian emphasis of mutual social responsibilities and acknowledged that there was such a thing as society, but argued that 'society is not the same as the state' (Cameron, 2005). Thus, in pursuing a distinctive and revamped policy agenda which seemed to have different priorities than past periods of Conservative government, Cameron displayed pragmatism and appeared to detach himself from the ideological certainties of the Thatcher era. This revised 'post-bureaucratic' viewpoint regarding the role of the state thus desired to reduce centralised political control and challenge welfare dependency, while in the process advocating fiscal conservatism to 'balance the books' within a smaller state. On this premise, it was a legitimate conservative-orientated argument that spending cutbacks were financially necessary to maintain national economic credibility. Yet critics highlighted that the Conservatives had limited representation in the urban, poorer areas with the highest concentration of welfare benefit recipients, which led to accusations of their being out of touch with those most in need.

Subsequently, how effective and genuine this approach was in tackling the so-called 'broken society' has come under significant political scrutiny. Critics have argued that Cameron's revised version of conservatism in the early 21st century was merely a smokescreen for further ideologically driven policies within an atmosphere of austerity, with key 'welfare reforms' such as Universal Credit and the 'bedroom tax' being a byword for cutbacks and economic retrenchment which have created more hardship and resulted in the rapid growth of charitable foodbanks in Britain since 2010. This could be viewed as a further 'roll-back' of the state under the Conservative governments of both Cameron and his successor, Theresa May (since 2016), with negative consequences in terms of addressing long-term levels of poverty and social inequality. On this basis it therefore seems to have been an unconvincing revision of conservatism, and the vague Big Society agenda fizzled out, with limited impact. Yet, on a demographic level, and with a growing population living longer (a positive consequence of an expanding welfare state), there can be some justification for such a review of welfare provision in the UK, due the associated rising costs. Despite facing such difficulties, on another policy dimension Cameron had greater success in refreshing the image and perception of conservatism. This came in the form of a more socially liberal acceptance of alternative life-styles, culminating in his government's passing equal (same-sex) marriage legislation in 2013 – a development that would have shocked the New Right's neo-conservative advocates of the 1980s. Although there remained internal party opposition to this ground-breaking policy, such a development again showed the adaptable and flexible nature of conservatism as an ideology in the way it adapted to a changing public mood.

Comparative perspectives

During the 1980s the governments of both the UK and the US experimented with a reversal of state intervention and a concerted revival of conservative-inclined economic politics, which some commentators have actually described as being 'neoliberal' in nature. Such policies were often referred to as representing the New Right and being more ideological, and they had a significant impact on each country's welfare state. This was a particularly striking and significant development in terms of how the UK dealt with its more generous and expanding model of welfare delivery that had grown substantially since the end of the Second World War.

The basic analysis of the prevailing form of conservatism at this point in time was that the post-war welfare state had become too large and bloated, was unaffordable and, in the words of Margaret Thatcher, required 'rolling back'. Within this context, on the Conservatives being elected to office at the end of the 1970s, the Thatcher model of conservatism introduced significant cutbacks to public spending and reductions in state intervention, linked to Thatcher's belief that the levels of personal taxation to fund such state activity had become too high. While the American welfare model was never as expansive or as universal as the UK's, US President Ronald Reagan adopted a similar approach to trimming government spending and welfare provision wherever possible, while again focusing on delivering cuts in taxation.

While the state did reduce its influence and taxation dropped throughout this decade in both countries, many on the political Right proclaimed this revived version of conservatism as being a success in the way that it liberated people from state control and high government taxation. However, a consistent and growing criticism of this political approach was that this specific revival of conservatism and its more ideological format ultimately resulted in failing public services, a crumbling public infrastructure and a welfare model that became inadequate and unfit for public use. This critical argument claimed that the poorer and most vulnerable members of society, in particular, were negatively affected by such changes. On this basis, by the mid-1990s there was a popular electoral backlash against such a minimalist variant of conservatism, alongside a revived critique from the liberal Left that forcefully argued that state intervention was needed in much greater volume in order to restore an improved safety net as part of a more civilised, compassionate and balanced social structure. On this basis, some have argued that the New Right experiment with conservatism during the 1980s was ultimately a transatlantic failure.

Conclusion

This chapter has identified that conservatism is a core ideology with a rich and varied set of influences and traditions. Within a mainly British context, there have traditionally been two rival variations of conservatism, in the form of the paternalistic One Nation variant of Disraeli and his successors, versus the laissez-faire (free market) alternative, which was witnessed during much of the Victorian era, and also more recently in the form of the New Right agenda. However, such traditions of conservatism have also been broadly evident in other Western liberal democracies, including the US, and, on this premise, such tensions within conservatism have had an international dimension. Over the years, these differing versions have offered alternative solutions and approaches to dealing with deep-rooted social and economic issues, and it could be argued that each particular tradition has been more suited to specific periods of history. Central to this debate within conservatism has been how to deal with the demands of an increasingly democratised society and a growing welfare state, and the significant public demands that stem from such developments. A natural instinct of conservatism has traditionally been to cut down and trim welfare provision, with a largely economic justification, when wielding national political power – primarily due to the strain it places on government spending and, in turn, the performance of the national economy. However, some conservatives have instead embraced a more explicitly socially themed policy agenda and sought to invest in the welfare state to varying degrees. Consequently, tensions are likely to continue within conservatism as the 21st century develops (with economic pressures continuing to be of significance), specifically between its pragmatic tendencies and its more avowedly ideological traditions.

Key features of conservatism

• Conservatism embraces a pessimistic and negative view of human nature and argues that people are ultimately driven by individualism and selfish motives in their behaviour. This particular viewpoint was a key influence behind of the New Right policy agenda of the 1970s and 1980s and its focus on personal enrichment, low taxation and a 'shrunken state'.

- Conservatism traditionally believes in a natural social order or hierarchy where the higher social classes govern in the interests of all, including the lower social classes, in a form of paternalistic rule (linked to the ideas of 19th-century prime minister Benjamin Disraeli). Conservatism also tends to support the need for a clear and explicit 'rule of law' to provide for such social order and stability, a viewpoint that is often linked to the ideas of Thomas Hobbes in the 17th century.

- Conservatism does not believe that social equality is possible or desirable, and holds that inequality is a natural state of everyday society. However, what levels of inequality are acceptable is a source of disagreement within conservatism, while conservative politicians ultimately favour the concept of equality of opportunity as opposed to equality of outcome.

- Conservatism is cautious, and resistant to sudden or rapid change, and its advocates highlight the dangers of social and political revolution as outlined in the writings of Edmund Burke, in particular. Instead, conservatism has generally argued for slow, cautious or managed change, allowing an often-complex society to adapt and evolve in an 'organic' manner.

- Conservatism is often associated with pride in the nation and patriotism, featuring unity across social classes who will, ideally, work cooperatively together for the national good, while being bound together by the system of capitalism and its values. It is also broadly pragmatic in its approach to responding to political and social issues that arise and is therefore inclined to reject ideological motives as the basis for action.

Critical questions

1 How does the conservative focus on controlling and managing societal change differ from the socialist and liberal ideological positions?

2 How can this 'controlling' element of the conservative position be seen to influence the social work and social care fields? What are the challenges to this?

3 Think of examples of how Thatcher's desire for a small welfare state impacted on those experiencing difficulties and requiring support.

4 How is the privatisation of care provision related to the conservative ideological perspective? Can you think of examples of this?

5 Think of examples of how current social work and care provision is affected by conservative ideology; how would different ideological positions vary in their approach to your examples?

Further reading

- Gamble, A. (1988) *The Free Economy and the Strong State: The Politics of Thatcherism*, London: Palgrave.

- Norman, J. (2010) *The Big Society: The Anatomy of the New Politics*, Buckingham Press, University of Buckingham.

- Oakeshott, M. (1962) *On Being Conservative in Rationalism in Politics and Other Essays*, London: Methuen and Company.

- Thatcher, M. (1993) *The Downing Street Years*, London: Harper Press.

- Williams, B. (2015) *The Evolution of Conservative Party Social Policy*, London: Palgrave.

Andrew Gamble's text is viewed as one of the key academic studies relating to an objective analysis of Thatcherism and its impact on British politics and society. It effectively complements Margaret Thatcher's own more subjective memoirs as outlined in *The Downing Street Years* and the two books together offer an in-depth commentary of the significant historical period when Thatcher was British Conservative prime minister (1979–90). Both books ultimately focus on the ideological nature of Thatcher's new form of conservatism and its links to the specific ideology of the New Right. By contrast, Oakeshott's text provides the opposite perspective and variant – namely, how conservatism has traditionally been viewed as having a non-ideological and pragmatic political approach which is instinctively in tune with everyday human nature. Jesse Norman's more recent book offers a contemporary summary of what post-Thatcher conservatism represents, in particular its revived focus on community, society and cooperative action. With similar views to David Cameron, Norman's work is seen as being an influential source behind conservative social policy and associated attitudes in the early 21st century. As a summary overview of this renewed policy narrative, Williams' text provides some wider-ranging evidence and analysis of how conservatism has developed social policy in particular for modern British society, with particular focus on the UK Conservative Party's return to national political office between 2010 and 2015.

References

Burke, E. (1790) *Reflections on the Revolution in France* [political pamphlet, not conventionally published].

Cameron, D. (2005) Leadership acceptance speech, 6 December, https://www.theguardian.com/politics/2005/dec/06/toryleadership2005.conservatives3

Disraeli, B. (1845) *Sybil: Or The Two Nations*, London: Henry Colburn.

Friedman, M. (1962) *Capitalism and Freedom*, Chicago: University of Chicago Press.

Gamble, A. (1988) *The Free Economy and the Strong State: The Politics of Thatcherism*, London: Palgrave.

Hayek, F.A. (1944) *The Road to Serfdom*, Abingdon: Routledge Press.

Hobbes, T. (1651) *Leviathan* [political pamphlet, not conventionally published].

Macmillan, H. (1938) *The Middle Way*, London: Random House.

Major, J. (1999) *The Autobiography*, London: HarperCollins.

Oakeshott, M. (1975) *On Human Conduct*, Oxford: Oxford University Press.

Thatcher, M. (1987) Interview in *Woman's Own*, 23 September, https://www.margaretthatcher.org/document/106689

UK Public Spending website: https://www.ukpublicspending.co.uk/index.php

Willetts, D. (1994) *Civic Conservatism*, London: The Social Market Foundation.

4

Neoliberalism

Ian Cummins

Introduction

From the mid–1970s onwards, neoliberalism has been the most influential political ideology. This influence has been exercised in several ways. In the global North, neoliberal ideas have underpinned the electoral success of politicians such as Margaret Thatcher and Ronald Reagan. Following their successes, progressive opposition parties such as New Labour under Tony Blair shaped their policies in response to a new political, economic and social landscape that had been created. In the global South, following neoliberal economic policies became a condition of receiving support from supranational institutions such as the World Bank. Finally, the emerging economies of the post–Soviet bloc followed key elements of neoliberal ideas. Neoliberalism is almost all-pervasive. Harvey's (2007) book *A Brief History of Neoliberalism* has on its cover, alongside Reagan and Thatcher, pictures of the Chilean military dictator, Pinochet, and the Chinese Communist leader Deng Xiaoping – testament to the reach, influence and flexibility of this political and economic ideology.

Neoliberalism has at its core a belief in the supremacy of the market. Any interventions that prevent the operation of a free market should be resisted. The electoral successes of parties such as the Tories under Thatcher and Republicans under Reagan have meant that there is a danger that these are seen as inevitable (Stedman-Jones, 2012) – inevitable because they were seen to reflect the alleged fact that there was ultimately no alternative to the market. This is certainly the view that was put forward by Thatcher – 'there is no alternative' (Young, 2014) – at the time, and by Conservative analysts such as Sandbrook (2013) and Moore (2014). This is part of the mythology of Thatcherism.

Hayek

The Austrian economist Friedrich Hayek (1899–1992) is the key thinker in the development of neoliberalism. Hayek wrote the key text in neoliberal political economy, *The Road to Serfdom*, which was published in 1944. He and his followers never accepted the developments that led to the establishment of institutions of the modern welfare state in the UK, such as the NHS and the expansion of public education. In 1950 Hayek moved from the London School of Economics and Political Sciences to the University of Chicago. From that point onwards, Chicago has been the centre for the development of neoliberalism – occasionally referred to as the Chicago School. In the 1950s and 1960s Western liberal democracies followed broadly similar social democratic economic, social and political policies. In the area of economics, Keynesian policies were followed which focused on public investment and the need to maintain full employment. The state was seen to have a positive role in intervening to rectify the failings or inadequacies of the market. Hayek and free marketeers were opposed to any such interventions. He was thus very much outside of mainstream thought during this period.

Hayek's work played a key role in the providing an intellectual case against social democratic trends. His work became a key influence in the development of the anti-statism that contributed to preparing the ground for the subsequent successes of Thatcher in the UK. His influence can be seen in the work of libertarian think-tanks such as the IEA. Wacquant (2009) outlines the way that think-tanks, alongside conservative journalists and publications, helped to shape public opinion and create an anti-welfare state narrative. The IEA would float ideas that initially were out of step with mainstream thinking but then were taken up by conservative columnists.

Key neoliberal ideas

This section will examine the main features of neoliberal thought. One of the key arguments that is put forward here is that neoliberalism has to be understood as a political and social project, not simply a technocratic economic one. The view that the market is the most effective form for the organisation of the distribution of resources leads to broader views about the role of the state and so on.

There are two key beliefs at the heart of neoliberal thinking. The first is the *supremacy of market*. The second is a commitment to *liberty*. Liberty is generally defined in this school of thought as freedom from state or other interference. Hayek (2001) argued that the role of the state should be limited to ensuring that the markets can operate. There is also a role for the state in guaranteeing a legal system to ensure that commercial contracts can be enforced. Nozick (1974), in setting out a philosophical support of neoliberalism, argued for a minimal or 'nightwatchman' state in which there is a limited role for the state in the market but there is a key role in protecting the individual citizen – that is, law and order – and in the defence of the realm. For individual liberty to flourish, then, there need to be effective sanctions against those who breach its rules in whatever sphere of life.

Neoliberalism holds that state intervention – either in the form of legislation or by the state control of assets – distorts the functioning of the market. Hayek and other key neoliberals such as Friedman were influenced by the classical economist of the Scottish Enlightenment, Adam Smith. Smith (1776) argued that an economy will function if individuals are allowed to trade freely among themselves without government interference. The market and the laws of supply and demand, alongside competition, will determine the price of goods. Smith's notion of the 'invisible hand' of the market is used to explain that in laissez-faire capitalist societies there is no overall control. Entrepreneurs start businesses with ideas for products or services that they think consumers will want. Consumers then decide by the choices that they make whether those entrepreneurs are successful. All these individual decisions result in needs being met. Thus, the unintended common good is the result of the activities of individuals in pursuit of their own interests. The mantra of choice is a key feature of neoliberal approaches. There should be few, if any, restrictions placed on the choices that adults can make. Neoliberalism is dynamic. Its libertarian wing's commitment to personal freedom extends from the market outwards to other areas. This creates a tension or clash with more traditional conservative positions in areas such as sexuality.

In practical political terms, neoliberalism provides a very clear template. The role of the state in the economy is to be reduced. This means that state assets will be sold, leading to the privatisation of utilities, telecommunications and other major industries. The Thatcher government followed these policies. The argument here is that state enterprises are sheltered from competition – and in that sense they are outside the disciplines of competition. Competition ensures that organisations have always to be looking at ways to become more efficient, as well as developing new products. Public sector bureaucracies, it is argued, become bloated and inefficient. These state concerns are monopolies and so they are not subject to the discipline of the market – consumers cannot exercise choice and use another provider. In addition, public sector workers are seen as overpaid and ineffective bureaucrats enjoying generous pay and pensions – certainly in comparison to workers in the private sector. Alongside the introduction of competition, it was argued that the sale of public assets would be the start of the creation of a share-owning democracy. Political and economic visions are intertwined here.

As noted above, individualism and the exercise of choice are highly prized within neoliberal thought. Markets operate on the basis of choice. We make decisions about the purchase of goods and services based on our own needs and tastes, but also on price and other factors. In the neoliberal economic model individuals are rational actors. Becker's (1968) work on Rational Choice Theory is important here. He argued that it was possible to apply economic models to all areas of human behaviour. For example, he argued that crime and offending needs to be understood as the result of a cost-benefit analysis. An offender when deciding to commit a crime makes the decision on the basis of a number of factors – the value of the goods stolen, the likelihood of being caught and any potential punishment. If the rewards are greater, then it is worth taking the risk. This model has the advantage of recognising the agency of offenders. However, there are huge debates about whether it really reflects the nature of most offending – for example, the impact of drugs and alcohol on decision making.

Public sector organisations are a statement of collectivism that Hayek (2001) strongly opposed. Areas such as education and health where the state had been forced to intervene because of market failings were not excluded in this analysis. For neoliberals, these should be viewed as commodities or services like any other. Therefore, they could and should be bought and sold. Friedman (2002), whose *Capitalism and Freedom* had a key influence on the Thatcher and Reagan governments, was a strong proponent of the introduction of a voucher system for schools. This system has never been introduced but is an excellent example of the thinking in this area. Such a scheme would give parents vouchers to spend on their children's education at a school of their choice, rather than have them attend their local school. Parents would also have the option of using their vouchers in the private sector – they would need to top them up to meet the cost of fees. Such approaches crystallise neoliberal thinking, as they extend the market into areas where it did not previously have a foothold. In addition, a school voucher scheme would, it is argued, break the power of educational bureaucrats. Michael Gove, when UK Education Secretary, argued that he was fighting 'the Blob', a group of bureaucrats, unions and academics who were committed to opposing his reforms. This discourse of the individual against the over-mighty but also elitist and distant state bureaucrat is a powerful trope in neoliberal social policy.

Neoliberalism and the state

The role of the state is a key question in the discussion of any political ideology. Political theory at its core is concerned with the relationship between the individual and wider society. Neoliberalism's key intellectual thinkers, Hayek, Friedman and Nozick, are fundamentally committed to a 'small state'. The role of the state is to be reduced. This means that neoliberals are inherently suspicious of what might be seen as state intervention or interference in the lives of citizens. Like all liberals, they are suspicious of an over-mighty state or state functions that restrict the rights of individuals. This libertarian strand in political thought would be opposed to measures such as the introduction of identity cards and would be very concerned about the potential for the state to monitor individual citizens. In the broader political field, the libertarian view opposes any restrictions on free speech. It is also concerned that equality and diversity legislation give special protections to particular groups – thus restricting the freedom of or disadvantaging others. As well as these concerns about the potential exercise of state power, this school of thought is very vexed by what it sees as the intrusion of the state into the daily lives of citizens. In a whole range of areas, from public health advice on diet and exercise to government guidance on parenting, it is argued that the state is seeking to restrict choice. The term 'nanny state' captures the feeling that bureaucrats have too much power.

Neoliberalism is committed to a small state and personal freedom. The economic and political are intertwined here. One of the key policies in both the Thatcher and Reagan governments was the reduction in the levels of income tax – particularly on higher earners. There are two elements to the argument supporting low income tax. The first is that entrepreneurs and risk takers need to be rewarded – it is argued that high levels of personal taxation stifle initiative and so on. There is no incentive to work harder if any rewards are lost because of higher rates of taxation. Nozick (1974) argued that taxation could be seen as akin to forced labour. The second element to this argument is that the funds raised by taxation are spent by public sector bodies. These are, as noted above, inevitably inefficient. In this model, individuals and families make better choices about how to spend money – even if they make poor choices, that is their responsibility. The reduction in the rates of personal taxation was one of the most influential elements of Thatcherism. New Labour under Blair made it clear that they too were committed to these relatively low levels of personal taxation.

Giroux (2011) highlights the way that neoliberal ideas have been able to set the agenda across social, political, economic and cultural fields. Bauman (2008) describes a culture of 'hyperindividualism' which leads to a loosening and weakening of social and community ties. It is an error to view neoliberalism as an economic project. It is clearly a political one which aims to recast the role of the state. In this regard, it has been very successful. From both the radical Right and Left there are concerns about the role of the state. For the Right, it is the destroyer of individual freedom; for the Left, it should be seen as a protector of vested interests and a barrier to radical social progress. From the 1980s onwards the role of the state has undergone a radical change. The expansion of the market or market mechanisms into a range of areas has seen the state become an equal player – in the jargon, 'a stakeholder' – alongside others. Thus, we see the involvement of private companies such as G4S and Serco in areas such as prisons and the criminal justice system that were previously seen as public sector areas.

Skelcher (2000) outlines the development of new models of the state. These are:

- 1960–1970s – an *overloaded* state
- 1980s–early 1990s – a *hollowed-out* state
- late 1990s – a *congested* state.

In the *overloaded* state of the 1960s and 1970s key industries such as mining and telecommunications were held in public ownership. Trade unions had a key role in the workplace and also in the broader development of economic policy. These features were of particular concern to neoliberals. Trade unions, because of collective bargaining, were seen as distorting the market. In addition, they were seen as restrictive of individual freedom – particularly where a closed shop operated. Under a closed shop, management agreed that workers had to be members of a trade union. Closed shops were outlawed in the UK in 1990. The role and influence of trade unions in UK public and industrial life changed significantly from the late 1970s onwards. The Thatcher governments saw trade unions not as partners in the development of industrial strategy but as a militant opposition. This political shift was accompanied by a decline in manufacturing industries – mining, steel, shipbuilding and cars – that had been the base of the trade union movement. The subsequent rise of the finance and service sectors, alongside more part-time and short-term contract work, made it more difficult for trade unions to recruit members – particularly in the private sector. The number of trade union members dropped dramatically. Alongside legislation to reduce the power of trade unions, the move to the *hollowed-out* state of the 1980s involved the sale of assets that were held in public ownership. In the UK this included the sale of council houses at discounted rates to their occupiers, and of shares in gas and electricity companies.

Theoretically, neoliberalism seeks to limit the role of the state. However, one of the paradoxes of this period was the development of new systems of regulation and audit. Pollitt and Bouckaert (1999) describe the rise of processes that are termed New Public Management (NPM). NPM can be understood as a means by which elements of the market were introduced into the public sector. It should be noted that these reforms were a hybrid – they cannot be seen as complete privatisation. In health and social care the National Health Service and Community Care Act 1990 led to a purchaser/provider split to end monopolies.

As well as structural changes, there was an important shift in the use of language. Patients, parents and passengers became customers. Policies were shot through with the language of consumerism and choice. These shifts were probably most apparent in the fields of health and education. For example, the introduction of league tables for schools was meant to give parents more choice and involvement in decision making about their children's education. These changes led a new system of regulation and inspection for public bodies – inspection of schools by Ofsted (the Office for Standards in Education) being the most high-profile example. Opposition to these moves was based on the cost and burdens that the new regimes placed on staff. The measurement and evaluation of the performance of any organisation is complex. In the field of health and social care it is a particularly difficult task. One of the key concerns was that the Key Performance Indicators (KPIs) that were chosen to measure performance across public services such as health, social care and education were crude measures unable to capture the complexity of the work involved. In addition, the collection and analysis of data became a hugely bureaucratic exercise in itself. Neoliberal thought has a very strong iconoclastic streak within it. This is evident in its distrust of experts – public servants, academics and so on. These are seen as a group with a vested interest who are trying to restrict the freedom of individuals because of a paternalist assumption that they know best.

Garland (2014) notes that all states are 'welfare states', as they are involved in one way or another in the provision of services that address the welfare needs of their citizens. It would be bizarre in the modern world if they did not. Garrett (2017) demonstrates the way that, in modern political discourse, welfare has taken on almost wholly negative meanings. Welfare has come to mean benefits paid to those who are not in work, rather than the whole range of support that citizens access across their lifetime. This is an important point, as it disguises the real nature of distribution of benefits (Hills, 2014). The myths about the generous nature of benefit payments and who receives them is an important part of the political attack on the notion of the welfare state. Neoliberalism is suspicious of any state organisation, and particularly suspicious of welfare state systems for social and economic reasons. The welfare state can be funded only via taxation, so the more generous the state, the higher the rates of taxation on either individuals or corporations. Either route will result in the restriction of choice. Neoliberalism views what it terms the dynamism of the free market as one of its most attractive features. In this model, it is important to recognise that in markets there are winners and losers, and that skills and talents are valued differently. Economic inequality is thus an inevitable outcome of a market economy. Any attempts to create more equal societies will fail because they do not recognise or accept this fact. Any attempt to create more equal societies leads to a loss of liberty or freedom – Hayek (2001) argued that any government committed to equality would need to use totalitarian powers to bring it about.

The welfare state is also viewed as creating dependency. As noted above, this is a particular use of the term 'welfare'. It does not cover the biggest area of welfare spending, which is pensions, in the UK. These ideas are most closely associated with Murray (1990) and his concept of the 'underclass'. Murray argues that the welfare state, because of its generosity, has created a class that is cut off economically, socially and, very importantly in his terms, morally from the wider society. In this schema, the welfare state rewards rather than punishes antisocial behaviour. Murray has a very traditionally conservative view of morality and personal relationships. For example, he sees the increase in the number of one-parent families as a huge social problem and the cause of a whole range of other problems such as poor educational performance and offending. The welfare state seeks to tackle these issues, but its interventions make a bad situation worse.

Austerity

Neoliberal ideas and approaches have become deeply embedded in the wider political culture. The realities of government and day-to-day politics mean that, even though there have been huge changes in the UK since the election of the first Thatcher government in 1979, for many neoliberals the state remains too large. In areas such as education and health, from this perspective, there is still huge scope for the extension or the introduction of the market and market mechanisms. Alongside this, the neoliberal and libertarian focus on individualism has seen it at the forefront of the backlash against what they term identity politics.

In 2008 the New Labour government, in response to the financial crisis, made the decision that the banks were 'too big to fail'. The resultant bailout of the banks cost an estimated £141 billion (Oxfam, 2013). This is clearly a huge sum of money. The irony was, of course, that the most vocal proponents of neoliberal economics were turning to state aid. In the 2010 general election, and ever since, David Cameron and opposition parties argued that the country faced a national emergency because of the profligacy of the New Labour governments. The 2010 Coalition government introduced a range of spending cuts that amounted to the biggest cuts in state spending since the Second World War (Crawford, 2010). These include the loss of over 900,000 public sector jobs between 2011 and 2018 (Institute for Fiscal Studies, 2012). It is important to note that austerity measures were also part of a recasting of the welfare state in line with neoliberal views about its nature and role. These measures included the trebling of university tuition fees to £9,000 per annum. Annual increases in a range of benefits such as Jobseekers' Allowance and Child Benefit were limited to 1% – an effective cut – for three years. These are not simply financial decisions that have a detrimental impact on the poorest people in society; they are also hugely symbolic statements. These measures are an attack on the vestiges of the social state – a second wave of Thatcherism. The Cameron administration introduced a series of policies that followed classic neoliberal arguments. These included cuts in the rates of personal taxation to encourage individuals to work harder or become more innovative (the idea being that higher rates of taxation discourage people from doing so as the state will take a greater share of their income), and cuts in the rates of welfare spending – apart from on pensions – to tackle the alleged problems of welfare dependency.

Comparative perspectives

The neoliberal perspective sees the market as the most effective system for the distribution of resources. Interfering in the market is, therefore, to be avoided or reduced to the minimum. Neoliberalism does not oppose individual acts of charity – this is an individual exercising choice. However, it is opposed to the involvement of the state. This is on the grounds of cost, and also a moral position that sees the welfare state as damaging and rewarding antisocial behaviour and poor choices. Neoliberalism argues that the state should provide very minimum levels of protection. The welfare system should operate in such a way that it deters claims, and those who do make claims should be subject to strict conditions. Esping-Andersen (1990), in his models of welfare capitalism, outlined three types of regime: *liberal, conservative* and *social democratic*. He saw the UK regime as something of a hybrid regime with elements of all three types. The *liberal* regime as outlined by Esping-Andersen would come closest to the neoliberal ideal. It is a residual model of welfare in which market solutions should be sought in most circumstances and any state services will be at a very basic level. There is a clear divide between the public and private sectors. The polar opposite of this would be the social democratic model of welfare most commonly associated with Scandinavian countries, in which public services are funded by comparatively high levels of personal taxation. Public services are not seen as inferior or stigmatising.

The marketisation and privatisation of health and social welfare services that has taken place since 1990 has been heavily influenced by the neoliberal belief in free markets. Alongside these moves, policies of increased welfare conditionality have been introduced across the benefits system. For example, claimants have to search and apply for a set number of jobs per week and so on. Failure to do so leads to sanctions, including reduction in benefit payments. These processes are designed to deter claims, but they also play on a range of stigmatising attitudes toward those who are in receipt of benefits, such as that they are feckless and workshy.

Conclusion

Policies influenced by the neoliberal approach have been adopted across the world by political parties of both the Right and the Left. One of the most profound impacts of neoliberal ideas has been not only their reach but also the way that they have shaped the political discourse. In the UK, for example, New Labour as a political project can only be really understood in the context of the Labour Party's catastrophic general election defeats of the 1980s and 1990s. There is no doubt that neoliberalism has been a successful political ideology in that it has underpinned the thinking and policies of governments across the world. There are clearly historically and culturally influenced variations of the form these policies take. If we focus on the UK, we can see the long-term influence of Thatcherism in a number of areas. The privatisation of key services and utilities is one key example. The argument put forward that this has led to vastly improved services has to be weighed against the monopoly conditions that have been created where a small number of firms exert control. In addition, the chief executive officers of these companies are now paid salaries that dwarf those paid to the heads of any nationalised concerns. Privatisation did not produce the dream of a share-owning democracy, as share ownership remains concentrated in institutions.

The critics of neoliberalism argue that it simply ignores or glosses over the failings of the market. If we cast success or failure in individual terms, we take no account whatsoever of the huge structural factors and inequalities that form the context in which these occur. The economic policies of neoliberalism, it is argued, have done great social and economic damage. Deindustrialisation has seen the rise of a service economy very reliant on financial and related services. Alongside this has been the development of precarious forms of employment (Standing, 2011). Many workers are on short-term or zero-hours contracts in low-paid work. The UK has become a much more unequal society and the division between rich and poor is increasingly stark. Garthwaite's (2016) work on foodbanks illustrates the impact of these shifts in patterns of employment. Employment was seen as the answer to poverty, but the period of austerity has seen a rise in in-work poverty.

The neoliberal concern for the potential for an over-mighty state has been outlined above. The state, far from being 'rolled back' in this period, has been recast and re-engineered. In the economic sphere the state has always had a key role (Chang, 2013). In the modern state, private companies have taken on what were previously seen as key state functions – prisons and roles in the criminal justice system being prime examples – and made significant profits. Wacquant (2009) outlines what he terms a 'centaur state'. The state has retreated from some roles, for example, the regulation of markets and the provision of social protections for workers. Elites in both their work and private lives are much less likely to be subject to state regulation or sanction. However, the state is more heavily involved in the lives of some groups of citizens – particularly people living in poverty. For example, the rate of imprisonment has more than doubled in the UK since the mid-1980s.

The late Stuart Hall (1932–2014) proved to be one of the earliest and most perceptive critics of neoliberalism. He is credited with coining the term 'Thatcherism'. His major works, such as *Policing the Crisis* and *The Politics of Thatcherism*, remain key texts for the analysis of the rise and success of neoliberal ideas. One of the most important themes in Hall's work is that an economic explanation is never in and of itself. The rise of Thatcherism and neoliberalism cannot be explained solely by the economic crisis of the mid-1970s. This is undoubtedly a very important factor, but on its own it does not offer a complete explanation. In the cultural sphere, neoliberalism, anti-statism and an appeal to individualism were in tune with broader social attitudes. These have been become much more deeply entrenched since that period. In an interview with *The Guardian* in 2012, Hall summed up his approach thus:

> "I got involved in cultural studies because I didn't think that life was purely economically determined. I took all this up as an argument with economic determinism. I lived my life as an argument with Marxism and with neoliberalism. Their point is that, in the last instance, economy will determine it. But what is the last instance? If you are analysing the present conjuncture, you can't start and end at the economy. It is necessary but insufficient." (Williams, 2012)

In 1979, Hall published 'The great moving right show', the article where he coined the term 'Thatcherism' – before Thatcher had been elected. In this analysis, he shows how neoliberal anti-statism was used as the rhetorical device that allowed Thatcher to pose as 'being with the people'. As he noted, the appeal here is grounded in the fact that for many ordinary people their experience of the state is not a positive one. The agencies of the state are experienced as punitive, uncaring, bureaucratic or a combination of all of these. Neoliberalism cannot be seen as simply an economic project. It is clearly rooted in economic ideas but it has a much broader social, political and cultural influence. Its key themes have seeped into many areas.

Key features of neoliberalism

- Markets and competition are the key to generating wealth and an efficient economy.
- Individuals should be able to make choices free from state interference.
- Personal taxation needs to be kept low to reward effort and innovation.
- The welfare state creates dependency.
- The state has become too large, bureaucratic, inefficient and wasteful.

Critical questions

1 How does neoliberalism define freedom and individual choice?
2 How does neoliberalism argue that the markets and competition make organisation more efficient?
3 Why does neoliberalism argue for a 'smaller state'?
4 Why is neoliberalism so critical of the welfare state?

Further reading

- Chang, H. (2013) *Economics: The User's Guide*, London: Pelican.
  An excellent introduction to the economic theories that underpin social and public policy.

- Cummins, I. (2016) 'Reading Wacquant: social work and advanced marginality', *European Journal of Social Work*, vol 19, no 2, pp 263–74.
  This article examines the work of Loic Wacquant, one of the key critics of neoliberal social and welfare policies.

- Garrett, P.M. (2010) 'Examining the "conservative revolution": neoliberalism and social work education', *Social Work Education*, vol 29, no 4, pp 340–55.
  This article explores the impact of neoliberal thinking on social work education.

- Garrett, P.M. (2016) *Words Matter: Deconstructing 'Welfare Dependency' in the UK*, https://blogs.lse.ac.uk/politicsandpolicy/%EF%BB%BFwords-matter-deconstructing-welfare-dependency-in-the-uk/
  An excellent blog that examines the politics of the term 'welfare dependency'.

- Hyslop, I. (2018) 'Neoliberalism and social work identity', *European Journal of Social Work*, vol 21, no 1, pp 20–31.
  This article explores the impact of neoliberal ideas on broader approaches to social work practice. It argues that social work needs to develop more collective responses to social problems.

References

Bauman, Z. (2008) *The Art of Life*, Cambridge: Polity Press.

Becker, G.S. (1968) 'Crime and punishment: an economic approach', *Journal of Political Economy*, vol 76, pp 169–217.

Chang, H. (2013) *Economics: The User's Guide*, London: Pelican.

Crawford, R. (2010) *Public Services: Serious Cuts to Come*, Emergency Budget, June 2010 briefing, London: Institute for Fiscal Studies, www.ifs.org.uk/budgets/budgetjune2010/crawford.pdf

Esping-Andersen, G. (1990) *The Three Worlds of Welfare Capitalism*, Cambridge: Polity Press.

Friedman, M. ([1962] 2002) *Capitalism and Freedom* (49th anniversary edn), London: University of Chicago Press.

Garland, D. (2014) 'What is the welfare state? A sociological restatement', London School of Economics and Political Science, www.lse.ac.uk/website-archive/newsAndMedia/videoAndAudio/channels/publicLecturesAndEvents/player.aspx?id=2695

Garrett, P.M. (2017) *Welfare Words: Critical Social Work and Social Policy*, London: Sage.

Garthwaite, K. (2016) *Hunger Pains: Life Inside Foodbank Britain*, Bristol: Policy Press.

Giroux, H. (2011) 'Neoliberalism and the death of the social state: Remembering Walter Benjamin's Angel of History', *Social Identities: Journal for the Study of Race, Nation and Culture*, vol 17, no 4, pp 587–601.

Hall, S. (1979) 'The great moving right show', *Marxism Today*, vol 23, no 1, pp 14–20.

Harvey, D. (2007) *A Brief History of Neoliberalism*, New York: Oxford University Press.

Hayek, F. ([1944] 2001) *The Road to Serfdom* (Routledge Classics), London: Routledge.

Hills, J. (2014) *Good Times, Bad Times: The Welfare Myth of Them and Us*, Bristol: Policy Press.

Institute for Fiscal Studies (2012) *Reforming Council Tax Benefit*, IFS Commentary 123. Available online: www.ifs.org.uk/comms/comm123.pdf [accessed 5 February 2018].

Moore, C. (2014) *Margaret Thatcher: The Authorized Biography, Volume One: Not For Turning*, London: Penguin.

Murray, C.A. (1990) *The Emerging British Underclass (Choice in Welfare)*, London: Institute of Economic Affairs.

Nozick, R. (1974) *Anarchy, State and Utopia*, Oxford: Blackwell.

Oxfam (2013) *Truth and Lies About Poverty: Ending Comfortable Myths About Poverty*, Cardiff: Oxfam Cymru. Available at: http://policy-practice.oxfam.org.uk/publications/truth-and-lies-about-poverty-ending-comfortablemyths-about-poverty-306526

Pollitt, C. and Bouckaert, G. (1999) *Public Management Reform: A Comparative Analysis*, Oxford: Oxford University Press.

Sandbrook, D. (2013) *Seasons in the Sun: The Battle for Britain, 1974–1979*, London: Penguin.

Skelcher, C. (2000) 'Changing images of the state: overloaded, hollowed-out, congested', *Public Policy and Administration*, vol 15, no 3, pp 3–19.

Smith, A. (1776) *An Inquiry into the Nature and Causes of the Wealth of Nations*, Volume One, London: printed for W. Strahan; and T. Cadell, 1776.

Standing, G. (2011) *The Precariat: The New Dangerous Class*, London: Bloomsbury.

Stedman-Jones, D. (2012) *Masters of the Universe: Hayek, Friedman, and the Birth of Neoliberal Politics*, Oxford: Princeton University Press.

Wacquant, L. (2009) *Punishing the Poor: The Neoliberal Government of Social Insecurity*, Durham, NC: Duke University Press.

Williams, Z. (2012) 'The Saturday interview: Stuart Hall', www.theguardian.com/theguardian/2012/feb/11/saturday-interview-stuart-hall

Young, H. (2014) *One of Us* (final edn), London: Pan Books.

5

Feminism

Lucy Mort

Introduction

Feminist theories of our social and political world retain their relevance in a contemporary context of persistent gender inequality. An exploration of how gender inequality impacts upon social work practice is necessary when we consider that women are more likely, for instance, to be in poverty (IFSW, 2012) and to be the focus of social work interventions and surveillance (Morriss, 2018).

Feminist theory and practice has often started with the 'always place women first' approach (Featherstone, 2001). However, an important and critical caveat is offered by Featherstone (2001) in her exploration of feminist social work practice, as she (analysing theoretical developments) cautions that social work needs to be 'wary of exploring women in isolation' and to interrogate traditional feminist theory and practice that has understood women only as victims and men only as problems. This chapter will situate these theoretical and practical tensions in their socio-political context.

To understand the current context of gender relations and their implications for social work we must first look to the historical context of gender theory, the emergence of feminist ideology and the developments therein. Two sections then follow, the first of which charts the theoretical context, including an outlining of key terms, an exploration of the emergence of the feminist movement and the subsequent 'waves' of feminism in the 20th century and an overview of the ideological underpinnings of the multiple schools of feminist thought. This section and the events and ideas that it narrates are historically contextualised, with a particular focus on how feminist action was in tension or harmony with the prevailing political ideology of the time.

The second of these two sections looks specifically to the implications of gender theory and formation, gender inequality and feminism for social work practice. The role of social work in addressing (and perpetuating) gender inequality will be explored, particularly in relation to poverty and inequality, oppression and discrimination and gendered violence. The chapter concludes with a comparative international case study, suggested further reading and critical questions that ask you to reflect on the relevance of feminist theory and action for contemporary social work practice.

Understanding gender

In discussing feminism it is first necessary to understand the concept of gender and the way in which it has been formulated across time and space, how it has been constructed, contested, problematised and reified. Gender is differentiated from 'sex', which is understood (not without controversy) to be determined by socially agreed-upon biological criteria for classifying people as male or female at birth (West and Zimmerman, 2002). In Western society, the notion of men and women as having very distinct psychological and behavioural attributes has been prolific and is perhaps exemplified by one of the most famous (and still popular) self-help titles: *Men Are from Mars, Women Are from Venus*. Though contemporarily this view may be less favoured, these differences have historically been conceptualised as natural and biologically determined.

Social theorists have analysed gender as learned behaviour, as socially constructed and as performative. While 'gender roles' have a behavioural element (in that they are enacted by an individual), the roles are usually conceived of as determined and moulded by societal norms and expectations. Moreover, gender is not only a role that is played by an individual but is ascribed to us by others when they determine whether we are male or female. In this way, gender is also relational. Gender works to distinguish and inscribe difference between boys and girls, men and women. Such difference is essentialised, so that we become acutely aware of what it is to be masculine and what it is to be feminine. Some feminists have theorised that gender has been constructed for the benefit of patriarchy, that is, the structural domination and oppression of women by men.

Gender is ascribed from a young age, and this impacts on how children are treated, with children being confronted by an array of vastly gender-specific toys, for instance. Such labelling, in childhood and throughout our lives, affixes static notions of gender roles that are premised on a heteronormative framework. Heteronormativity – a position whereby cultural, legal and institutional practices maintain normative assumptions that 'there are two and only two genders, that gender reflects biological sex, and that only sexual attraction between these "opposite" genders is natural or acceptable' (Schilt and Westbrook, 2009, p 441) – does not factor in people who fall outside of gender norms and expectations, such as gay, lesbian, transgender and non-binary people. Later in the chapter the contestation of established gender norms and roles will be further critiqued in relation to the emergence and increased concern for non-binary and transgender issues in the current socio-political context.

Defining patriarchy

In discussions of feminism the term 'patriarchy' is often employed to describe the system of oppression that controls gendered power relations. Walby (1990, p 20) defines patriarchy as 'a system of social structures and practices in which men dominate, oppress and exploit women'. She explains that these social structures have six components: the patriarchal mode of production (that is, men as 'breadwinners' have innate power in the family unit, while women's household labour is unpaid and undervalued for its productive quality), patriarchal relations in paid work, patriarchal relations in the state, male violence, patriarchal relations in sexuality and patriarchal relations in cultural institutions. These relations happen at an intrapersonal and state level, and Walby argues that 'the state is patriarchal as well as being capitalist and racist ... the state has a systematic bias towards patriarchal interests in its policies and actions' (Walby, 1990, p 21).

Patriarchy as a concept has, however, been critiqued for its totalising approach and its blindness to other forms of oppression, such as race, class, disability, age and so on. Patil (2013, p 847) highlights criticism that names patriarchy as a 'homogenous, monolithic account' of gender oppression. 'Patriarchy', it is argued, does not recognise the 'differences and power relations within each category' (Patil, 2013, p 850). That is, it does not account for differences that abound within the category 'man' or 'woman'. As Featherstone (2001) noted: 'many of the men who come to the attention of social services are marginalised and impoverished. They are not straightforwardly powerful...'.

Despite theoretical disagreement on the usefulness of patriarchy as a concept, it is still widely employed, and it retains centrality in feminist theorising. Later in the chapter, the concept of 'intersectionality' will be introduced, a theoretical development that extends the concept of patriarchy through attention to multiple and concurrent differences and inequalities (such as gender, race, class, disability and so on).

Feminist movement(s)

The history of feminism is usually metaphorically illustrated as having occurred in 'waves'. The first of these occurred throughout the 19th century and into the early half of the 20th century. The second wave spanned the 1960s to the late 1980s. The dates for the third and fourth waves are more contested. The third can generally be said to be from the 1990s through to the late 2000s/early 2010s, and the fourth has been mooted since 2009 (Solomon, 2009) and was declared by Kira Cochrane (2013) more assuredly in her book titled *All the Rebel Women: The Rise of the Fourth Wave of Feminism*.

It is important to note the limitations of this metaphor, which gives the impression that the fight for women's rights in the last couple of centuries has at times been active (when the tide is in) and at others has receded from public view. Each wave is credited with particular ideas, theoretical developments and actions, but the movement for women's rights cannot be neatly apportioned into distinct time periods – in this sense it is important to remember the fluidity of waves. For instance, while we will see below that the third wave is credited with attending to the differences *between* women, it was a century earlier that Sojourner Truth, a black woman in America emancipated from slavery in 1927, who asked 'Ain't I a woman?' and who has inspired many of the most prominent intersectional feminist activists. The metaphor of waves also presumes that the feminist movement has been evenly distributed geographically (that is, it is Western-centric) and does not adequately account for differences and nuance within a given time period. With these caveats in mind, we now turn to consider the historical context of feminism in Britain, and the associated ideological developments of feminism.

First wave feminism

The first wave of feminist action for women's rights was a period of huge division, change and advancement. This was the era of women's suffrage and of two world wars. Women's demands were firmly directed at the public sphere. That is, they implored that they should have greater rights in relation to enfranchisement (the right to vote), employment and education.

The suffragette movement called for the rights of women to vote – sometimes (and notoriously) through civil disobedience, direct action and violence. 'Deeds not words' was a rallying cry adopted by the Women's Social and Political Union (WSPU) – a women-only political movement founded in Manchester by the Pankhurst family. The suffrage movement (headed by the National Union of Women's Suffrage Societies) was broader in motive and tactics, however, with many preferring to adopt more traditional lobbying and less violent means to reach their goal.

Recent articulations of this history at the centenary celebrations in 2018 have pointed out that the Representation of the People Act 1918 was a win for only *some* women (Attwood Hamard, 2018). The contributions of working-class women have often been overlooked in historical representations of the women's suffrage movement. Textile mill workers, trade unionists, seamstresses and other labouring women also called for greater political representation – though they were not always at ease with more radical means of achieving this, as Jackson (2018) notes:

> As the WSPU's actions became more focused on civil disobedience and violence, some working-class women were dismayed. While many ... were prepared to risk arrest, assault and brutal force feeding, many others felt the price was too high. Often they had children to care for, and as breadwinners a spell in prison could mean that they lost their job. Without rent their family could easily lose their home.

After the First World War and following the integration of many more women into the workforce (working-class women were already working in higher proportions than their middle-class counterparts), societal perceptions of the role of women changed. As they filled the gaps left behind by men sent to war, women were seen to be employable in fields (such as munitions factories) beyond what was traditionally understood as 'women's work'. This, coupled with a successful campaign based on zealous patriotism (the suffrage movement – both radical and moderate – called a halt to most political action during the war), meant that the rights of women to vote were viewed more favourably in the post-war period.

In 1918 women over the age of 30 and who owned property were permitted to vote. Despite a societal shift in perceptions, the enfranchisement of working-class women remained elusive. It was not until a decade later, in 1928, and after women had defended their position in civic and political spheres, that women gained equal voting rights to men. All men and women over the age of 21 could now vote, and with this 'first wave' feminism achieved a defining moment for the feminist movement.

It can be noted that the first wave of feminism was a largely liberal feminist movement, with its focus on gaining women access to the same opportunities as men in the public realm. Classical liberalism, a product of the Enlightenment and notions of rationality, was a mobilising force in arguing for greater rights for women, as it was argued that they too – like men – were rational beings and therefore should have equal access to education, employment and political decision making (Saulnier, 1996). Left out of this approach is any meaningful focus on the work that women did (and do) in the home – the labour of childcare and housework that was not seen to be as valuable as work done in the public sphere. The next wave of feminism set about offering a corrective to this blind spot.

Second wave feminism

Counter to the first wave of feminism, which was primarily concerned with the public realm and women's presence within it, the second wave positioned its feminist action more firmly within the private sphere. Emblematic of the second wave is the rallying slogan: 'the personal is political'. That is, the home and women's intimate relationships are also a site of inequity such as that seen in the public sphere. McLaughlin (2003, p 1) notes that

> Second wave feminism, in different ways, connected the continued gaps in the rights and opportunities women suffered in the public realm to the roles they played in the private sphere. The focus on the private sphere brought a new range of issues into activism and the development of feminist ideas. The new areas included sexuality, reproduction, domestic labour and domestic violence.

Continuing theoretical developments in feminist thought were a feature of the second wave, with three key ideologies mobilised to explain women's oppression and ascertain priorities for feminist struggles. Introduced above, liberal feminist thought was one such development, alongside socialist (also referred to as Marxist) feminism and radical feminism.

Liberal feminist action continued in the second wave as women fought within their workplaces for equal pay and conditions to their male counterparts. This was epitomised, for instance, in the film *Made in Dagenham*, which shows the Ford

Motor factory in London as a key site of struggle for women who were employed in roles seen as 'unskilled' (such as sewing car interiors) in comparison to their 'skilled' male co-workers. A 15% disparity in pay led to strike action in 1968, and, following support from Barbara Castle MP, the Equal Pay Act was passed into legislation in 1970, prohibiting unequal pay and working conditions between men and women in the workplace (Sisterhood and After Research Team, 2013).

However, legislative gains did not signal the end of inequality in the workplace. The Grunwick Film-Processing Laboratories strike in 1976, for instance, highlighted the continuing inequalities experienced by working-class Asian women in the workplace. The women of Grunwick – a majority Asian workforce in a London firm – experienced lower wages, exploitative overtime practices and racism in the workplace. The discrimination they experienced was a consequence not only of gendered relations and inequality but of racial and class inequality too.

This example points to some of the limitations of second wave feminism, particularly that which is 'radical' in ideology – which focused on the differences between men and women at the expense of recognising the differences between women themselves. McLaughlin (2003, p 8) writes:

> Radical feminism argued that 'women as a social group are oppressed by men as a social group and that this oppression is the *primary* oppression for women' (Rowland and Klein, 1996: 11, original emphasis). This claim appears to rule out that for some women, 'race' or class may be the oppression they consider their primary barrier.

Radical feminist thought privileges the concept of the patriarchy at the expense of all other modes of oppression. For radical feminists, it is 'men, rather than the social organisation of masculinity or the processes whereby men become men [which] are problematised' (Dominelli, 2002, p 25). Radical feminism typically focused on the home, reproductive rights and women's relationships with men as a site of oppression and violence, exposing the unequal power relationships that it suggests typify male–female relationships and which, it is argued, sustain the patriarchy (Dominelli, 2002).

A defining achievement of radical feminist action in this period was the establishment of women-only services, such as Women's Refuges and Rape Crisis Centres. These are key spaces for social care and social work practice, though a counter-argument that posits the 'women only' model reifies essentialist understandings of gender as an issue that has continued significance in contemporary debates about the exclusion of transgender people (and which will be returned to below).

Socialist (or Marxist) feminism was another ideological and theoretical development arising from the second wave of feminism. Barbara Ehrenreich, writing on what it was that she saw as defining socialist feminism, said of the two ideologies:

they are critical ways of looking at the world. Both rip away popular mythology and 'common sense' wisdom and force us to look at experience in a new way … There is no way to have a Marxist or feminist outlook and remain a spectator. To understand the reality laid bare by these analyses is to move into action to change it. (Ehrenreich, 2018)

To be a socialist feminist was (and is) to challenge the status quo of capitalist *and* patriarchal relations. For socialist feminists, the liberal mode of feminism – in which more women might be elected to power, for instance – is not sufficient in the current political system.

The second wave of feminism was concerned with many issues and had many contestations and differing perceptions of both the problem and the solutions to gender inequality. While there are critiques of the way in which much second wave feminism tended to essentialise the category of 'woman', Phillips and Cree (2014, p 941) find that much social work research is still informed by this period and its concerns and argue that this is possibly because 'the broader social justice agenda for social work has persisted, for example: poverty; gender inequality; domestic violence; child abuse and neglect. As these social problems persist, frameworks for analysis and practice logically persist with them.' McLaughlin (2003), however, also cautions against the compartmentalisation of feminist theory into three distinct ideologies; feminist thought – historically and contemporarily – is much more dynamic than this triptych would have us believe.

Third wave feminism

A key element of the third wave was its demand for an appreciation of the multiple perspectives and experiences among women. Mainstream feminism had been seen to be largely in the interests of white, middle-class women – and, as such, did not adequately address the conditions and multiple inequalities experienced by the majority of women.

In the 1990s Kimberlé Crenshaw coined the term 'intersectionality', building on the several decades of Black feminist thought and activism which had responded to the exclusionary nature of much liberal feminism (Salem, nd). Intersectionality has become a key motif in contemporary feminist theorising, as it provides a framework for understanding how multiple oppressions and identities – such as race, class and gender – shape an individual's experience. Following a period of research in domestic abuse refuges, Crenshaw (1991) illustrates the intersectional experience of oppression vividly in an article exploring violence against women:

Race and culture contribute to the suppression of domestic violence … Women of colour are often reluctant to call the police, a hesitancy likely due to a general unwillingness among people of colour to subject their private lives to the scrutiny and control of a police force that is frequently hostile. (Crenshaw, 1991, p 1257)

And:

Immigrant women are ... vulnerable to spousal violence because so many of them depend on their husbands for information regarding their legal status. Many women ... suffer abuse under threats of deportation by their husbands. Even if the threats are unfounded, women who have no independent access to information will still be intimidated by such threats. (Crenshaw, 1991, p 1248)

Intersectionality, then – here described in terms of race, gender, class and immigration status (but which can also take into account age, disability, sexuality, among others) – posits that it is necessary to consider patriarchal oppressions alongside racism, classism, disablism, heteronormativity, xenoracism and so on. These do not affect people in isolation – they are intimately and irrevocably intertwined.

The relevance of intersectionality for social work is evident, as it asks that we attend to issues of 'race', class, disability, and so on in tandem with gender (see, for instance, Case Study 5.1 on p 73). Gringeri et al (2010, p 402) argue that thinking intersectionally is important for social work practice that moves away from 'binary thinking' and instead engages 'more fully with emancipatory practice and the pursuit of social justice' as the people that social workers support are enabled to define themselves and their experiences not only in terms of 'tick-box' categories.

The current context

Fourth wave feminism

Currently, it has been argued (and contested) that we are experiencing a 'fourth wave' of feminism. This is said to be distinctive by its mobilisation on social media and the internet, which has propelled various feminist campaigns into popular consciousness.

Feminism has also been caught up in the tide of neoliberalism and capitalism as it has become 'palatable' and 'profitable' (Rivers, 2017, p 19). This can be typified, for instance, by the wearing of T-shirts with the slogan 'This is what a feminist looks like' by politicians such as Ed Miliband and Nick Clegg, and which were later found to have been manufactured in exploitative conditions in a factory in Mauritius that paid women employees 62 pence per hour.

However, it is a disservice to the current state of feminist activism to portray it as something that is only individualistic or commercialised in nature. For instance, the #MeToo movement has mobilised many women across the world in a shared revolt against sexual violence and harassment in multiple and wide-ranging spheres – from the film industry to politics to domestic workers in the US.

Trans and non-binary

Though the dichotomisation of male/female categorisation has been contested and disrupted throughout the ages and across cultures and continents (Yeadon-Lee, 2016), increased fluidity in the construction of genders has gained increased social recognition in the last decade (Manners, 2019), posing a challenge to the heteronormativity of society. This rise in recognition for those who define as non-binary – that is 'those who identify as both genders or neither' (Yeadon-Lee, 2016, p 19) – and as transgender has been accompanied by resistance from some feminists, particularly those from a radical tradition which, as noted earlier, is premised on there being two genders – one of which oppresses and the other which is oppressed.

In the current socio-political context, transgender people – despite experiencing greater social acceptability and visibility – simultaneously face discrimination, marginalisation and violence (Rogers, 2019). Trans people experience inequality in relation to hate crime, mental health outcomes, health service treatment and employment opportunities (Hudson-Sharp, 2018). A report by the Department for Education (Hudson-Sharp, 2018) found that, while there is limited evidence about the experiences of transgender people in relation to social work and social care, the existing evidence suggests that:

> many professionals lack appropriate information about transgender people's general needs (Hines, 2007), and that professionals can sometimes be insensitive to the needs of transgender service users, partly due to a failure to accept their acquired gender (Whittle et al, 2007). In line with this, transgender people report widespread transphobia within social and care settings (Alleyn and Jones, 2010). (Hudson-Sharp, 2018, p 23)

The issue of transgender access to traditionally women-only spaces, such as domestic abuse refuges, is one that has become salient in recent times, and particularly so in light of a 2018 government consultation on the Gender Recognition Act 2014, which Finlayson et al (2018) note became 'a focal point for a heated and often toxic debate over what we as a society owe to trans people.' In the fourth-wave age of feminism the conflict between those who are supportive of greater access and those who are not has played out on the social media stage.

Important for social workers to note is that the inequality experienced by trans and non-binary people means that though this may be, relatively, a minority issue (approximately 1% of the population are thought to be transgender (Hudson-Sharp, 2018)), in a context of increased trans and non-binary self-definition in young people and adults, this is a gendered inequality issue that has resonance within spaces of social work and social care.

Feminism and social work practice

For social work, an understanding of gender inequality and awareness of feminist theory and action are vital. As noted in the introduction, women are more likely to be in poverty and to be the beneficiaries of welfare and social work interventions. As well, transgender young people and adults are more likely to experience inequality and to experience barriers to effective welfare, health and social care provision when necessary. This section will briefly highlight some of the areas in which gender inequality is evident, and the role of social work – both in perpetuating and in addressing inequality.

Austerity

In the period of austerity since 2010, it has been well evidenced that women have been the worst hit by austerity measures implemented by the Conservative–Liberal Democrat Coalition government and the Conservative government, with poverty and inequality increasing as a result (Women's Budget Group, 2016). Taking an intersectional approach, whereby the category 'woman' cannot be understood in isolation, we also see that migrant and Black and Minority Ethnic people have faced disproportionate effects of austerity (Sandhu et al, 2013), as have those who are long-term sick and disabled (Garthwaite, 2014), people with mental health issues (Mattheys, 2015), women and children who experience domestic abuse (Sanders-McDonagh et al, 2016), mothers (de Benedictis, 2012), families (O'Brien and Kyprianou, 2017), benefit claimants (Patrick, 2017), older people (Lymbery, 2014) and young people (Blackman and Rogers, 2017). Though this is not an exhaustive list, the scale of austerity and its reach into the lives of all those that social workers serve is clear.

While austerity has presided over a severe scaling back of public services, it has also been argued that austerity has meant that the state (through social service functions) has extended 'its reach into the lives of disadvantaged or "troubled" families' (Crossley, 2016, p 193) through increased interventions in the home (rather than in publicly available provision such as Sure Start centres – now much reduced in number). Austerity then presents a significant issue for social work and those whom it serves. This is true both in terms of how it affects service users and also how it affects the (predominantly female) workforce, as the balance between care and control is tipped in favour of the latter, leading to a 'disjuncture between … personal and professional values and the demands of austerity', moral judgements about the deservingness of service users and the potential risk of burnout (Grootegoed and Smith, 2018, p 1942).

> **CASE STUDY 5.1: GENDERED PRACTICE: FAILING TO MEET NEEDS**
>
> A migrant woman with no recourse to public funds (a visa condition that means one cannot access 'public funds' such as welfare benefits or housing, though remains entitled to social services provision if other statutory criteria are met) leaves her partner due to domestic abuse and sexual violence. She takes her two children with her, one of them a young baby. On the advice of a friend she goes to a social services office for help. She cannot speak English well and, after hours of waiting without food or drink, a male interpreter is provided. When no refuge will accept her, the mother and children are put up in bed and breakfast accommodation for the night, given £10 and told to return to the office the next day for further assessment. The immediate emotional, psychological and physical needs of the woman and her children are not addressed.

Mothers and care proceedings

In research concerned with child protection processes in the UK, Morriss (2018) highlights how gender inequality is manifest in relation to care proceedings in the Family Court. Morriss highlights how parents – 'normally mothers' (2018, p 817) – are at increased risk of reappearing in care proceedings if a child is removed from their care and then, for instance, they become pregnant again. Noting the state abandonment experienced by mothers whose children are removed (and who have often experienced trauma and abuse themselves), whereby therapeutic support is rarely provided and welfare and housing are placed at risk, Morriss suggests that 'it is perhaps understandable that the women (re)turn to drugs and alcohol, remain in violent relationships, or indeed, become pregnant again as a way to ameliorate their grief' (Morriss, 2018, p 818).

Morriss goes on to highlight the intersectional inequalities experienced by often young, working-class women who find themselves as 'failed' mothers who are perceived to have 'moral flaws of class, gender and sexuality' (Morriss, 2018, p 819) and whose circumstances are not considered in the broader context of the 'deep poverty' and inequality that many subject to care proceedings experience (Morriss, 2018, p 820).

The practice examples in this section, alongside those relating to domestic abuse woven throughout this chapter, ask us as social workers to consider a key dilemma of social work: care versus control. Feminist theory and action can help social workers to navigate this terrain. In this chapter we have seen that feminism has a long history of organising, campaigning, critical analysis and listening to the experiences of those who experience inequality and injustice. Employing an 'ethics of care' alongside a commitment to social justice (Orme, 2002) enables social workers both to respond ethically in everyday practice with service users and to challenge the status quo of structural inequality.

Comparative perspectives

The *New York Times* dedicated an article on International Women's Day 2019 to Sweden: 'one of the best places to be a woman' (Salam, 2019). This is because Sweden was the first government – in 2014 – to use the word 'feminist' when talking about policy development, with women's rights placed centrally in decision making; it has the most generous paid parental leave policy in the world; government schools avoid organising their classes by normative gender patterns (and higher education is free); gender-neutral pronouns have been incorporated into the national culture; and it has ensured that explicit consent to sex is enshrined in law. However, while the list no doubt elicits admiration and celebration, this does not guarantee equality for all women in Sweden. A rise in neoliberal policies and far-right political support threatens the fabric of purported state feminism for the most marginalised – poor and migrant – women in Sweden (see Mulinari and Neergaard, 2017).

Conclusion

This chapter has illustrated the complexity and expansive nature of feminist ideology, theory and action historically and contemporarily. By situating gender as something that has been constructed and contested over time, the chapter has sought to offer a theoretical appreciation of the changing tide from binary thinking to more fluid and inclusive forms of feminist theorising. Feminist practice in social work, then, is not only a case of thinking about women – though this is crucial. It should also include consideration of the intersectional diversity within the category of 'woman'; consider the socially constructed nature of gender and pose a challenge to heteronormativity; be aware of the unequal position of trans and non-binary people in society; and – just as we deconstruct the category of 'woman' – should do the same also for the category of 'man' so that we can move beyond simplistic and dualistic notions that fix women only as victims and men only as villains, and instead consider the full range of gendered relations (Featherstone, 2001).

Key features of feminism

- Feminism is concerned with challenging the inequality, oppression and discrimination inherent within gendered systems of power.

- The concept of patriarchy as a defining structure within society is central for many feminist analyses, though for some this is a limited analysis of structural inequality.

- There are many ideologies and perspectives within the feminist movement and in feminist theory. These may overlap and they may oppose one another.

• While there have been many feminist gains, there are continuing and active struggles for the rights of marginalised people.

Critical questions

1 If a woman is elected to political power who must then preside over severe austerity measures that detrimentally and disproportionately affect women, is that a feminist achievement?

2 How can theories of intersectionality be used in social work practice? Does it promote social justice and empowerment? If so, how?

3 How can each of the four 'waves' of feminism and their accompanying ideologies and theories be related to social work theory and practice?

4 A feminist analysis asks us to consider how gender inequality is shaped by the political, economic and social dimensions of austerity. How can the feminist theories described in this chapter help you as a social worker to understand the oppression experienced by the woman in the case study above? How could a feminist approach to practice be used? What needs to change at a structural level and at an interpersonal level?

5 In the article described above, Morriss speaks about the transformative power of group work for women who have experienced state removal of their children, as it enabled participants to challenge dominant discourses that suggest 'child neglect is a result of parental pathology' and instead to look at the 'structural inequalities and poverty in which many vulnerable families live' (Morriss, 2018, p 828). Do you think group work can facilitate a feminist approach to social work? If so, why?

Further reading

• Dominelli, L. (2002) *Feminist Social Work Theory and Practice*, Basingstoke: Palgrave Macmillan.
An overview of key issues in social work and feminism (though slightly out of date).

• Featherstone, B., Rivett, M. and Scourfield, J. (2007) *Working with Men in Health and Social Care*, London: SAGE.
An introduction to feminist social work with men.

• Fraser, N. (2013) *Fortunes of Feminism: From State-managed Capitalism to Neoliberal Crisis*, London: Verso.
An in-depth critical analysis of feminism historically and contemporarily.

• hooks, b. (2014) *Feminism is for Everybody: Passionate Politics*, New York: Routledge.
An accessible introduction to intersectional feminism.

References

Attwood Hamard, R. (2018) 'Before you celebrate the centenary of women voting, remember that it isn't actually the triumph you think it is', *The Independent* (5 February). Available at: https://www.independent.co.uk/voices/100-years-centenary-anniversary-women-vote-britain-not-all-women-a8195381.html [accessed 20 September 2018].

Blackman, S. and Rogers, R. (2017) *Youth Marginality in Britain: Contemporary Studies of Austerity*, Bristol: Policy Press.

Cochrane, K. (2013) *All the Rebel Women: The Rise of the Fourth Wave of Feminism*, London: Guardian Shorts.

Crenshaw, K. (1991) 'Mapping the margins: intersectionality, identity politics, and violence against women of color', *Stanford Law Review*, vol 43, no 6, pp 1241–99.

Crossley, S. (2016) 'From the desk to the front-room? The changing spaces of street-level encounters with the state under austerity', *People, Place and Policy Online*, vol 10, no 3, pp 193–206.

de Benedictis, S. (2012) 'Feral parents: austerity parenting under neoliberalism', *Studies in the Maternal*, vol 4, no 2, pp 1–21.

Dominelli, L. (2002) *Feminist Social Work Theory and Practice*, Basingstoke: Palgrave Macmillan.

Ehrenreich, B. (2018) 'What is socialist feminism?', *Jacobin Magazine,* 30 July. Available at: https://jacobinmag.com/2018/07/socialist-feminism-barbara-ehrenreich [accessed 20 September 2018].

Featherstone, B. (2001) 'Where to for feminist social work?', *Critical Social Work*, vol 2, no 1. Available at: www1.uwindsor.ca/criticalsocialwork/where-to-for-feminist-social-work [accessed 20 September 2018].

Finlayson, L., Jenkins, K. and Worsdale, R. (2018) '"I'm not transphobic, but…": A feminist case against the feminist case against trans inclusivity', blog post, *VERSO*, 17 October. Available at: www.versobooks.com/blogs/4090-i-m-not-transphobic-but-a-feminist-case-against-the-feminist-case-against-trans-inclusivity [accessed 7 August 2019].

Garthwaite, K. (2014) 'Fear of the brown envelope: exploring welfare reform with long-term sickness benefits recipients', *Social Policy and Administration*, vol 48, no 7, pp 782–98.

Gringeri, C., Wahab, S. and Anderson-Nathe, B. (2010) 'What makes it feminist?', *Affilia*, vol 25, no 4, pp 390–405.

Grootegoed, E. and Smith, M. (2018) 'The emotional labour of austerity: how social workers reflect and work on their feelings towards reducing support to needy children and families', *British Journal of Social Work*, vol 48, no 7, pp 1929–47.

Hudson-Sharp, N. (2018) *Transgender Awareness in Child and Family Social Work Education*, Research Report, London: Department for Education.

IFSW (International Federation of Social Workers) (2012) 'Poverty eradication and the role for social workers', 23 February. Available at: https://www.ifsw.org/poverty-eradication-and-the-role-for-social-workers/ [accessed 20 September 2018].

Jackson, S. (2018) '"Women quite unknown": working-class women in the suffrage movement', *British Library* (6 February). Available at: https://www.bl.uk/votes-for-women/articles/women-quite-unknown-working-class-women-in-the-suffrage-movement [accessed 20 September 2018].

Lymbery, M. (2014) 'Austerity, personalisation and older people: the prospects for creative social work practice in England', *European Journal of Social Work*, vol 17, no 3, pp 367–82.

Manners, P. (2019) 'Trans inclusion in women only spaces', *CONCEPT*, vol 10, no 1, pp 1–18. Available at: http://concept.lib.ed.ac.uk/article/view/3000/3986

Mattheys, K. (2015) 'The Coalition, austerity and mental health', *Disability and Society*, vol 3, no 3, pp 475–8.

McLaughlin, J. (2003) *Feminist Social and Political Theory: Contemporary Debate and Dialogues*, Basingstoke: Palgrave Macmillan.

Morriss, L. (2018) 'Haunted futures: The stigma of being a mother living apart from her child(ren) as a result of state-ordered court removal', *The Sociological Review Monographs*, vol 66, no 4, pp 816–31.

Mulinari, D. and Neergaard, A. (2017) 'Doing racism, performing femininity: women in the Sweden Democrats', in M. Köttig, R. Bitzan and A. Petö (eds), *Gender and Far Right Politics in Europe*, Basingstoke: Palgrave Macmillan.

O'Brien, M. and Kyprianou, P. (2017) *Just Managing? What It Means for the Families of Austerity Britain*, Cambridge: Open Book Publishers.

Orme, J. (2002) 'Social work: gender, care and justice', *British Journal of Social Work*, vol 32, no 6, pp 799–814.

Patil, V. (2013) 'From patriarchy to intersectionality: a transnational feminist assessment of how far we've really come', *Signs*, vol 38, no 4, pp 847–67.

Patrick, R. (2017) *For Whose Benefit? The Everyday Realities of Welfare Reform*, Bristol: Policy Press.

Phillips, R. and Cree, V. (2014) 'What does the "fourth wave" mean for teaching feminism in twenty-first century social work?', *Social Work Education*, vol 33, no 7, pp 930–43.

Rivers, N. (2017) *Postfeminism(s) and the Arrival of the Fourth Wave: Turning Tides*, Basingstoke: Palgrave Macmillan.

Rogers, M. (2019) 'Challenging cisgenderism through trans people's narratives of domestic violence and abuse', *Sexualities*, vol 22, no 5–6, pp 803–20.

Salam, M. (2019) 'This is what a feminist country looks like', *New York Times*. Available at: https://www.nytimes.com/2019/03/08/world/europe/international-womens-day-feminism.html [accessed 3 April 2019].

Salem, S. (nd) 'Sisterhood', *International Political Economy of Everyday Life*. Available at: http://i-peel.org/homepage/sisterhood/ [accessed 20 September 2018].

Sanders-McDonagh, E., Neville, L. and Nolas, S.-M. (2016) 'From pillar to post: understanding the victimisation of women and children who experience domestic violence in an age of austerity', *Feminist Review*, vol 112, no 1, pp 60–76.

Sandhu, K., Stephenson, M.A. and Harrison, J. (2013) *Layers of Inequality: A Human Rights and Equality Impact Assessment of the Public Spending Cuts on Black Asian and Minority Ethnic Women in Coventry*, Coventry: Coventry Women's Voices, Coventry Ethnic Minority Action Partnership, Foleshill Women's Training and the Centre for Human Rights in Practice, School of Law, University of Warwick.

Saulnier, C. (1996) *Feminist Theories and Social Work: Theories and Applications*, New York: Routledge.

Schilt, K. and Westbrook, L. (2009) 'Doing gender, doing heteronormativity: "gender normals", transgender people, and the social maintenance of heterosexuality', *Gender and Society*, vol 23, no 4, pp 440–64.

Sisterhood and After Research Team (2013) 'Equal pay and equality legislation', *British Library* (8 March). Available at: https://www.bl.uk/sisterhood/articles/equal-pay-and-equality-legislation#authorBlock1 [accessed 20 September 2018].

Solomon, D. (2009) 'Fourth wave feminism', *New York Times*, 9 November. Available at: www.nytimes.com/2009/11/15/magazine/15fob-q4-t.html?_r=0 [accessed 20 September 2018].

Walby, S. (1990) *Theorising Patriarchy*, Oxford: Basil Blackwell.

West, C. and Zimmerman, D. (2002) 'Doing gender', in S. Fenstermaker and C. West (eds), *Doing Gender, Doing Difference: Inequality, Power and Institutional Change*, London: Routledge, pp 3–24.

Women's Budget Group (2016) *A Cumulative Gender Impact Assessment of Ten Years of Austerity Policies*. Available at: https://wbg.org.uk/wp-content/uploads/2016/03/De_HenauReed_WBG_GIAtaxben_briefing_2016_03_06.pdf [accessed 20 September 2018].

Yeadon-Lee, T. (2016) 'What's the story? Exploring online narratives of non-binary gender identities', *The International Journal of Interdisciplinary Social and Community Studies*, vol 11, no 2, pp 19–34.

PART II

Social and political contexts of practice

Introduction to Part II

Sarah Pollock

The second part of this book explores how the different political ideologies presented in the first part influence contemporary social work practice. Each chapter explores a different area of social work provision and encourages readers to think critically about the role undertaken by social workers and care professionals.

Since the creation of the welfare state after the Second World War, local authorities have consistently reorganised the way support is provided. Many factors have influenced these restructurings, including political ideology, child deaths, the media and the economic climate.

Historical context

The creation of the post-war welfare state in Britain was based on the principle of secure 'cradle-to-grave' care for all who required it. The Beveridge Report, published in 1942, identified the 'five giant evils of society': want, squalor, disease, idleness and ignorance. The author, William Beveridge, proposed that the development of a welfare state was necessary to eliminate these evils and, following the end of the Second World War, the newly elected Labour government introduced a number of laws in order to develop his proposals and form the welfare state:

- the Education Act 1944
- the Family Allowances Act 1945
- the National Health Service Act 1946
- the New Towns Act 1947
- the National Insurance Act 1948
- the National Assistance Act 1948.

In combination, it was hoped this legislation would ensure that education, health, care and adequate housing were provided to the whole population, alongside introducing measures to protect people financially during periods of unemployment. In addition, the Children Act 1948 established children's services as a separate provision, soon followed by the creation of local authority mental health departments.

The 1950s and 1960s are often described as a period of 'social consensus', with the social democratic welfare state operating to ensure security for the people of Britain and social work services for children, adults and mental health support provided separately (Alcock and May, 2014). However, reports began to indicate that inequality still existed, particularly in relation to the existence of poverty, which the welfare state had hoped and government had pledged to eliminate. Abel-Smith and Townsend (1965) suggested that the redefinition of poverty as relative to the community, rather than absolute (that is, not having enough resources to survive), revealed that the problem remained hidden rather than reduced, disguising the failure of the social democratic welfare state system. The authors discovered a substantial number of families living in poverty, including working people, and poverty specifically affecting children and older people.

The increased presence of activism and equal rights campaigning throughout the 1960s further indicated the presence of inequality within the social democratic system, with the disability rights movement having particular relevance for social work. In 1965 the conclusions of the Seebohm Report challenged the ideology of social consensus and recommended the uniting of social work services into generic social services departments in order to support families more holistically. These recommendations were enshrined in the Local Authority Social Services Act 1970.

Throughout the 1970s and 1980s media attention focused on the deaths of children in receipt of social work support, including Maria Colwell in 1973 and Jasmine Beckford in 1985, directing the focus of children and families work towards child protection and away from generic practice. Adult protection, on the other hand, remained excluded from statutory duties until the introduction of the Care Act 2014. The introduction of the Children Act in 1989 and the National Health Service and Community Care Act (NHSCCA) in 1990 further established the division between the two services and introduced competition into service provision in the adult care sector.

Adult social care has always differed from children and families and mental health provision in its means-tested nature. This means that, unlike other forms of support, adults in need of care are required to contribute to the costs on a scale based on their income. The introduction of the NHSCCA 1990 by the Conservative government enabled independent organisations to bid for contracts to provide this funded care on a larger scale and introduced the role of 'care coordinators' to manage this externally provided support.

The media in the early 2000s continued to highlight child deaths, including those of Victoria Climbié (2000), Peter Connelly (Baby P) (2007) and Daniel Pelka (2012), increasing public awareness and centring publicity on the social work profession (Butler and Drakeford, 2005). The interaction between political ideology and the media is encapsulated in the public firing of Sharon Shoesmith (Director of Haringey Children's Services at the time of Peter Connelly's death) by then Secretary of State Ed Balls during a press conference in 2008.

Current context

Since the Conservative-led Coalition government's decision to implement a regime of austerity in 2010, local authorities, voluntary and charitable organisations have felt the impact of significant cuts in funding. This has seen the reduction of some services and the closure of others, with local authorities attempting to make the required 'efficiency savings' by merging provision and selling premises.

The introduction of the Care Act 2014 in England and Wales advanced previous policies that encouraged adult social care and health to integrate. Local authorities have undertaken this task in many different ways, with some choosing to collocate and merge completely with health colleagues and others retaining separate spaces and closer links with children's services, including in some cases shared management structures. Critics of integration have associated this with financial motives rather than the wellbeing of those receiving services (Beresford, 2014) and have levelled the same criticism at initiatives such as strengths- and asset-based practice. These methods involve connecting people with community provision; however, many such services have closed, due to austerity measures, leading critics to question the integrity and motivation of such schemes.

Contemporary social work practice is a challenging landscape in which austerity measures have hit those living in precarious circumstances hardest (see Part III of this volume), both by increasing poverty levels and forcing cuts to the services they depend on. Since their introduction, welfare state services have been structured to function separately, restructured to align together, separated to focus on different challenges and, currently, integrated with health and other allied professions while undergoing strict efficiency savings and seeing an increase in the numbers of those requiring support.

Chapters in this part

The chapters in this part explore the challenges described above in more detail for each area of practice; however, it is important to remember that in order to maintain best practice as a professional it is essential to understand the overlaps between practice arenas. The findings of serious case reviews and inquiries are consistently that communication has failed between and within organisations, and readers are therefore advised to consider the chapters as interconnected in their approach.

Themes such as poverty, austerity, use of power and the impact of different ideological perspectives on how power is used are common across each chapter. Theorists such as Bourdieu, Hall and Foucault describe how the distribution of capital, development of discourses and the perpetuation of systems of representation oppress those with limited access to resources. These social constructionist theories are applicable across the different fields of social welfare and are often seen in combination, with families and individuals experiencing multiple disadvantages.

References

Abel–Smith, B. and Townsend, P. (1965) *The Poor and the Poorest, A New Analysis of the Ministry of Labour's Family Expenditure Surveys of 1953–54 and 1960*, London: G. Bell & Sons Ltd.

Alcock, P. and May, M. (2014) *Social Policy in Britain*, 4th edn, London: Palgrave Macmillan.

Beresford, P. (2014) *Personalisation*, Bristol: Policy Press.

Beveridge, W. (1942) *Social Insurance and Allied Services (The Beveridge Report)*, London: HMSO.

Butler, I. and Drakeford, M. (2005) *Scandal, Social Policy and Social Welfare*, 2nd edn, Bristol: Policy Press.

Seebohm, F. (1968) *Report of the Committee on Local Authority and Allied Personal Social Services (The Seebohm Report)*, London: HMSO.

6

Social work with adults

Alex Withers and Sarah Pollock

Introduction

This chapter is not intended to be a complete history of social work practice with adults – comprehensive historical accounts can be found elsewhere. Rather, this is an attempt to explore how social work practice has reflected and been influenced by politics and ideology since 1945. It hardly needs saying that British society has undergone a complete transformation since 1945 and the social work practice which takes place in this society has been transformed with it. This chapter will provide some of the background to practice: the prevailing political ideologies of these times.

Harris (2008) states that 'changes to social work are never purely professional matters. They always connect with wider social, economic and political currents.' In some sense, you might say, the history of political ideology from 1945 onwards demonstrates how social work came to be shaped in the way that it has been. Social work does not take place in a vacuum but in a living, dynamic society. Examining the course of what has taken place in that society since 1945 helps us to move towards an understanding of our current position and will also, hopefully, encourage critique. We certainly don't wish to denigrate the undoubted successes and advances of 1945 but, as Hall ([1960] 2017) beautifully illustrates, 'If we find an old people's home where there are carpets on the floor, we think – 'Good: this is what it should be like.' But is it? Suppose we stopped and asked 'Is that good enough? Is that what old age should look like for the thousands in our institutions?'' There is no place for complacency, and we believe that the critique of the welfare state is in some senses the critique of social work which takes place within its borders. Should we, as social workers, ask for further-reaching and comprehensive change to society, or to settle with what we are given?

We will explore how developments in policy and legislation reflect dominant ideology (for instance, the individuating effect of the Care Act 2014) in the era of neoliberalism and contrive to produce potentially positive impacts for service users that move away from the universal approach of the welfare state. Given the stated intention of putting people's wellbeing at the centre of practice, can such developments be said to contribute to the precarity of service users – again leading to the question whether social work is merely a reflection of the dominant political ideology? Yet the idea that social work has blindly followed prevailing ideological trends is far from correct. Often the ideologies of the era pushed social work into places that were a poor fit with its stated values or intentions, and so, we will investigate ways in which social work has been part of or has followed alternative discourses distinct from the prevailing political ideologies since 1945.

Social work and the welfare state development (1945–75)

Beveridge

The Labour government established the welfare state from 1945 onwards, the government's programme putting the following major pieces of legislation in place:

- the Family Allowances Act 1945
- the National Health Service Act 1946
- the National Insurance Act 1948
- the National Assistance Act 1948.

As Green and Clarke (2016) set out, social work was very much an afterthought, as opposed to an integral part of the new system. Its position was as part of the state and yet outside of it, part of state apparatus and yet opposed to it, paternalistic but, as time went on, incorporating ideas such as feminism and empowerment that were diametrically opposed to this position. Social work's development in this way can be attributed to Beveridge's belief in cradle-to-grave comprehensive provision, which excluded the notion of social work (Payne, 2005). The financial expediency of the government was also influential (spending on the welfare state reached only 10% of gross domestic product by 1950, significantly below spending in Belgium and West Germany (Payne, 2005)). This all had an impact on social work's development and how it interacted with the dominant ideologies of the era within which it functioned. The way in which social work as a profession developed, in a piecemeal fashion, can be said to reflect its ambiguous position within the welfare state.

Post-war developments

Many developments shaped the way that social work progressed. However, three key recommendations were central.

1. In 1957 Younghusband recommended that a 'general purpose social worker' be introduced, in response to what was perceived as a complicated profusion of services that often replicated each other's roles (Younghusband Report, 1959).
2. The Seebohm Committee of 1965 proposed that the merger of existing social services into specific social services departments should take place (Payne,

2005). The Seebohm Report (1968) sought to move social work from its original position 'to the centre of social welfare and to widen citizenship entitlement to social work, seen as part of the evolution towards more social rights' (Payne, 2005).

3. As part of this move of 'social work' to a cohesive, regulated profession the British Association of Social Workers (1970) and the Central Council for Education and Training in Social Work (1971) were established.

Critique of consensus

It is undoubtedly the case that the welfare state, as created and sustained by social democracy and the post-war settlement, lessened precarity for millions of people and transformed how British society functions. Despite the massive and substantive achievements of this era, the British post-war consensus is not closed to critique. It can be argued that the consensus was limited in promoting widespread social change. Hall ([1957] 2017) states: 'The welfare state had valid but limited objectives in as much as it tried to redress the balance of forces in the community without affecting the hierarchies in the UK. Certain groups in society remained privileged and some oppressed. There were clearly changes to the lives of many but ultimately there was not substantial structural change to the way in which society was structured.'

For those unable to contribute, the state and state functionaries such as social workers would provide. Compared to the days of the workhouse and the Poor Law, this was a quantum leap forward, but what was provided was a safety net, and often, until the 1990s, this meant large-scale institutional care for adults. Arguably, implicit in meeting need in this way is the idea that social work was 'done to' rather than 'done with', a one-size-fits-all response to people's situations, with ideas of individuation and personalisation being ignored in favour of universal provision. As the experiences of people with disabilities and/or mental health issues and the elderly demonstrate, experiencing abuse, institutionalisation and neglect by the institutions of the welfare state through its apparent 'golden age' (Beresford, 2016), there was a sense that little had changed post-1945 (Bamford, 2015).

Homogeneity or diversity?

Beresford (2016) argues that, for all its benefits, the welfare state was 'implemented by a narrow white male political and policy elite' and that it therefore 'perpetuated the exclusion from and marginalisation of women, gay, bisexual [...] black and minority ethnic groups and disabled people'. This author goes on to describe how women were seen as inferior in the labour market and consequently were paid less. In addition, people with disabilities were restricted to 'marginal roles' (Beresford, 2016). The old orders of class, race, gender and inequality remained intact in this context.

Disengagement theory

An example of how social work has been complicit in the economic expediency that is arguably inherent in the welfare state is disengagement theory. Scragg (2012) states that 'disengagement theory described the assumed natural process of decline as the older person disengaged from society'. Disengagement theory perpetuates the idea that a sense of usefulness becomes outlived in a person's life cycle. While critique of disengagement theory exists, the theory arguably reflects the notion of utility (inherent in the idea of the welfare state) that as someone moves towards death they themselves compensate for their lack of 'use' by withdrawing from the public and family life in which they live. Scragg (2012) makes this link more explicit in his assertion that a view exists that 'older people are wealth consumers rather than wealth creators', and goes on to set out how concerns about the ageing UK population and talk of pension crises have led to increases in the age of retirement.

Care versus control

McLaughlin (2008, p 142) states that 'there is no getting away from the fact that Social Work, in the main, is an activity that takes place within a state agency with one of its functions as being responsible for maintaining the status quo'. He refers to the work of Davies (1981, in McLaughlin, 2008), who characterises the role of social work as being inherently conservative, concerned as it is with maintaining society by 'providing provision for those who are unable to provide for themselves'. 'Social work' is, arguably, a conservative part of the state apparatus, developing and evolving as the state that fostered it matures.

Yet there was also a contradiction here, which put social work in a curious position. As Parry and Parry (1979, in McLaughlin, 2008) set out, 'Social workers were to be neither autonomous professionals nor bureaucratic functionaries; social work was to exist in its own right, within the shell of local government administration, as a form of bureau-professionalism.' Independent yet not quite, part of the state but also not. Social work can be said to reflect the limitations of the welfare state itself. On the one hand, social work (and the welfare state) can be said to sustain: it provides support for people at critical points in their lives and, at its best, it helps to empower and promotes equality; on the other hand, social work (and the welfare state) regulate and restrict, and promote social control.

Adult social work and neoliberalism (1975–2008)

This period had profound and far-reaching consequences for British society and social work. The year 1975 marks the beginning of the shift away from the dominance of British political ideology and public life by the post-war consensus and social democracy and, arguably, marks the beginning of the end of the 'welfare state settlements of the post war period' (Bamford, 2015). (For a full discussion of neoliberalism and a definition refer to Chapter 4.)

Thatcherism and social work

On coming to power in 1979 Thatcher's Conservative government ensured that the market became the focus; the state would be rolled back and, with it, welfare provision, as individual responsibility, choice and freedom were to be prioritised. The domination of political ideology by neoliberalism meant that the politics of Thatcherism had an extremely wide-ranging effect on society, resulting in mass unemployment and greater inequality across society.

The government waged war against the trade unions, culminating in the miners' strike of 1985, and set about privatising industries, and changing employment law and trade union legislation (Ferguson, 2008). The defeat of the miners and collectivism – something that had defined politics since 1945 (Ferguson, 2008) – led, arguably, to the wholesale dismantling of the post-war consensus, including ideas implicit in it such as the 'one-size-fits-all' traditional welfare response (Ferguson, 2008). Social work taking place in this new terrain changed too, in response both to the change in political ideology and to the subsequent changes in society.

The Barclay Commission

After Thatcher's election in 1979, as Rogowski (2010) outlines, there were few changes for social work. The then Secretary of State commissioned an inquiry into the roles and tasks of social workers, and the recommendations of the Barclay Commission were published in 1982 as the Barclay Report. The Barclay Commission identified two main areas of social work: relationship-based work with individuals and community social work in 'communities', which went beyond the idea of just helping individuals themselves. These fitted in with structuralist interpretations of the world implied in social democracy, but also undercut the centralisation and bureaucracy inherent in services (Rogowski 2010; Bamford, 2015). Many in social work thought that the Barclay Report vindicated the idea of community social work, although its recommendations were not universally deployed (Rogowski, 2010).

The Griffiths Report and National Health Service and Community Care Act (NHSCCA) 1990

As the 1980s progressed, attention focused on public sector services and how they operated. Profound change for work with adults came in the form of the NHSCCA 1990. Sir Roy Griffiths had been asked to produce a report on the problems of the NHS. In 1988 he produced a Green Paper called 'Community Care: Agenda for Action', commonly known as the Griffiths Report (Griffiths,

1998). Griffiths' background as chairperson of the supermarket Sainsbury's is crucial, as the report itself can be said to reflect the market-driven neoliberal agenda of the business world (Ferguson, 2008). The report led to the NHSCCA 1990.

The introduction of the Act marked fundamental change for how social work was practised with all adults, and the environment that it operated in. The main changes were:

1. a move from residential care to care at home
2. a move from social services' role as a provider of care to a commissioner of care, otherwise known as the purchaser/provider split.

This introduced the concept of the market into social provision for the first time. Ferguson (2008) demonstrates how social work reflects the prevailing ideology of neoliberalism by the change in the role of social workers and their characterisation as 'care managers' 'managing' packages of care for 'clients'. Implicit in this idea of managing care packages is a shift away from the standardisation of social work provision in the era of social democracy. Gone is the idea of 'universal provision' as a response to structural inequality (Green and Clarke, 2016), replaced by the notion of individualisation that is inherent in neoliberalism.

New Labour (1997–2010): risk and risk management

New Labour sought to move welfare from the 'one-size-fits-all statist approach' to one that was increasingly centred around the individual. Harris (2008) sets out how this was a development from individualist approaches to practice which coincided with the move towards psychodynamic practice in the late 1950s. These had been challenged in the 1970s by the radical social work movement which identified that the issues that people experienced were caused by structural disadvantages in society. Yet increasingly in the New Labour era, those who were not 'fixed' were seen as 'to blame' for their own shortcomings, something that mirrored the individualistic ideology of neoliberalism. This focus on the individual was reflected by the perception that social work was a way in which people's 'problems' could be managed. This is illustrated by the increasing preoccupation during the New Labour era with risk and risk management. Whilst neoliberal ideology assumes that individuals will make rational choices about their wellbeing (Bamford, 2015) this approach takes little or no account of the structural reasons why people may be indulging in 'risk' behaviour in the first place, stressing instead their own agency to address the issues.

CASE STUDY 6.1: SOCIAL WORK WITH ADDICTION

In the field of social work with addiction, New Labour's massive investment in drug treatment was part of the national drug strategy, Tackling Drugs to Build a Better Britain (1998). It can be argued that, by funding services to deliver treatment to individuals, and despite the strategy's stated intention of addressing underlying social issues associated with drug use, New Labour's adoption of neoliberal economic policies exacerbated the conditions that led to addiction in the first place.

Current practice (2008–present)

The Human Rights Act 1998 and the Mental Capacity Act 2005

The Mental Capacity Act is a key piece of legislation used by social workers with adults in England. The central rationale of the Act is to enshrine the rights of the individual and help to protect them against abuse. Social workers can use the legislation to consider people's previously expressed wishes in instances where they do not have capacity to make specific decisions – for example, about housing or finances. Even in situations where someone is profoundly affected the person can still be involved in the planning of their care.

If we compare social work in the neoliberal era in the context of the Care Act 2014 and the Human Rights Act 1998 with the social democratic era of the National Assistance Act 1948, we can contrast social work practice 'done with' service users and social work 'done to' service users. For example, section 47 of the National Assistance Act 1948 'gives power to a local authority to apply to a magistrates' court to remove a person from home on the grounds that: the person is suffering from grave chronic disease or being aged, infirm or physically incapacitated is living in unsanitary conditions'. The invasiveness of this should be immediately apparent, and can be said to reflect the paternalist statist approach to mainstream 'social work' in the social democratic era – 'done to', not 'done with'. The Human Rights Act 1998 and the Mental Capacity Act 2005 can be said to reflect the move from the 'universalist' or collectivist approach of the social democratic era to the individualism of the neoliberal era.

The introduction of this legislation could be viewed as a further advancement of the 'individual'. However, neoliberalism is not about the advancement of individual rights as it claims. As Heartfield (2002) states of the Conservative era in Britain: 'Political assessments of the Thatcher era are confused in taking at face value the Conservative claim to have been the party that stressed individual liberty [...] the Conservatives showed an instinctive hostility to civil liberties across the board.' Neoliberalism in fact seeks the opposite.

Self-neglect and the Mental Capacity Act 2005

In my career as a social worker working with adults with substance misuse issues, the Mental Capacity Act 2005 (MCA) has been one of the pieces of legislation that has most shaped my practice. My work frequently brings me into contact with people who are experiencing very significant issues around self-neglect.

Prior to the Human Rights Act and MCA, on encountering people in such situations, technically, I would have been able to use the National Assistance Act to *make* changes in their lives. My social work response *could* have been a 'one-size-fits-all' approach to their situation, but since the MCA there exist a series of checks and balances that aim to safeguard the individual and ensure that their wishes and feelings are taken into account. Under the MCA, 'people have the right to make eccentric or unwise decisions'. In a case where a person does not have the capacity to make a specific decision the primacy of the individual and their rights is further safeguarded by the appointment of an Independent Mental Capacity Advocate, who is appointed to act for the person as part of the best interest process.

Direct Payments

Service user movements can also be said to reflect the concern of neoliberalism with 'the individual', but for service user movements this is about the 'rights' of a person and is concerned, among other issues, with independent living, self-organisation and 'people wanting to speak for themselves' (Green and Clarke, 2016), as opposed to promoting 'the individual as the best way to advance the needs of the market' (Ferguson, 2008). For two decades before their introduction, part of the demand of disability activists had been for Direct Payments. Direct Payments (DPs) are where 'social service departments give money directly to individuals to buy the support they had been assessed as needing instead of providing the services themselves' (Rogowski, 2010). This again moves social work practice to the realm of 'done with' as opposed to 'done to' as, at least hypothetically, the service user can choose their carer and have a greater degree of autonomy than before (Ferguson, 2008). However, numerous issues can be taken with this position.

Service users with DPs have to take over the responsibility of running their own care package, with all that this entails, such as finding, recruiting and managing carers and managing budgets (Rogowski, 2010). While the locus of social work has been moved away from the universalist state to the individual, this is far from a universally positive situation. While it could be said that with the introduction of DPs the state seeks to empower individuals, it is more arguable that this is a way of removing what the state perceives as dependence and exposes people with complex needs to a new level of issues. The experience of service users here also demonstrates that, contrary to the individualisation of neoliberalism, the 'collective' approach is still vital. Heartfield (2002) states that 'collective organisations are not a barrier to individual self-assertiveness. On the contrary, most people use such collective bodies as an arena in which their personal ambitions are advanced.' It is through collective action that individual lives are transformed. Commentators such as McLaughlin (2008) have argued that the state's co-option of activists' demands has disinvested the claims of their radical agenda.

Austerity

The financial crisis of 2008 saw a major worldwide challenge to capitalism and neoliberalism. While there was a significant challenge as set out, this moment had far-reaching ramifications. Hall explains that 'The financial crisis has been used by many western governments as a means of further entrenching the neoliberal model. They have adopted swingeing austerity measures which they claim are the only way of reducing the deficits [...] they have launched an assault on the incomes, living standards and conditions of life of the less well off in society [...] it has encouraged private capital to hollow-out the welfare state and dismantle the structures of health, welfare and education' (Hall et al, 2015).

Austerity has had major implications for social work since the financial crisis as 'the disintegration of public services reached destructive levels' (Rustin, 2017). As Cooper and Whyte (2017) state: 'in the first 5 years of austerity local authority budgets were cut by 40 percent amounting to an estimated £18bn in care provision'. This was the new context for social work. It is important that austerity is seen as an ideological choice in the same way that neoliberalism is. While austerity can exist separately from neoliberalism, and vice versa, it is vital that austerity is seen in the context of the small-state, personal-responsibility ethos put forward by neoliberalism.

The Care Act 2014 and strengths-based approaches

The Care Act

In current practice the Care Act 2014 is central to social work with adults. Wellbeing is the underpinning principle of the Act. Stanley (2016) writes that 'Wellbeing is at the heart of the Care Act, and I think best conceptualised through a human-rights and asset-based lens.' He goes on to say: 'ostensibly, the Care Act 2014 is something that promotes individualism from a rights perspective and helps social work to practise in way that sees people as individuals away from a one size fits all welfare statist approach'. However, in the age of government-imposed austerity it can also be seen as a matter of good practice obscuring bad ideology. Looking at people's 'assets' or 'strengths' has been a part of social work practice since the late 19th century. Bamford (2015) writes that 'We see the beginnings of what would today be termed a strengths-based approach, building resilience by a focus on the positive elements in the social situation rather than the deficit of individuals.'

Strengths-based approaches

In the application of strengths and wellbeing, we need to be mindful of the economic and social context in which social work currently takes place. The approach has much political and practice-based support, with the Principal Social Worker for Adults in England, Lyn Romeo, a key advocate. However, since the advent of neoliberalism many of the resources that people have drawn on as assets in their communities have disappeared. Since the late 1970s there has been a systematic dismantling of organisations like trade unions, an increase in precarity in people's employment, increases in homelessness and huge reductions in public spending, as illustrated above. Yet social workers and service users are now expected to look for sources of support in these communities. As Gray (2011) states, this takes an 'optimistic view of community and social capital,' as the resources in themselves have to exist. This point is powerfully illustrated in *Maerdy: 30 Years On* (Coalfields Regeneration Trust, 2016), a documentary about a Welsh coalmining town which explores the legacy of the closure of its pit. In the video there is a scene where two women discuss the subsequent closure of local resources or 'assets', including the local library. It is hard to see how asset-based social work can take place in such a context, in a community that, in the year 2016, does not have something as basic as a *library*. In 2016 the Library Campaign, a national charity championing the need for local libraries as community assets, reported over 1,000 local library closures since 2009.

Three conversations

Strengths-based models such as 'Three Conversations' (http://partners4change. co.uk/) also undermine any sense of collective responsibility for the issues and areas in which social work finds itself. The question from the model 'How can I connect you to things that will help you get on with your life – based on your assets, strengths and those of your family?' asks the person to seek support from contacts that in the current context are likely not to be able to provide support. Eribon (2018) states: 'Any philosophy or sociology that begins by placing at the centre of its project the point of view of the actors […] does nothing more than perpetuate the world as it stands.' In addition, the use of models of practice created by private companies and commissioned by local authorities with little by way of independent, peer-reviewed evidence echoes the neoliberal ethos of social workers as care coordinators.

We must stress, again, that seeking to work with individuals' lived experience is a positive approach, but it is clearly an approach which stresses the role of the individual away from the collective responsibility of the state and that can be said to not address the structural explanations of poverty, class and gender which all influence the person and their experience. The individual may change, but the underlying issues remain the same.

CASE STUDY 6.2: DISABILITY RIGHTS AND THE LAW

The idea that the Care Act 2014 enables good practice to disguise bad politics is illustrated by the case of Luke Davey.[1]

Davey is a quadriplegic man who was in receipt of a care package of £1,651 per week, including a contribution of £730 through the Independent Living Fund (ILF). However, after the ILF closed Oxfordshire Council proposed reducing his budget to £950 per week.

The social worker said in their assessment that the best way for Luke to reduce his anxiety was for him to increase his independence, including spending time alone. Mr Davey said that the proposed personal budget would not meet his needs and told the court that two of the council's reasons for making the cut posed a risk to his wellbeing. He argued that the change would be in breach of the council's duties under the Care Act 2014, including the section 1 requirement to promote a person's wellbeing when making decisions about their care.

The judge ruled against Davey, setting out that the council had met its duty under the Care Act.

The Disabled People Against Cuts campaign group was formed in response to the cuts in funding and subsequent care provision. In response to Luke Davey's case in 2017 they stated that the case clearly showed that in the age of austerity, when local authorities have to find significant savings, the provisions of the Care Act 2014 concerned with notions of choice and control 'do not have teeth'. They stated further that the case showed the limitations of 'wellbeing duty'. Again, in Davey's case it is possible to see how, while the Act may assert that it is about the rights of the individual, at worst, it can be said to be a cover for neoliberal ideology and government-imposed austerity.

During the case, Oxfordshire Council accepted that Davey had experienced anxiety when left alone in the past. However, his social worker said that she had assessed that Davey's need, and the best way to reduce his anxiety was to develop greater independence rather than to never spend time alone. Justice Morris acknowledged that Davey had suffered 'serious anxiety and panic attacks' when left alone in the past, but he was satisfied that the council had considered the risk to his psychological wellbeing. He concluded the council had met its duty under section 1 of the Care Act and that the social worker's assessment could not be 'Wednesbury' unreasonable[2] as this was a matter for her professional judgement. On the risk of Davey losing his established care team due to his having to reduce their pay and conditions, Justice Morris found that the council had met its section 1 duty to 'have regard' to all of the individual's circumstances. He found that the council had 'consistently recorded' that it was important to Davey to retain his existing care team. He added that there was 'no sufficient evidence' that the changes in pay and conditions had resulted, or would result, in the break-up of that team.

Conclusion

This chapter has explored the historical context within which contemporary social work practice has been based. The move from social democratic models of support, through neoliberal care management to the strengths-based focus of current practice has been explored and connected to the political and ideological developments in the landscape of social care and more generally. Social work with adults is unique, as empowerment and the prioritising of choice and control are crucial to good practice. However, the economic and ideological restrictions on practitioners mean that they are challenged in fulfilling these value-based requirements. The Luke Davey case exemplifies these challenges and the detrimental effects that they can have on those relying on the support of social workers.

Critical questions

1 As a social worker who are you responsible to: the person you are working for or the organisation you are working for?

2 Think about the different areas of social work. Consider how work in these areas may be construed as control. How might this conflict with social work values of empowerment and anti-discriminatory practice?

3 Consider that while you may work for an employer, you are an independently registered professional, who signs up to a code of conduct that is entirely separate from, and may contradict, what your employer wants you to do. How do you think you would or could manage this conflict?

4 The underpinning principle of the Care Act 2014 is the wellbeing principle. Considering this, does the case of Luke Davey fit in with the stated aims of the Care Act? Does Mr Davey's case contradict this?

5 How does Luke Davey's case fit in with the strengths approach? What positives and negatives does it demonstrate about this approach?

Further reading

- Beresford, P. (2016) *All Our Welfare: Towards Participatory Social Policy*, Bristol: Policy Press.
  This text by Peter Beresford, a well-known academic and activist for users' rights, presents an alternative to the current welfare system. The book challenges existing welfare regimes in order to advocate fully participatory social policies that acknowledge lived experience and expertise.

- Ferguson, I. (2008) *Reclaiming Social Work*, London: Sage.
  Despite being written over a decade ago, Ferguson's book presents a clear, accessible and lasting message about the tensions between social work values and the current neoliberal social welfare system. This book offers guidance on managing these tensions and focuses on the social justice aspects of social work practice.

- Fook, J. (2016) *Social Work: A Critical Approach to Practice* (3rd edn), London: Sage.
  Fook's text explores critical social work and the contribution that this approach can provide for social work practitioners. This third edition provides up-to-date discussions about the current context of practice, and considers the theoretical underpinning of the critical social work movement, presenting ideas to inform new practices informed by social justice and rights-based positions.

- Hall, S. (2017) *Selected Political Writings*, Durham, NC: Duke University Press.
  Stuart Hall was a sociologist, cultural theorist and activist who advanced theory relating to power, identity and discrimination, among many other academic and social justice-related disciplines. This book is a collection of his explicitly political writings that will be of interest to readers wanting to explore how theory can be applied to political decision making and how this is influenced by issues such as ethnicity, 'race' and power.

References

Bamford, T. (2015) *A Contemporary History of Social Work: Learning From The Past*, Bristol: Policy Press.

Barclay Report (1982) *Social Workers: Their Role and Tasks*, London: Bedford Square Press.

Beresford, P. (2016) *All Our Welfare: Towards Participatory Social Policy*, Bristol: Policy Press.

Coalfields Regeneration Trust (2016) *Maerdy: 30 Years On*. Available at: https://www.bing.com/videos/search?q=maerdy+30+years+on&view=detail&mid=2C251108669DB2F6CF902C251108669DB2F6CF90&FORM=VIREyoutube [accessed 13 June 2019].

Cooper, V. and Whyte, D. (2017) *Austerity Demands That We Die Within Our Means* (23 May). Available at: https://www.opendemocracy.net/uk/vickie-cooper/government-austerity-demands-that-we-die-within-our-means [accessed 12 July 2018].

Eribon, D. (2018) *Returning to Reims*, London: Allen Lane.

Ferguson I. (2008) *Reclaiming Social Work*, London: Sage.

Gray, M. (2011) 'Back to basics: a critique of the strengths perspective in social work', *Families in Society: The Journal of Contemporary Human Services*, vol 92, no 1, pp 5–11.

Green, L. and Clarke, K. (2016) *Social Policy for Social Work Placing Social Work in its Wider Context*, Cambridge: Polity Press.

Griffiths, R. (1988) *Community Care: Agenda for Action*, London: HMSO.

Hall, S. ([1957]/2017) 'The new Conservatism and the old', in *Selected Political Writings* (ed S. Davison, D. Featherstone, M. Rustin and B. Schwartz), Durham, NC: Duke University Press, pp 18-27.

Hall, S. ([1960]/2017) 'The supply of demand', in *Selected Political Writings* (ed S. Davison, D. Featherstone, M. Rustin and B. Schwartz), Durham, NC: Duke University Press, pp 47–69.

Hall, S., Massey, D. and Rustin, M. (2015) *After Neoliberalism? The Kilburn Manifesto*, London: Lawrence and Wishart.

Harris, J. (2008) 'State social work: constructing the present from moments in the past', *The British Journal of Social Work*, vol 38, no 4, pp 662–79.

Heartfield, J. (2002) *The 'Death of The Subject' Explained*, Sheffield: Sheffield Hallam University Press.

McLaughlin, K. (2008) *Social Work, Politics and Society: From Radicalism to Orthodoxy*, Bristol: Policy Press.

Payne, M. (2005) *The Origins of Social Work: Continuity and Change*, Basingstoke: Palgrave Macmillan.

Rogowski, S. (2010) *Social Work: The Rise and Fall of a Profession?*, Bristol: Policy Press.

Rustin, M. (2017) 'Are real changes now possible? Where next for Corbyn and Labour?', *Soundings*, vol 66, pp 7–22.

Scragg, T. (2012) *Social Work with Older People: Approaches to Person-Centred Practice*, Maidenhead: Open University Press.

Seebohm Committee (1968) *Report of the Committee on Local Authority and Allied Personal Social Services*, Cmnd 3703, London: HMSO.

Stanley, T. (2016) 'A practice framework to support the Care Act 2014', *Journal of Adult Protection*, vol 18, no 1, pp 53–64. Available at: https://doi.org/10.1108/JAP-07–2015–0020

The Younghusband Report (1959) *Journal (Royal Society of Health)*, vol 79, no 4, doi.org/10.1177/146642405907900401

7

Child protection social work

Kate Parkinson

Introduction

This chapter examines the contemporary policy and practice of child protection social work in England. It explores the current context of child protection practice and the post-war development of child protection services, in relation both to political ideology and to the social construction of women, children and those living in poverty.

The chapter discusses the impact of poverty and inequality on child protection practice and explores Lapierre's (2007) theory of 'mother blaming' in domestic abuse cases and the low levels of engagement of fathers in child protection processes.

A discussion on the role of the media in shaping attitudes towards both social workers and families that are engaged in social work services is also presented. This discussion is followed by a case example from practice and some critical questions for students relating to the case study.

It is acknowledged that this chapter explores the above ideas and concepts only briefly and at a fundamental level. Therefore, some further reading is listed which should enable students to explore these ideas and concepts in greater depth.

Before the discussion commences, it is important to refer to the impact of devolution on social work practice. No longer is it pertinent to refer to social work in the UK as a single entity. There are now significant differences in child protection processes and practice among the devolved countries of the UK. For example, Scotland, Wales and Northern Ireland have a greater focus on early intervention and family support. The focus in England, however, appears to be on responding to risk, with high thresholds for social work intervention and a scaling back of family support and early intervention services (Vincent et al, 2010; Parton, 2014; Devaney and McConville, 2016). However, that having been said, McGhee et al (2017) in their comparative research examining child protection systems in the four countries of the UK found that, despite the different legislative, policy and practice contexts, since 2005 all four countries have shown an increasing orientation towards child protection for younger children, particularly under the category of emotional abuse. While this chapter focuses only on child protection processes in England, some further reading on child protection in the devolved countries is provided at the end of the chapter.

The current context of child protection social work

There is much written about the current child protection system in England from a critical perspective. There are some who argue that the child protection system in England is a success because very few children die as a result of abuse and neglect, as compared to other countries (Featherstone et al, 2017). However, it is widely acknowledged among social work academics and commentators that the current system is 'broken'. Many suggest that current child protection processes fail to engage with children and families in a positive and empowering way and that responses to families are punitive (Ferguson, 2011; Featherstone et al, 2014; Parton, 2014; Featherstone et al, 2017; Cummins, 2018), failing to take into account the pervasive nature of poverty and inequality and their impact on parenting (Katz et al, 2007; Bywaters et al, 2016).

Since the death of Peter Connelly in 2007 (Warner, 2013), numbers of child protection investigations have risen. Figures from the Department for Education (DfE) demonstrate that child protection investigations in England and Wales increased by 79.4% between 2009/10 and 2014/15 (DfE, 2015). This is despite the fact that child deaths as a result of abuse and neglect have decreased significantly (Featherstone et al, 2018). Care applications are also on the increase and adoption is increasingly being promoted as the 'golden ticket' for children who are removed from their families (Featherstone et al, 2014).

Parton argues that this approach to child protection in England is a mechanism of what he refers to as 'the authoritarian liberal state' (Parton, 2014, p 139). On the one hand, neoliberal ideology is concerned with reducing the level of state-provided welfare, which is evident in the welfare reforms under the (at the time of writing) current Conservative administration. However, the rhetoric and practice of neoliberalism appears to be that when considering poor and marginalised members of society, who make up the vast majority of families who are subject to child protection processes (Bywaters et al, 2016), a directive and disciplinary approach is necessary to 'police' these groups and ensure that they behave appropriately. In this sense the state becomes a mechanism for coercive control (Parton, 2014). Thus, while liberal ideology has a focus on individual freedoms, the underlying assumption is that, in order to exercise these freedoms appropriately, one needs self-control and discipline, and that the poor and the marginalised need training in these areas (Parton, 2014). This construction of poor people as 'feckless' and lacking in moral stature, the cause of their own poverty and difficulties, is one that has existed for centuries (Macnicol, 1987), and it continues to permeate into child protection responses (Katz et al, 2007; Featherstone et al, 2014; Bywaters et al, 2016; Cummins, 2018).

Indeed, there is a clear relationship between poverty and inequality and child abuse and neglect (Bywaters et al, 2016). Studies in the UK and across the globe have emphasised the impact of poverty and associated stresses on parenting (Coulton et al, 2007; Cooper and Stewart, 2013; Donkin et al, 2014; Pelton, 2015). Furthermore, research suggests that those countries with lower levels of poverty and inequality have lower levels of referrals to child protection services (Bywaters et al, 2016). However, while poverty *can* lead to abuse and neglect, the vast majority of families living in poverty do not abuse their children and/or come to the attention of child protection services (Bywaters et al, 2016). Hence, it is not as simple as stating that child abuse and neglect are caused by poverty; rather, it is the relationship between poverty and other complex factors that can either contribute to or negate the impact of poverty and inequality on parenting (Bywaters et al, 2016). Other significant factors emphasised in the research include drug and alcohol misuse, the prevalence of family violence, mental ill-health, disability, lack of social networks and support, family experiences with services and feelings of stigma and 'shame' associated with being 'poor' (Hooper et al, 2007; Cleaver et al, 2011; Farmer and Callan, 2012; Jutte et al, 2014).

Following the election of the Coalition government in 2010 and the subsequent Conservative administrations, child poverty in the UK has continued to rise, alongside an increase in the gap between the wealthiest and the poorest members of society (Child Poverty Action Group, nd; Belfield et al, 2015). In 2015/16 there were four million children living in poverty in the UK – 30% of all children. Of these, 67% were living in a household where at least one person was working (Child Poverty Action Group, nd), hence challenging the centuries-old social construction that poverty is caused by laziness.

This has undoubtedly had an impact on the numbers of children subject to child protection responses. It has raised a question about social work responses to families in poverty and whether families are being unnecessarily penalised and accused of neglecting their children when they are struggling to adequately meet the needs of their children due to a lack of financial resources and social capital. Gupta et al (2016) argue that the current Conservative government seeks to 'demonise' families in poverty and 'rescue' children from poor families by speeding up the court process and focusing on increasing adoption rates, while at the same time reducing family support services and narrowing the role of the social worker. This is compounded by the Conservative government's policy of reducing state-provided benefits, which has ensured that an increasing number of families are living in poverty and struggling to meet their children's basic needs. Evidence of this can be found in the increase in the use of foodbanks since the full roll-out of the Universal Credit scheme began in 2016. Loopstra and Lalor (2018) found that those foodbanks that had been operating in a full Universal Credit area for a year or more had seen a 52% increase in the number of people using the service. Many of those using the services were families, and in 2017/18 approximately one third of emergency food supplies were given to children.

This increase in poverty and the subsequent reported impact on child protection referrals have led to calls for social work responses that recognise and challenge the impact of poverty on families and offer support to families to overcome the impact of poverty rather than 'punish' them for not being able to cope. Krumer Nevo (2016) developed the 'poverty aware paradigm', arguing that social workers need to understand the nature of the poverty that they are facing in order to make sound ethical judgements and adhere to the principle of social justice. Furthermore, Gupta et al (2016) argue that child protection social workers have a moral imperative to think differently about how they engage with families living in poverty. This is one of the biggest challenges in contemporary practice facing child protection social workers. However, managing the impact of poverty and inequality has long been a challenge for social workers, as discussed in the historical context below.

Post-war development of child protection services

Not only did the post-war period witness the development of the NHS and the welfare state, based upon the socialist principles of the Labour government of that time, it also brought with it a major change in the structure and organisation of services to protect children. The implementation of the Children Act 1948 created an administrative framework for all children who were deprived of a 'normal home life' and led to the creation of local authority children's services departments to provide accommodation for those children identified as being in need (Parton, 2014). At this time the role of the local authority was quite narrow and focused only on providing accommodation for those children unable to live at home. Family support was not provided, as the post-war welfare state was based upon the traditional, patriarchal model of the nuclear family and full male employment. The prevailing ideology at this time was that most of the 'welfare work' in a family would be undertaken by women and that the state's role was to support this arrangement. Hence the focus was on providing accommodation for children with no women to look after them adequately (Parton, 2014). However, during the 1950s professionals increasingly began to consider that the role of the local authority was much too narrow and that there should be a focus on intervening earlier in family life and providing support to enable families to stay together. This led to the Children and Young Persons Act 1963, which placed a duty on local authorities to provide community-based services for children in need (Horner, 2012). Research at this time began to highlight the relationship between deprivation and child neglect and it was felt that by tackling these issues in the community the numbers of children entering the care system would reduce (Parton, 2014). The Seebohm Committee, which was tasked with reviewing the welfare functions of the local authority, and its resulting report (1968), called for an organised and structured response to providing family support services so as to prevent the need for care. The result was the Local Authority Social Services Act 1970, which created a generic community and family service and the new role of social worker to support families and vulnerable people in the community (Thane, 2009). One of the clearly defined roles of the new service was to tackle the issue of the emerging 'problem family', a small number of families who were regarded as creating a disproportionate number of problems in the community. Hence the labelling of poor people as 'problem' citizens needing the intervention of well-meaning professionals clearly prevailed and created a social stigma about needing the support of social care (Parton, 2014), not unlike what is evident in the child protection social work context of the 2010s.

At that time social workers were optimistic that social work intervention could change the behaviours and attitudes of these 'problem families'. Social work responses were rooted firmly in the individual taking responsibility for their own behaviour and changing their behaviour to meet societal norms. While it was acknowledged that poverty and deprivation were linked with a range of 'social problems' such as drug and alcohol misuse and family breakdown (Shildrick and Rucell, 2015), little focus was placed upon changing environmental circumstances; rather, the attitude was that poor people were 'to blame' for their circumstances (Mack and Lansley, 1985). Furthermore, the focus was on balancing the *privacy* of the family with the *public* responsibility of the state, as the prevailing ideology was still that family life should be private and that the role of the state was to support the family (meaning women) to care for their children (Parton, 2014). However, it became increasingly apparent throughout the 1970s and 1980s that this approach was not adequate to manage the increasing complexity of child protection cases faced by local authorities. The death of Maria Colwell in 1974, killed by her step-father, who was subject to a supervision order and was visited by social workers on several occasions, marked a turning point in child protection practice (Parton, 2004). Maria's death was followed by 29 other child deaths between 1974 and 1985. This, followed by the Cleveland Affair (1987), when 121 children remained in hospital against the wishes of their parents, based on unfounded suspicions that they were being sexually abused, led to criticisms that social workers were failing to intervene adequately in some circumstances and being over-zealous and protectionist in others (Richardson and Bacon, 2018). At the same time, social, economic and political changes also had an impact on attitudes towards child protection social work. An emerging children's rights movement alongside a burgeoning civil rights movement took a critical stance on over-zealous state intervention in family life in the name of welfare. This was exacerbated by the neoliberal stance of the Thatcher government, elected in 1979, with its emphasis on individual responsibility and minimum state intervention in family life. The prevailing belief was that families should take responsibility for themselves and the state should intervene with a 'strong arm' as a last resort to protect the weak, the vulnerable and wider society (Kus, 2006). It was increasingly felt that local authorities and their social workers needed some guidance to enable them to make decisions that balanced the *privacy* of the family with the duty of the local authority to intervene in the *public* interest to protect children at risk. The result was the Children Act 1989.

This significant piece of legislation was an attempt to balance the private and the public fields. The focus of the Act is on family support and working in partnership with parents to enable children to remain in the care of their families where it is safe to do so. The Act is clear that compulsory statutory intervention should be a last resort and the 'no order' principle mandates that court orders should be used when all other options have been exhausted. The legislation attempted to create a balance between *preventative* work to support families to remain together and *protection* work to protect children and potentially remove them from their families when they are experiencing or at risk of *significant harm*.

The underlying philosophy that children should remain in the care of their families where possible is clearly aligned to the neoliberal rhetoric of that time, and now, that families should take responsibility for themselves. However, the focus on providing family support services did not fit neatly with the concept of minimum state intervention and concerns were raised at the time that financial resources would not be available to provide these services (Frost, 1992). This is indeed the case in child protection practice in the 2010s, where successive Conservative governments have implemented a policy of austerity which has led to severe spending cuts in children's social care (Gallagher, 2017).

The 1990s saw a struggle by local authorities to implement the Children Act 1989, and a narrow focus on child protection tended to prevail. The *refocusing debate* following the publication of findings from Department of Health research examining child protection practices (1995) emphasised the importance of local authorities moving away from punitive child protection practices and refocusing on family support and prevention. However, throughout the 1990s local authorities struggled to maintain this balance (Parton, 2014) and this situation was compounded in 1993, following the death of two-year-old Jamie Bulger by the hands of the ten-year-old boys Jon Venables and Robert Thompson. The subsequent media outrage and the political responses that followed suggested that societal views about childhood were in crisis (Valentine, 1996) and that there needed to be a rethink about the role that the state should play in family life.

The then Shadow Home Secretary coined the phrase 'tough on crime, tough on the causes of crime' (Hoyle and Rose, 2008), and this set the tone for the newly elected New Labour government to introduce a range of interventionist policies in 1998 to support families to raise their children and overcome the impact of poverty and deprivation. This process aligns itself to the socialist principles of the Labour Party, that is, that the state should play a key role in family life to support its citizens to achieve greater equality and encourage social inclusion. Policy for children's services was focused on early intervention and prevention, with an emphasis on the importance of the early years in determining outcomes for children (Allen, 2011). Perhaps one of the most defining policies for New Labour was the Sure Start initiative, which focused on providing a range of family support services to children under the age of five and their families, with a specific focus on families in more economically challenged areas. The notion of 'targeted universalism', that is, providing services for all but targeting those that need them most (Carey and Crammond, 2017), was a cornerstone of New Labour policy and is aligned to social democratic principles. However, the New Labour approach to welfare has been described as 'the Third Way', because it balances social democratic and socialist principles with neoliberal principles of individual responsibility. The emphasis was on *the investment state* (Parton, 2014), and that state welfare should be provided to citizens to enhance the capitalist principles of profit and productivity and focus on future benefit rather than immediate need. For example, while there was a focus on supporting families there was also an emphasis on the *responsible family* and *working families*, and policies such as Sure Start, free childcare for three-year-olds and the New Deal were aimed at encouraging mothers back to work (Hirsch and Millar, 2004). The New Labour administration were also clear that they wanted to restructure and refocus children's services, with a focus on integrative services and multi-agency working.

The implementation of the Children Act 2004 emphasised that protecting children is the responsibility of all public bodies and citizens. This legislation and subsequent policy guidance clearly defined the role of education, the police and the health service in taking responsibility alongside social work departments to safeguard and protect children, and the tag line 'safeguarding is everyone's responsibility' was adopted. The *Every Child Matters* (HM Treasury, 2003) Green Paper, which preceded the Act, also emphasised the collective responsibility of society to protect children. This document outlined five outcome areas that children need to achieve in order to be safe and meet their full potential. The approach was universal and emphasised that *all* children could be at risk at some time in their lives and that government policy should be aimed at keeping all children safe, with a specific focus on those that were most at risk. Hence, the social construction of children at this time was clearly that children are vulnerable and need protecting and that families need state-provided support to care for their children effectively, particularly poor and socially excluded families.

However, the death of Peter Connelly (Baby P), aged 17 months, in 2007 and the subsequent prosecution of two men in 2008 for causing his death and of his mother for being complicit in the abuse that he experienced caused a media outrage and widespread criticism of child protection policy and practice. Right-wing commentators argued that, in focusing on universal services for children and families, the New Labour administration had shifted the balance away from child protection services, which were failing to protect children as a result. Subsequent high-profile scandals involving children's social care followed in Birmingham, Kirklees and Doncaster, all pointing to institutional and system failure (Parton, 2014). These and other high-profile cases, such as that of Shannon Matthews in 2008, led David Cameron, the leader of the Conservative Party, to coin the phrase 'broken society', arguing that families with no morals, abusing alcohol and drugs, living off state benefits and indulging in antisocial behaviour meant that there needed to be a reform of state welfare and benefits so as to prevent the moral decline of society. Hence the 'state paternalism' of New Labour was completely reversed in 2010 with the election of the Conservative-led Coalition government. Since then, until the time of writing, with the election of successive Conservative governments a neoliberal policy of individualism and minimum state intervention has prevailed. Social service and welfare budgets have been significantly reduced and family support services marginalised. This includes the closure of children's centres, which were a major tenet in New Labour's child welfare policy.

Role of the media

One of the major factors shaping the development of child protection policy since the death of Victoria Climbié in 2000 has been the role of the media. Not only does the media play a significant role in shaping general societal attitudes towards those who are poor and marginalised and those who are engaged in child protection services, but media responses to high-profile cases such as that of Baby P have directly influenced government decision making and policy (Jones, 2014). Since the advent of reality TV there has been an increase in sensationalist documentaries on television about those who live on benefits and are not working (Jones, 2011). While TV channels and production companies state that their aim is not to 'shame' those who are the subject of these programmes, the result is the reinforcing of negative images and stereotypes and a 'mocking' in the mainstream media of those involved. Many refer to these programmes as 'poverty porn' due to their voyeuristic nature (Joseph Rowntree Foundation, 2013). The mainstream 'right wing' press paint a picture of poor people who are lazy and feckless, uneducated and 'stupid, abusing drugs and alcohol and if they are not abusing or neglecting their children, they are failing to control them and allowing them to cause anti-social behaviour in the community' (Chauhan and Foster, 2014). This context of shame and blame has a direct impact on the social work role. The pervasive impact of shame on individuals is well documented (Tagney and Dearing, 2004). Gupta (2015), in her study on the relationship between poverty and shame for those engaged with child protection processes, found that feelings of shame about poverty led to people feeling isolated, powerless, having low self-worth, wanting to hide from people and feeling disrespected. Clearly, all of these elements are likely to impact on the relationship between the social worker and the person they are working to support, potentially inhibiting the development of a constructive working relationship (Gibson, 2013). Perhaps more significantly, these factors are likely to impact on the emotional and mental health of an individual and potentially inhibit their capacity to care for their children effectively (Smith, 2004; Miller Prieve, 2016).

The direct impact of the media on child protection policy and practice is also significant and has an impact on child protection decision making (Jones, 2014). Following the death of Baby P, Ed Balls, the then home secretary, called on national TV for the sacking of Sharon Shoesmith, the then director of Haringey Children's Services, in response to media pressure. This action created a feeling of uncertainty among social work departments and social workers were left feeling under pressure, worrying that making the wrong decision could leave them without a job (Jones, 2014). The pervasive 'politics of outrage' and 'trial by media' (Greer and McLaughlin, 2010) saw the beginning of a media culture that is sensationalist, which blurs the line between the public and private spheres and focuses on 'scandals' (Ayre, 2001). This has created an uncomfortable environment for child protection social workers, whose role has become increasingly focused on child protection rather than family support in response to this changing culture. This media influence, combined with a neoliberal approach to welfare, has undoubtedly led to a child protection system which is risk averse and focused on protecting children in high–risk cases, rather than preventative work and family support (Featherstone et al, 2014).

Gender and child protection social work

A discussion on the politics of child protection social work would not be complete without focusing on the impact of the construction of gender roles on contemporary social work practice. Social work responses in child protection cases reflect traditional gender roles. The traditional construction of the role of women as carers of children prevails, as the focus is on engaging with mothers. Fathers, on the other hand, are not routinely engaged in decision making and planning processes (Scourfield, 2006; Featherstone and Peckover, 2007; Maxwell et al, 2012).

The construction of women as caring and maternal individuals is also firmly embedded in child protection processes and it has been argued that women who do not adequately care for their children or 'fail to protect' them from abuse and neglect are responded to in harsh and punitive ways, whereas fathers and their role in caring for children are largely negated or ignored (Scourfield, 2001; Featherstone, 2003; Mulkeen, 2012).

This is particularly significant in child protection cases involving domestic abuse. Lapierre (2007) introduced the concept of 'mother blaming' to understand social care responses to mothers experiencing domestic abuse. He argues that responses focus on the shortcomings of women when domestic abuse has occurred, as the focus is on 'blaming' the woman for not protecting her children from the impact of the abuse, and on her deficits as a mother. Indeed, standard child protection practice in domestic abuse cases is to tell women that they need to ask the abusive partner to leave the family home, otherwise their children will be at risk of becoming looked after by the local authority if they do not (Rogers and Parkinson, 2017). In other words, the responsibility is placed firmly on the shoulders on the mother and little attention is paid to her vulnerability in this context, the fear that she may have about asking her partner to leave and the potential repercussions. Featherstone and Peckover (2007) argue that local authorities are letting fathers 'get away with it' in these cases and little work is undertaken with them on addressing their abusive behaviour, despite the fact that they will still be having contact with their children.

Indeed, there is a large body of research which demonstrates the lack of engagement of fathers in child protection cases (Scourfield, 2006; Featherstone, 2010; Maxwell et al, 2012). Scourfield (2001) states that reasons for the lack of engagement of men could be attributed to the construction of men as violent, abusive and potential threats to women and children, including to mainly female social workers. This, coupled with the societal assumption that the responsibility of women is to care for children, has ensured that the focus of social work intervention is on women and their taking responsibility for ensuring that they are adequate parents, rather than on encouraging men to take responsibility for their behaviours (Mulkeen, 2012). Since the late 1990s there has been a focus on how local authorities and social workers can meaningfully engage with men; however, to date this is still proving to be a challenge. This situation is likely to be exacerbated in the current context of austerity as high case-loads, reduced resources and high thresholds of social care intervention are creating a difficult climate for social workers to reflect upon and modify their practice (Parton, 2014).

CASE STUDY 7.1: NEGLECT OR POVERTY?

The following case study is fictional, but is based on experiences that the author faced when a practising as a social worker.

Bethany (10 years), Kieran (8 years) and Connor (5 years) live with their mum, Sarah (28 years), in a small town in the north of England. The family live in private rented accommodation. Sarah's partner and the children's father, Tony, has moved out of the area and rarely sees the children and does not provide any financial assistance to Sarah because he is unemployed, due to the factory where he worked closing down. The family have no extended family locally. Tony's parents live in Spain and the children visit in the school holidays. Their flights are paid for by their grandparents. Sometimes Tony's parents help Sarah out with money, but she does not like to ask them because they are retired. Sarah's parents live in the south of England. Her mum has young-onset dementia and her dad has given up work to care for her, so they are struggling financially.

Sarah works three nights a week behind the bar at the local nightclub. She left school at 16 with no GCSEs and she has worked in bars ever since.

The family's next-door neighbour contacted the children's social care department expressing concerns that Sarah was leaving all three children on their own asleep in bed, while she went to work. The neighbour had previously raised this with Sarah, who had told the neighbour to mind their own business.

A social worker visited the family and Sarah admitted that she does leave the children while she goes to work because she has no one to look after them and this is the only job she can get. She says that she needs to work to pay the extra rent that is not covered under the 'bedroom tax' because her property is determined to be too big for her and her children (it has four bedrooms). She said that Bethany is 'grown up for her age', so she is capable of looking after the other children.

Bethany told the social worker that because her mum is tired after work she gets herself and her brothers ready for school and makes breakfast, and then gets her mum up to walk them to school.

When the school was contacted, the head teacher reported that the children are doing well at school, but they are often late.

The social worker observed a loving relationship between Sarah and all three of her children.

Conclusion

This chapter has provided an introductory discussion on the politics of child protection social work. It has by no means addressed all of the factors that have shaped contemporary practice; rather, it has provided a foundation for readers which can be built upon with further reading, some of which is listed below.

The chapter has introduced readers to the historical and contemporary, political and social factors that have shaped current practice and which continue to do so. It is hoped that readers will be left with the understanding that child protection social work is essentially political and that it is crucial that social workers have an in-depth understanding of the impact of politics on the families that they support and on the practice perimeters of their profession.

Critical questions

1 Taking into consideration the issues discussed in this chapter, what factors will shape how you would respond to the case presented in the case study?

2 Is the case neglect, the result of poverty or a combination of both factors?

3 Are the children at risk of significant harm?

4 What services could support the family?

Further reading

• Bywaters, P., Bunting, L., Davidson, G., Hanratty, J., Mason, W., McCartan, C. and Steils, N. (2016) *The Relationship Between Poverty, Child Abuse and Neglect: An Evidence Review*, York: Joseph Rowntree Foundation.
This report explores the relationship between poverty, child abuse and neglect. While the authors emphasise the complexity of the factors involved in this subject area,

their broad findings are that children living in poverty are more likely to be abused or neglected, and that those children who have been abused or neglected are more likely to experience poverty in adult life. The report goes on to make recommendations for future policy to reduce levels of family poverty in the UK and for social work practice which recognises the impact of poverty and inequality in assessment, decision making and intervention processes.

• Featherstone, B., White, S. and Morris, K. (2014) *Re-imagining Child Protection: Towards Humane Social Work with Families*, Bristol: Policy Press.
This book offers a critical perspective on the current child protection system in the UK. It argues that the current system is overly bureaucratic, resource led, punitive and overly risk focused. It proposes a new approach to child protection based upon a relationship-based approach and one that empowers families, recognising their strengths and uniqueness.

• Featherstone, B., Gupta, A., Morris, K. and Warner, J. (2018) 'Let's stop feeding the risk monster: towards a social model of "child protection"', *Families, Relationships and Societies*, doi: 10.1332/204674316X14552878034622
This article focuses on the risk-averse child protection system in the UK, proposing that the 'risk monster' does not work and that in fact it fails to meet the needs of children and their families, in many cases. It proposes a relationship-based model of child protection which draws on the strengths and resources in families, and one which recognises the economic, social and cultural barriers that many families face.

• Morris, K., Mason, W., Bywaters, P., Featherstone, B., Daniel, B., Brady, G., Bunting, L., Hooper, J., Mirza, N., Scourfield, J. and Webb, C. (2017) 'Social work, poverty, and child welfare interventions', *Child and Family Social Work*, doi: 10.1111/cfs.12423
This article, like the book above, emphasises the relationship between poverty, social work and child protection practice. It emphasises that poor families are more likely to be involved with children's social care. It makes recommendations for social work practice which effectively engages with and challenges the impact of poverty and inequality on children and their families.

• Parton, N. (2014) *The Politics of Child Protection: Contemporary Developments and Future Directions*, London: Palgrave Macmillan.
This book offers a comprehensive discussion on the relationship between social work practice and the political context in the UK. It discusses the development of British social work and demonstrates that social work legislation, policy and practice are inextricably linked to political ideology.

• Scourfield, J., Maxwell, N., Holland, S., Tolman, R., Sloan, L., Featherstone, B. and Bullock, A. (2013) *Improving the Engagement of Fathers in Child Protection*, Cardiff: National Institute for Health and Social Care Research.
This report discusses the low level of involvement that fathers have in current child protection systems. It emphasises the importance of social workers engaging with fathers and makes recommendations for future practice.

- Stafford, A., Vincent, S., Parton, N. and Smith, C. (2012) *Child Protection Systems in the United Kingdom: A Comparative Analysis*, London: Jessica Kingsley Publishers.

  This book compares the child protection systems in England, Wales, Scotland and Northern Ireland and presents a critical discussion on the different systems, which have seen increasing divergence following devolution in Scotland, Wales and Northern Ireland.

References

Allen, G. (2011) *Early Intervention: The Next Steps. Government Report.* Available at: https://www.gov.uk/government/publications/early-intervention-the-next-steps--2 [accessed 8 October 2011].

Ayre, P. (2001) 'Child protection and the media: lessons from the last three decades', *The British Journal of Social Work*, vol 31, no 6, pp 887–901.

Belfield,C., Cribb, J., Hood, A. and Joyce, R. (2015) *Living Standards, Poverty and Inequality in the UK: 2015*, Institute for Fiscal Studies.

Bywaters, P., Bunting, L., Davidson, G., Hanratty, J., Mason, W., McCartan, C. and Steils, N. (2016) *The Relationship Between Poverty, Child Abuse and Neglect: An Evidence Review*, York: Joseph Rowntree Foundation.

Carey, G. and Crammond, B. (2017) 'A glossary of policy frameworks: the many forms of "universalism and 'policy targeting'", *Journal of Epidemiology Community Health*, vol 71, no 3, pp 303–7.

Chauhan, A. and Foster, J. (2014) 'Reports of poverty in British newspapers: a case of "othering" the threat', *Journal of Community and Applied Psychology*, vol 24, no 5, pp 390–405.

Child Poverty Action Group (nd) *Child Poverty: Facts and Figures*,www.cpag.org.uk/content/child-poverty-facts-and-figures [accessed 10 October 2018].

Cleaver, H., Unell, A. and Aldgate, J. (2011) *Children's Needs: Parenting Capacity Child Abuse, Parental Mental Illness, Learning Disability, Substance Misuse, and Domestic Violence* (2nd edn), London: The Stationery Office.

Cooper, K. and Stewart, K. (2013) *Does Money Affect Children's Outcomes? A Systematic Review*, York: Joseph Rowntree Foundation.

Coulton, C.J., Crampton, D.S., Irwin, M., Spilsbury, J.C. and Korbin, J.E. (2007) 'How neighbourhoods influence child maltreatment: a review of the literature and alternative pathways', *Child Abuse and Neglect*, vol 31, nos 11–12, pp 1117–42.

Cummins, I. (2018) *Poverty, Inequality and Social Work*, Bristol: Policy Press.

Department of Health (1995) *Child Protection: Messages from Research*, London: HMSO.

Devaney, J. and McConville, P. (2016) 'Child neglect: the Northern Ireland experience', *Research, Policy and Planning*, vol 32, no 1, pp 53–63.

DfE (Department for Education) (2015) *Characteristics of Children in Need: 2014–2015*, London: Department for Education. Available at: www.gov.uk/government/uploads/system/uploads/attachment_data/file/469737/SFR41_2015_Text.pdf [accessed 10 October 2018].

Donkin, A., Roberts, J., Tedstone, A. and Marmont, M.(2014) 'Family socio-economic status and young children's outcomes', *Journal of Children's Services*, vol 9, no 2, pp 83–95.

Farmer, E. and Callan, S. (2012) *Beyond Violence: Breaking Cycles of Domestic Abuse: A Policy Report for the Centre of Social Justice*, London: The Centre for Social Justice.

Featherstone, B. (2003) 'Taking fathers seriously', *The British Journal of Social Work*, vol 33, no 2, pp 239–54.

Featherstone, B. (2010) 'Writing fathers in but mothers out!!!', *Critical Social Policy*, vol 30, no 2, pp 208–24.

Featherstone, B. and Peckover, S. (2007) 'Letting them get away with it: fathers, domestic violence and child welfare', *Critical Social Policy*, vol 27, no 21, pp 181–202.

Featherstone, B., White, S. and Morris, K. (2014) *Re-imagining Child Protection: Towards Humane Social Work with Families*, Bristol: Policy Press.

Featherstone, B., Morris, K., Daniel, B., Bywaters, P., Brady, G., Bunting, L., Mason, W. and Mirza, N. (2017) 'Poverty, inequality, child abuse and neglect; changing the conversation across the UK in child protection?', *Children & Youth Services Review*, vol 97, pp 127–33.

Featherstone, B., Gupta, A., Morris, K.M. and Warner, J. (2018) 'Let's stop feeding the risk monster: towards a social model of "child protection"', *Families, Relationships and Societies*, vol 7, no 1, pp 7–22.

Ferguson, H. (2011) *Child Protection Practice*, Basingstoke: Palgrave Macmillan.

Frost, N. (1992) 'Implementing the Children Act in a hostile climate', in P. Carter, T. Jeffs and M.K. Smith (eds), *Changing Social Work and Social Welfare*, Buckingham: Open University Press.

Gallagher, B. (2017) 'Fewer staff, dwindling services: how austerity has hit child protection', Social Care Network, *The Guardian*. Available at: https://www.theguardian.com/social-care-network/2017/jul/17/impact-austerity-child-protection [accessed 10 October 2018].

Gibson, M. (2013) 'Shame and guilt in child protection social work: new interpretations and opportunities for practice', *Child and Family Social Work*, vol 20, no 3, pp 333–43.

Greer, C. and McLaughlin, E. (2010) '"Trial by media": policing, the 24–7 mediasphere and the "politics of outrage"', *Theoretical Criminology*, vol 15, no 1, pp 23–46.

Gupta, A. (2015) 'Poverty and shame – messages for social work', *Critical and Radical Social Work*, vol 3, no 1, pp 131–9.

Gupta, A., Featherstone, B. and White, S. (2016) 'Reclaiming humanity: from capacity to capabilities in understanding parenting in adversity', *The British Journal of Social Work*, vol 46, no 2, pp 339–354.

Hirsch, D. and Millar, J. (2004) *Labour's Welfare Reform: Progress to Date*, York: Joseph Rowntree Foundation.

HM Treasury (2003) *Every Child Matters*, London: HMSO.

Hooper, C., Gorin, S., Cabral, C. and Dyson, C. (2007) *Living with Hardship 24/7: The Diverse Experience of Families in Poverty in England*, London: The Frank Buttle Trust.

Horner, N. (2012) *What is Social Work?*, London: Sage.

Hoyle, C. and Rose, D. (2008) 'Labour, law and order', *Political Quarterly*, vol 72, no 1, pp 76–85.

Jones, O. (2011) *Chavs: The Demonisation of the Working Class*, London: Verso Books.

Jones, R. (2014) *The Story of Baby P: Setting the Record Straight*, Bristol: Policy Press.

Joseph Rowntree Foundation (2013) *Poverty Porn? Who Benefits from Documentaries on Recession Britain?*, York: Joseph Rowntree Foundation.

Jutte, S., Bentley, H., Miller, P. and Jetha, N. (2014) *How Safe Are Our Children?*, London: NSPCC.

Katz, I., Corlyon, J., La Placa, V. and Hunter, S. (2007) *The Relationship Between Parenting and Poverty*, York: Joseph Rowntree Foundation.

Krumer Nevo, M. (2016) 'Poverty-aware social work: a paradigm for social work practice for people in poverty', *British Journal of Social Work*, vol 6, no 1, pp 1793–808.

Kus, B. (2006) 'Neoliberalism, institutional change and the welfare state: the case of Britain and France', *International Journal of Comparative Sociology*, vol 47, no 6, pp 488–525.

Lapierre, S. (2007) 'Taking the blame? Women's experiences of mothering in the context of domestic violence', PhD thesis, University of Warwick.

Loopstra, R. and Lalor, D. (2018) *Financial Insecurity, Food Insecurity, and Disability: The Profile of People Receiving Emergency Food Assistance from The Trussell Trust Food Bank Network in Britain*, London: The Trussell Trust.

Macnicol, J. (1987) 'In pursuit of the underclass', *Journal of Social Policy*, vol 16, no 3, pp 293–318.

Mack, J. and Lansley, S. (1985) *Poor Britain*, London: George, Allen and Unwin.

Maxwell, N., Scourfield, J., Featherstone, B., Holland, S. and Holman, R. (2012) 'Engaging fathers in child welfare services: a narrative review of recent research evidence', *Child and Family Social Work*, vol 17, pp 160–9.

McGhee, J., Bunting, L., McCartan, C., Elliot, M., Bywaters, P. and Featherstone, B. (2017) 'Looking after children in the UK – convergence or divergence', *The British Journal of Social Work*, vol 5, no 1, pp 1176–98.

Miller Prieve, V. (2016) 'Women, shame and mental health: a systematic review of approaches in psychotherapy', Sophia, the St Catherine University Repository website, https://Sophia.stkatd.edu/msw_papers/630 [accessed 10 October 2018].

Mulkeen, M. (2012) 'Gendered processes in child protection: "mother-blaming" and the erosion of men's accountability', *Irish Journal of Applied Social Studies*, vol 12, no 1, article 7.

Parton, N. (2004) 'From Maria Colwell to Victoria Climbie: reflections on public inquiries into child abuse a generation apart', *Child Abuse Review*, vol 13, no 2, pp 80–94.

Parton, N. (2014) *The Politics of Child Protection: Contemporary Developments and Future Directions*, London: Palgrave Macmillan.

Pelton, L.H. (2015) 'The continuing role of material factors in child maltreatment and placement', *Child Abuse and Neglect*, vol 41, pp 30–9.

Richardson, S. and Bacon, H. (eds) (2018) *Child Sexual Abuse: Whose Problem? Reflections from Cleveland*, Birmingham: Venture Press.

Rogers, M. and Parkinson, K. (2017) 'Exploring approaches to child welfare in the context of domestic violence and abuse', *Child and Family Social Work*, vol 23, no 1, pp 105–12.

Scourfield, J. (2001) 'Constructing men in child protection work', *Men and Masculinities*, vol 4, no 1, pp 70–89.

Scourfield, J. (2006) 'The challenge of engaging fathers in the child protection process', *Critical Social Policy*, vol 26, no 2, pp 440–9.

Seebohm Committee (1968) *Report of the Committee on Local Authority and Allied Personal Social Services* [chair Frederic Seebohm], London: HMSO.

Shildrick, T. and Rucell, J. (2015) *Sociological Perspectives on Poverty: A Review of Sociological Theories on the Causes of Poverty*, York: Joseph Rowntree Foundation.

Smith, M.(2004) 'Parental mental health: disruptions to parenting and outcomes for children', *Child and Family Social Work*, vol 9, no 1, pp 3–11.

Thane, P. (2009) 'History of social care in England', Memorandum for Health Committee Enquiry: Social Care. Available at: https://publications.parliament. uk/pa/cm200809/cmselect/cmhealth/1021/1021we49.htm [accessed 10 October 2018].

Valentine, G. (1996) 'Angels and devils: moral landscapes of childhood', *Environment and Planning D: Society and Space*, vol 14, no 5, pp 581–99.

Vincent, S., Daniel, D. and Jackson, S. (2010) 'Where now for child protection in Scotland?', *Child Abuse Review*, vol 19, no 6, pp 438–56.

Warner, J. (2013) 'Social work, class politics and risk in the moral panic over Baby P', *Health, Risk & Society*, vol 15, no 3, pp 217–33.

8

Mental health

Rich Moth and Scott Massie

Introduction

This chapter provides an overview of some of the key political processes shaping mental health policy and their implications for social work practice in this setting. It begins with a historical outline of policy responses to mental distress from the era of the asylum, through the 20th-century development of, first, hospital and then community care, and into the present period characterised by increasingly market-oriented and residualised service provision and individual responsibility placed on service users. In spite of these challenges from above, there remain a number of resources of hope for mental health social work. These emerge from person-centred initiatives and collective struggles 'from below' by social workers and service users to develop and extend support rooted in the values of social justice. The chapter gives examples of these and concludes with a case study to illustrate implications for practice.

Historical context of service provision

Mental health social work practice is significantly influenced by the policy context in which it takes place. Mental health policy in the UK is continually evolving, and shaped by a range of legal, professional and organisational strands (Glasby and Tew, 2015) within a wider context of neoliberal ideology (see Chapter 4). In order to understand social work in mental health in the present, it is necessary to reflect on the historical processes and institutions that have shaped it. There have been four key stages in the history of mental health service provision in the UK which, we argue, continue to exert an influence on contemporary policy and practice: the custodial asylum, the biomedical hospital system, community care and the current neoliberal period. In this section we outline the first three of these historical stages of mental health policy and practice. In the following section we then describe the main contours and dynamics of the contemporary neoliberal era and its implications for mental health social work.

Custodialism and the asylum

The primary response to mental distress in Britain during the Victorian era and before would have been either the removal of the person to a small-scale private 'madhouse' or segregation into one of the large-scale public asylums that had emerged by the early 19th century (Porter, 1987). Many of those committed to the latter institutions were classed as 'paupers' under the reforms that culminated in the Poor Law Amendment Act 1834. The predominant practice within the asylum system was *custodialism*, with inmates confined within a highly regimented and restrictive regime (Rogers and Pilgrim, 2001). Conditions were influenced by the wider context of the barrack-like regimes of the new sites of industrial production – the factory and mill – and, most importantly, by the harsh and punitive regime of the workhouse for the 'able-bodied' poor and destitute. The design of the buildings reflected this and, in spite of their grand facades, the interiors of asylums were modelled on prisons in terms both of a concern with security and the culture of staff (Busfield, 1986). The Lunacy Act 1890 served to reinforce this custodial orientation. Although it would be some time before a formal role for social work was designated in mental health law, the specialist magistrate's function under this legislation might be regarded as a forerunner of the approved mental health professional (explained further below) (Hill et al, 2015).

Biomedical treatment in hospital

By the first half of the 20th century there had been a significant growth in state intervention around social policy. The initiatives included public health, housing, social insurance and pensions schemes and, most relevant for this chapter, *hospital provision*. The Maudsley psychiatric hospital in London opened in 1915 and this was followed by the 1924–26 Royal Commission on Lunacy and Mental Treatment Act 1930. These reforms marginalised the custodial asylum doctor and heralded a new emphasis on medical care and cure via biomedical treatments[1] within the hospital setting (Rogers and Pilgrim, 2001). The opening of the Tavistock Clinic around this time was also emblematic of a significant expansion of psychiatric hospital and outpatient clinic provision that challenged the Victorian-era custodial approach (Coppock and Hopton, 2000). Alongside this, a new emphasis on the role of the environment developed, with a growth in the influence of psychological ideas and treatments (Busfield, 1986). Psychiatric social work too began to develop from the 1920s, with practitioners based in hospitals such as the Tavistock Clinic utilising psychotherapeutic methods (Ramon, 2006).

The 1950s saw a further shift towards biomedical treatments with the introduction of new neuroleptic medications such as Haloperidol and Chlorpromazine, the so-called 'anti-psychotic' treatments. This was the backdrop to the Mental Health Act 1959, which reinforced the dominant notion of mental disorder as a form of illness to be treated medically, though the role of psychiatry in deprivation of liberty was also retained (Rogers and Pilgrim, 2001).

Social care in the community

After the Second World War a new consensus based on public sector provision of welfare began to emerge. Though the biomedical model endured, new approaches to the community treatment of mental distress became both acceptable and feasible in the expanding welfare state (Busfield, 1986). But, while psychiatric hospitals were reorganised to integrate with the new NHS, large populations still remained in the old asylums. It was not until health minister Enoch Powell's 1961 'water towers' speech that the move from asylums to *community care* began to take shape. The plan was for the replacement of asylums with new forms of community provision alongside acute treatment in District General Hospital (DGH) units. The promise of further community service development was held out by two key provisions in the Mental Health Act 1959: a requirement for out-patient follow up of discharged patients and a legislated role for social work (Glasby and Tew, 2015).

However, while DGH units increased in number, community provision expanded slowly. Despite some social work involvement in community service development, competing funding obligations deterred local councils from investing in residential facilities (Bamford, 2015). Nonetheless, by the 1980s a new institutional network of mental health service provision in the community had emerged as the last of the asylums approached closure. This included hostels, group and nursing homes and NHS- and social services-run day centres, as well as moves towards the creation of multidisciplinary community teams (Rogers and Pilgrim, 2001).

In spite of the slow progress of community care, there were two other highly significant features of this period: (i) the emergence of service user/survivor[2] movements and (ii) alternative ways of understanding mental distress. These will be briefly outlined.

Service user/survivor movements

The contemporary mental health service user/survivor movement began to take shape in the 1970s. The movement identified a range of challenges facing users but had a particular focus on two related concerns within services. These were the continued dominance of a biomedical model of illness, and emphasis on psychiatric drug treatments at the expense of alternative approaches (Beresford, 2012). The movement drew attention to the inequalities of power experienced by service users both within the psychiatric system and in wider society, highlighting the relationship of these to experiences of mental distress. This translated into a focus on recognising and addressing power imbalances in services and inspiring the growth of user involvement and user-led services, as well as highlighting material issues such as cuts to welfare and services (Ferguson, 2008). In broader terms, the focus on power foregrounded the *social* nature of mental distress, that is, the role of social and environmental factors in causing and exacerbating mental health issues, in contrast to the psychiatric focus on biological causes within the individual. In this way user movements significantly contributed to the promotion of alternatives to biomedical orthodoxy (Beresford, 2012).

Alternative models for understanding mental distress

As we have seen, the community care era heralded new forms of mental health provision beyond the hospital. Occupations such as social work and psychology and their knowledge bases began to gain greater prominence, alongside the promotion by user movements of experiential standpoints. Consequently, alternative ways of understanding mental distress, such as psychological and psychotherapeutic frameworks, and social perspectives informed by sociological theory and service user perspectives, began to challenge the authority of psychiatry and the dominance of the biomedical model as noted above (Rogers and Pilgrim, 2014). This led to inter-professional and user–professional contestation and conflict (Colombo et al, 2003). The social work profession tended to promote social approaches and to align with initiatives to strengthen user involvement and advocacy within multidisciplinary services (Tew, 2005).

Current context, including legislation and policy

This historical overview has indicated some of the most significant developments in mental health policy and provision between the Victorian era and the 1980s. We now turn to more recent reforms shaping contemporary mental health social work. In the first part of this section we describe UK mental health policy developments since the 1990s. That point marked a transition from the comprehensive welfare state consensus of the community care era towards a neoliberal policy agenda. However, as a result of devolution there has been some divergence and so, in the second part of this section, we note some areas of difference in mental health policy and practice across the devolved nations.

The neoliberal era: markets, risk, responsibility and austerity

Neoliberalism has significantly reshaped mental health policy and practice in the UK since the 1990s. However, neoliberal reforms have been implemented through a diverse range of policy strategies including: marketisation and managerialism, risk, recovery and austerity. While these four agendas are not highly coordinated, they share a market-oriented and individualised directional momentum and their trajectories interweave, overlap and occasionally come into conflict in the context of contemporary practice (Moth, 2020).

The first policy agenda is *marketisation and managerialism*. This was initially embedded in mental health (and other) services through the Conservative administration's National Health Service and Community Care Act (NHSCCA) 1990. The legislation promoted a 'mixed economy of care', establishing competition and the profit motive (particularly in care) and developing a business culture in health and social care services. This agenda mobilised the concepts of increased choice and consumer rights (Clarke et al, 2007) and was implemented through organisational changes such as the purchaser/provider split and the creation of internal and external markets to promote service commodification and marketisation. Consequently, social workers began to focus more on care management than on direct provision (Harris, 2003).

This was accompanied by the 'universalisation of management', with performance indicators and target regimes to create quasi-market disciplines. This 'modernising', target-oriented approach was extended under the subsequent New Labour governments from 1997 to further embed market norms (Ferguson, 2008). *New Ways of Working* reforms were an important aspect of this, promoting more generic and flexible working practices to align with market demands. This resulted in dilution of the mental health social work role, for example the loss of the Approved Social Worker specialism to Approved Mental Health Professional (AMHP) under the Mental Health Act (MHA) 2007 (Bailey and Liyanage, 2012). While the NHSCCA 1990 has now been superseded by the Conservative-led Coalition government's Care Act (CA) 2014, the latter legislation further embeds in law the duty on local authorities to promote 'efficient and effective' markets in care (DH, 2014).

The second policy trajectory, emerging in the mid–1990s, is the *risk agenda*. This involved an increased focus on the danger to the public purportedly posed by mental health service users, following several high-profile public cases during this period such as the killing of Jonathan Zito by Christopher Clunis.[3] Despite evidence that homicides by people experiencing mental distress had actually been reducing over the previous three decades, there was a resultant shift in policy discourse away from viewing people with mental health needs as vulnerable and towards a focus on the concept of dangerousness and risk containment (Pilgrim and Ramon, 2009). The increasingly coercive policy measures that followed reflected a wider 'punitive turn' in social policy under neoliberalism (Wacquant, 2010; Hart et al, 2019).

The most prominent policy response by the New Labour government was reform of the MHA 1983. This proved controversial because it included restrictive measures such as Supervised Community Treatment (SCT) via community treatment orders (CTOs), which were ultimately implemented in spite of a high-profile campaign by the umbrella group the Mental Health Alliance.[4] CTOs were originally promoted as a safety net for those considered at high risk in the community and to address 'revolving door' hospital admissions (Godefroy, 2015). However, in practice they functioned as a means to treat individuals under compulsion, outside hospital, so as 'to pursue the successful coercive social control of prospective risk' (Pilgrim and Ramon, 2009, p 274). CTOs are now widely used, despite little evidence of their effectiveness, impact in reducing hospital readmission rates or positive outcomes (Maughan et al, 2014). Annual application numbers in England are considerably higher than original estimations (Lawton-

Smith, 2010). A further concern is the disproportionate imposition of CTOs on people (particularly men) from Black and Minority Ethnic (BME) groups. BME men are four times more likely than white men to be detained in hospital under the MHA 1983 (CQC, 2018a) and nine times more likely than white men with similar symptoms to be placed under SCT (NHS Digital, 2017). This reflects wider issues of institutionalised racism in the mental health system (Centre for Mental Health, 2013), with policy echoes of the custodialism noted earlier in the chapter.

A third policy shift is the promotion of *recovery* since the early 2000s (DH, 2001). The recovery model was initially developed as a (mainly) service user-led approach and was welcomed by many in survivor movements, due to its critique of pathologising biomedical perspectives on mental distress and appearing to meet aspirations for more social perspectives in provision. However, the most prominent definition in official policy, of recovery as a personal journey, is highly individualised, with the onus on the service user to alter their attitudes, beliefs and behaviours in order to achieve recovery outcomes (Pilgrim and McCranie, 2013). The most visible manifestation of this philosophy in the NHS is the 'Recovery College', a service model that first emerged in 2009. Recovery Colleges emphasise the individual service user's responsibility to engage in educational work to improve their skills in self-managing symptoms as a precursor to return to employment (Perkins et al, 2018). This 'responsibilisation' of the user marginalises the role of social factors such as poverty, inequality and discrimination in mental distress and implies that the required locus of change is within the person rather than society. Recovery thus aligns with neoliberal tenets by de-emphasising the collective provision of longer-term, therapeutically oriented mental health services and promoting the reduced consumption of services by users (Harper and Speed, 2012), prompting criticism from service user/survivor-led activist groups such as Recovery in the Bin (Recovery in the Bin, nd).

The fourth and most recent policy intervention is the *austerity programme* that followed the global financial crisis of 2007/08. Austerity has two main features: reductions in service and welfare provision, alongside a strong focus on welfare to work. The first of these, mental health service delivery, has been significantly reconfigured and reduced. There have been swingeing cuts to local authority budgets in England, resulting in a 37% reduction in the number of adults with mental health needs accessing adult social care support between 2010 and 2015 (Burchardt et al, 2015). Alongside this, in the NHS, between 2012 and 2016 there was a 15% cut in mental health in-patient beds. One consequence of this has been local bed shortages, resulting in some service users being transported hundreds of miles for in-patient admission, so-called out-of-area treatments. These can have harmful effects by taking people away from their support networks and hindering recovery (Carter, 2018). As well as bed reductions there have been significant cuts to support in the community (CQC, 2018b). Between 2012 and 2016 the total number of service users supported fell by 7%, community staff levels were reduced by 4%, while community contacts with service users were down 6% (Centre for Mental Health, 2017).

The other main feature of the austerity era has been welfare 'reform'. This has involved policy changes to limit access to and levels of benefit support. Examples include freezing of benefit rates and redrawing eligibility criteria to reduce the access of claimants with mental health needs to disability benefits such as Personal Independence Payment (Beatty and Fothergill, 2016; Roulstone, 2015). The conditions attached to claiming benefits have also increased. A prominent form of welfare conditionality involves 'behavioural conduct' – for instance, requirements to engage in activities such as job search, mandatory courses or workfare. However, 'psychological conditionality' has also become increasingly integral (Watts and Fitzpatrick, 2018). This requires that claimants modify their attitudes, dispositions or personality in order to return to or find work, underpinned by the notion of unemployment as a product of individual/psychological deficits. This punitive escalation of various types of conditionality, combined with sanctions for non-compliance, has been dubbed 'psychocompulsion' (Friedli and Stearn, 2015). In combination, these reforms have caused significant harm, exacerbating the 'benefits distress' experienced by service users and claimants (Moth and Lavalette, 2017).

However, the direction of travel is not only towards cutting benefits and mental health services, but also reconfiguration of the remaining provision to more closely align its practices and priorities with those of the welfare to work agenda (Moth and McKeown, 2016). The most significant example is the Improving Access to Psychological Therapies (IAPT) programme, involving large-scale delivery of short-term counselling services within primary (GP settings) rather than secondary care (mental health services). This approach has attracted significantly increased investment (NHS England, 2016). However, while expanding access to psychological support might be seen as welcome, there are significant concerns that, with a primary focus on reducing sickness absence and returning to work, the service user's own therapeutic goals are marginalised (Walker, 2015). Similarly, the mechanised and short-term nature of IAPT therapies leads to poor outcomes for users and burnout for staff (Cotton, 2017; Scott, 2018).

We have highlighted four mental health policy agendas implemented during the neoliberal era. These interact to produce a more restrictive and punitive context both for users of services and for social workers (and other practitioners) within them. However, while these four policy trends are broadly applicable across the four nations of the UK, there is some policy variation as a result of devolution.

Devolution trends

While the Westminster government continues to set the wider policy and funding context for the UK, the devolution settlements of 1999 have produced some distinct differences in the management of health and social care in Scotland, Wales and Northern Ireland. In this section we highlight three areas of divergence from England: marketisation; universalism; and human rights and specialism in mental health legislation.

The three devolved territories rely on a block grant from the UK government but, since 1999, have taken an independent direction in decisions on how to manage funding to meet localised need (Birrell, 2007). Arguably the most visible symbol of policy difference is the rejection of *marketisation* introduced in England through NHSCCA 1990. The Scottish authorities phased out the NHS internal market in 1997 even before formal devolution. The Welsh government too has abolished the purchaser/provider split (Bevan et al, 2014). Unlike the CA 2014 in England, the equivalent 2014 statute in Wales – the Social Services and Well-being (Wales) Act 2014 – eschews provider competition, instead developing integrated regional Partnership Boards (Welsh Government, 2015).

Another area of divergence from England relates to *universalism* in health and care provision. The Scottish government introduced free universal personal care in 2002, making Scotland a unique forerunner in aligning care with a 'health' rather than a 'social' need. From 2011 Scotland has also joined Northern Ireland and Wales in offering free prescriptions, in contrast to England (Triggle, 2011). These trends indicate the rejection of the greater selectivity and conditionality seen in England and a more universalist approach to welfare state provision in the devolved territories (Simeon, 2003).

A third area of difference is in *mental health law*. While legislation regarding mental capacity is relatively standardised across the UK,[5] in mental health legislation there have been more diverse initiatives. The MHA 1983, amended by the MHA 2007, applies to both England and Wales. However, Scotland has long had a completely separate system of mental health law and amended its legal framework with the Mental Health (Scotland) Act 2015. The Scottish legislation is regarded as less punitive than that in England and Wales, with a greater emphasis on the human rights of service users (Mental Health Foundation et al, 2016) and more focus on social perspectives (Hothersall et al, 2008). Moreover, Scotland and Northern Ireland (NI) have not adopted the generic approach of the AMHP, with NI maintaining the Approved Social Worker role and Scotland having its equivalent in the Mental Health Officer (MacIntyre, 2018).

In this section we have provided a historical overview of the context of mental health social work practice, highlighting the complex and politically contested nature of this environment. Neoliberal reform has reshaped services and foregrounded market mechanisms and individual responsibility in the context of service retrenchment and more punitive policy measures. Despite significant changes over time, elements of older institutional structures such as custodialism and biomedical treatments also endure or continue to exert an influence on contemporary practice, while devolution trends suggest a growing divergence in policy.

An alternative political agenda for contemporary practice

Having highlighted a number of constraints on and challenges for mental health social work arising from top-down neoliberal policy reforms, we now turn to discussion of possibilities for an alternative politics of mental health provision 'from below'. These proposals draw on research identifying the efforts and aspirations of mental health social workers[6] to practise in ways commensurate with their social justice value base within the challenging policy contexts of neoliberalism (Moth, 2020). We propose four components[7] of a progressive mental health social work, highlighting various 'resources of hope' that offer examples of, or inspiration for, more transformative forms of practice.

Relationship and values-based practice

We described above the constraints faced by mental health social workers in a neoliberal practice context that is dominated by targets and markets. The first of our socially just alternatives involves maintaining a commitment to good individual casework practice in this setting. This has two components: (i) relationship-based practice with service users that is respectful and empathic, seeking to gain a holistic picture of the needs of the person-in-context; and (ii) values-based practice that is sensitive to issues of power in the user–worker relationship, that takes account of rights, discrimination and oppression in service users' lives and that is committed to supporting users to address inequalities and injustices. To achieve this requires working in partnership with service users by respecting their preferred framework for understanding and responding to their mental distress, raising consciousness of and challenging discrimination and utilising professional discretion and advocacy skills to access resources as appropriate and to maximise positive outcomes. In this way, striving for good casework practice constitutes a form of politicised social work under neoliberalism. However, while we consider good casework to be an important basis for effective social work, we consider it necessary to go beyond the individual level and develop a mode of practice that is informed by social and political perspectives that incorporate community, dialogic and collective action dimensions.

Family and community development approaches

There is substantial evidence of an important role for social and environmental factors in causing and contributing to mental distress (Rogers and Pilgrim, 2014). Such determinants include social class (poorer people in economically unequal contexts are more likely to experience mental distress), as well as social divisions based on characteristics such as gender, race and sexuality. The latter have adverse implications for mental health, due to experiences of relative disadvantage, discrimination and oppression faced by women, people from ethnic minority groups and LGBT communities (Tew, 2011). Social experiences at the level of families, workplaces, communities and societies can further exacerbate or mitigate the development of mental distress (WHO, 2014).

Consequently, it is important to go beyond regarding the service user as an isolated individual, and to recognise the value of supporting people in the context of both (i) their familial/social networks and/or (ii) wider communities. An example of the former is Open Dialogue, which offers support to the service user in their home, alongside and in dialogue with key members of their family and social support network, rather than in an institutional setting. This was developed in Finland and has been trialled in six NHS Mental Health services in the UK since late 2017 (adapted to include a peer-support dimension) (Razzaque and Stockmann, 2016).[8]

An example of a community-based approach is Sharing Voices Bradford, a voluntary sector project organised by and for BAME communities to address inequalities, including over-representation in more restrictive forms of mental health provision and lack of availability of culturally appropriate services. The project utilises a community development approach, seeking to support and empower BAME communities through peer support and campaigning. This orientation is underpinned by a social perspective which identifies the key causal factors for mental distress as poverty, unemployment, racism and sexual trauma, rather than individual biology (Bracken and Thomas, 2005).

Democratic and dialogic alternatives

However, as well as practice that mobilises family and community networks of support, service users and survivors have foregrounded the importance of valuing lived experience and understanding and defining mental distress within users' own frames of reference. One prominent example of this has been the emergence of the Hearing Voices Network (HVN), an approach which has an increasing profile within NHS mental health services and beyond. The HVN approach challenges the dominant biomedical model that automatically pathologises unusual experiences such as voice hearing (Tew, 2011) by promoting instead acceptance and development of a more constructive relationship with voices within an informal, peer-led group setting. Approaches such as this[9] also undermine traditional hierarchies between the dominant professional as expert and the passive user as recipient, offering a more democratic and egalitarian alternative in which expertise by profession and expertise by experience can operate in a collaborative and mutually supportive way in the context of a survivor-led model (Longden et al, 2018).

Campaigning and collective action

As Chapter 1 of this text has noted, politically progressive developments within social work have often been shaped by wider social struggles such as the civil rights, LGBT and disabled people's movements (Ferguson and Woodward, 2009). The fourth component is therefore engagement with collective forms of political action and social movements. This recognises the necessity of more systemic forms of political transformation in order to confront the structural causes of mental distress such as poverty, inequality and oppression faced by service users (WHO, 2014).

In the current mental health practice context the role of contemporary movements against austerity and inequality (for example, Occupy) is of particular relevance. For example, in light of the cuts to welfare and services noted above, the disabled people's and mental health service user/survivor movements have played a central role in resistance. Practitioner-led groups such as SWAN[10] have contributed through political work alongside service user-led campaigns such as Disabled People Against Cuts and Mental Health Resistance Network. This has taken the form of joint campaigning and direct action at the local level – for instance challenging austerity-related mental health service closures (see Moth et al, 2015) – and 'agitational' interventions such as the SWAN Mental Health Charter calling for alliances of resistance against austerity (Moth and Lavalette, 2019). Getting involved in a trade union is also important, as these offer the potential for collective action to defend and improve rights and conditions at work. Moreover, many trade union branches have also been active in building cross-sectional alliances between practitioners and service user groups to campaign for 'more and better' mental health services and support (Moth and McKeown, 2016).

Getting involved in trade unions and campaigning networks such as SWAN at both local and national level, and being part of movements against austerity and for wider progressive social change, are important ways that practitioners can build alliances with service users and contribute to making 'another social work possible'.[11]

The following case study illustrates how the four components of an alternative progressive mental health social work might be applied in practice.

CASE STUDY 8.1: PROGRESSIVE MENTAL HEALTH PRACTICE

Phil had been a user of his local Community Mental Health Team (CMHT) for five years, following experiences of low mood and stress related to his beliefs about the police continually following and monitoring him, which his psychiatrist viewed as 'paranoid thoughts'. However, he was recently discharged, following sustained improvements in his mental wellbeing. He was in agreement with the discharge and had positive plans for the future. These included continuing to attend the local day service, where he has a number of friends. Phil's access to the service was costed on his care plan and reviewed annually by the social work team.

Following his discharge a number of situations impacted upon Phil's mental health. These included the following:

- Phil had to move out of his family home, due to increased rent through the 'bedroom tax'. He is now living in a one-bed flat in an area he does not know.

- He was called to a work capability assessment with the Department for Work and Pensions (DWP), after which his benefits were greatly reduced, with the DWP arguing that his mental health was no longer a barrier to paid work.
- The local authority reduced funding to the day service he attends (due to austerity). The service now operates only two days per week and attendees have to meet activity targets to be able to attend. The informal social groups have had to end.

As a result of these issues, Phil's mental distress increased. He stopped attending the day service, feeling highly anxious about pressure from day service activity targets and DWP expectations that he return to paid employment. Phil self-referred to the Crisis Team one evening, feeling extremely low and distressed. However, he was told they could not see him, as his case was no longer open to the CMHT, and should attend the emergency department at his local hospital instead.

Phil contacted the social work team the following day and team member Jane arranged a visit. Together Phil and Jane developed the following plan of support.

- A full holistic reassessment offered Jane an opportunity to explore with Phil, in a person-centred way, how his current circumstances were impacting on his distress, and also what 'recovery' meant to him. Jane used this to build a case and advocate for extended day service support. Working with the legislation, specifically the CA 2014, Jane identified outcomes based upon Phil's definition of what he called 'moving forward' and argued for suitable services to meet his needs. Jane also linked Phil with a welfare rights advocacy service for support to appeal the benefits decisions based on his changed circumstances, as well as advice on housing. Jane reassured Phil that she would write supporting letters to the DWP as necessary and ensure that he was supported to attend benefits assessments.
- Jane organised a review meeting with Phil at the day service, including fellow users and other colleagues. She drew on research to argue that social and emotional contact would be equally (if not more) valid as fixed activity sessions in respect of improving wellbeing. The service identified time slots where rooms in the building could be used for this purpose. Phil and some fellow users set up a peer-led support group.
- Phil had heard about a local 'unusual beliefs group' (a user-led approach linked to HVN) where he could share his beliefs in an accepting and supportive peer-group setting and explore coping strategies to reduce his distress. Jane supported Phil to make contact with the group.
- Jane was concerned about the impact of cuts to services and benefits on Phil and many other CMHT service users. She made contact with like-minded practitioners within her service to discuss strategies for raising concerns about reducing care packages. To support her case Jane and colleagues identified research evidence (including user-led research) detailing the impact of issues such as isolation on

longer-term mental wellbeing. This enabled the presentation of an evidence-based case to funding panels – for instance, detailing the increased longer-term costs for the local authority as a result of short-term reductions in care packages.

- Jane joined campaigning initiatives by her trade union branch and got involved in her local SWAN group, where she worked alongside local service user and disability activist groups to challenge cuts to day service provision.

Conclusion

This chapter has presented two visions of mental health social work. The first is a neoliberal, top-down approach shaped by markets, targets and risk management, where the onus to 'recover' is placed on the individual. We advocate an alternative approach from below that places relationships and values at its core, foregrounds social perspectives and views egalitarian practice and political alliances between experts by profession and experts by experience as essential elements in realising this vision.

Critical questions

1 What are some of the main perspectives or models of mental distress in mental health services? Why might they lead to conflict in multidisciplinary teams?

2 What do we mean by social determinants of mental distress? In what ways do these impact on mental health?

3 Does current mental health law and policy strike a good balance between service users' rights and issues of risk?

4 Why have there been criticisms of the way in which the recovery approach has been implemented within mental health services?

Further reading

- Rogers, A. and Pilgrim, D. (2014) *A Sociology of Mental Health and Illness* (5th edn), Maidenhead: Open University Press.
  This text offers a comprehensive overview of sociological approaches to mental health and illness, including useful material on stigma, class, gender and race and the sociology of the mental health professions.

- Tew, J. (2011) *Social Approaches to Mental Distress*, Houndmills: Palgrave Macmillan.
  This book provides a holistic overview of the impact of social factors on mental health and social approaches for responding to mental distress. The text includes helpful frameworks for applying these ideas in practice.

- Ferguson, I. (2017) *Politics of the Mind: Marxism and Mental Distress*, London: Bookmarks Publications.

  Ferguson's book is a concise but sophisticated Marxist analysis of mental distress, with chapters on medicalisation, Freud, anti-psychiatry and alienation.

- Beresford, P. (2010) *A Straight Talking Introduction to Being a Mental Health Service User*, Ross-on-Wye: PCCS Books.

  This short text gives an indispensable account of the mental health service user/survivor movement written by a leading activist within it. The book presents users' critiques of current mental health service provision and outlines survivor-led alternatives.

References

Bailey, D. and Liyanage, L. (2012) 'The role of the mental health social worker: political pawns in the reconfiguration of adult health and social care', *British Journal of Social Work*, vol 42, pp 1113–31.

Bamford, T. (2015) *A Contemporary History of Social Work: Learning From the Past*, Bristol: Policy Press.

Beatty, C. and Fothergill, S. (2016) *The Uneven Impact of Welfare Reform: The Financial Losses to Places and People*, Project Report, Sheffield: Sheffield Hallam University.

Beresford, P. (2012) 'Psychiatric system survivors: an emerging movement', in N. Watson, A. Roulstone and C. Thomas (eds), *Routledge Handbook of Disability Studies*, London and New York, NY: Routledge, pp 151–64.

Bevan, G., Karanikolos, M., Exley, J., Nolte, E., Connolly, S. and Mays, N. (2014) 'The four health systems of the United Kingdom: how do they compare?', The Health Foundation and the Nuffield Trust. Available at: www.nuffieldtrust.org. uk/files/2017–01/4–countries-report-web-final.pdf [accessed 4 August 2018].

Birrell, D. (2007) 'Devolution and social care: are there four systems of social care in the United Kingdom?', Socialist Health Association. Available at: www. sochealth.co.uk/national–health–service/devolution–in–health/devolution–social-care/ [accessed 16 August 2018].

Bracken, P. and Thomas, P. (2005) *Postpsychiatry: Mental Health in a Postmodern World*, Oxford: Oxford University Press.

Burchardt, T., Obolenskaya, P. and Vizard, P. (2015) 'The Coalition's record on adult social care: policy, spending and outcomes 2010–2015', Social Policy in a Cold Climate working paper, SPCCWP17, London: CASE/LSE.

Busfield, J. (1986) *Managing Madness: Changing Ideas and Practice*, London: Unwin Hyman.

Carter, R. (2018) 'AMHPs are being left to improvise solutions to system failures', *Community Care*, 27 March. Available at: www.communitycare. co.uk/2018/03/27/amhps-left-improvise-solutions-system-failures/ [accessed 6 June 2018].

Centre for Mental Health (2013) *The Bradley Commission: Black and Minority Ethnic Communities, Mental Health and Criminal Justice*, London: Centre for Mental Health.

Centre for Mental Health (2017) *Briefing 52: Adult and Older Adult Mental Health Services 2012–2016*, London: Centre for Mental Health.

Clarke, J., Newman, J., Smith, N., Vidler, E. and Westmarland, L. (2007) *Creating Citizen-Consumers: Changing Publics and Changing Public Services*, London: Sage.

Colombo, A., Bendelow, G., Fulford, B. and Williams, S. (2003) 'Evaluating the influence of implicit models of mental disorder on processes of shared decision making within community-based multi-disciplinary teams', *Social Science and Medicine*, vol 56, no 7, pp 1557–70.

Coppock, V. and Hopton, J. (2000) *Critical Perspectives on Mental Health*, London: Routledge.

Cotton, E. (2017) 'The Future of Therapy. Surviving Work', www.thefutureoftherapy.org

CQC (Care Quality Commission) (2018a) 'Monitoring the Mental Health Act in 2016/17', APS Group. Available at: www.cqc.org.uk/sites/default/files/20190108_mhareport2017_amend_1.pdf

CQC (Care Quality Commission) (2018b) 'Mental Health Act 1983: approved mental health professional services', www.cqc.org.uk/sites/default/files/20180326_mha_amhpbriefing.pdf [accessed 25 May 2018].

DH (Department of Health) (2001) *The Journey to Recovery – The Government's Vision for Mental Health Care*, London: Department of Health.

DH (2014) *Care and Support Statutory Guidance*, London: Williams Lea.

Ferguson, I. (2008) *Reclaiming Social Work: Challenging Neo-liberalism and Promoting Social Justice*, London: Sage.

Ferguson, I. and Woodward, R. (2009) *Radical Social Work in Practice: Making a Difference*, Bristol: Policy Press.

Friedli, L. and Stearn, R. (2015) 'Positive affect as coercive strategy: conditionality, activation and the role of psychology in UK government workfare programmes', *Medical Humanities*, vol 41, no 1, pp 40–7.

Glasby, J. and Tew, J. (2015) *Mental Health Policy and Practice* (3rd edn), Basingstoke: Palgrave Macmillan.

Godefroy, S. (2015) *Mental Health and Mental Capacity Law for Social Workers: An Introduction*, London: Sage.

Harper, D. and Speed, E. (2012) 'Uncovering recovery: the resistible rise of recovery and resilience', *Studies in Social Justice*, vol 6, no 1, pp 9–25.

Harris J. (2003) *The Social Work Business*, Routledge: London.

Hart, E., Greener, J. and Moth, R. (eds) (2019) *Resist the Punitive State: Grassroots Struggles Across Welfare, Housing, Education and Prisons*, London: Pluto Press.

Hill, D., Penson, B. and Charura, D. (2015) *Working with Dual Diagnosis: A Psychosocial Perspective*, Houndmills: Palgrave Macmillan.

Hothersall, S., Maas-Lowit, M. and Golightly, G. (2008) *Social Work and Mental Health in Scotland*, Exeter: Learning Matters.

Lawton-Smith, S. (2010) *Briefing Paper Two: Supervised Community Treatment*, London: Mental Health Alliance.

Longden, E., Read, J. and Dillon, J. (2018) 'Assessing the impact and effectiveness of hearing voices network self-help groups', *Community Mental Health Journal*, vol 54, no 2, pp 184–8.

MacIntyre, G. (2018) 'Mental health services', in V. Cree and M. Smith (eds), *Social Work in a Changing Scotland*, Abingdon: Routledge, pp 161–70.

Maughan, D., Molodynski, A., Rugkasa, J. and Burns, T. (2014) 'A systematic review of the effect of community treatment orders on service use', *Social Psychiatry and Psychiatric Epidemiology*, vol 49, pp 651–63.

Mental Health Foundation et al (2016) *A Review of Mental Health Services in Scotland: Perspectives and Experiences of Service Users, Carers and Professionals*, Mental Health Foundation, Vox Scotland and The Scottish Government.

Moth, R. (2020) *Understanding Mental Distress: Knowledge, Practice and Neoliberal Reform in Community Mental Health Services*, Bristol: Policy Press.

Moth, R. and Lavalette, M. (2017) *Social Protection and Labour Market Policies for Vulnerable Groups from a Social Investment Perspective: The Case of Welfare Recipients with Mental Health Needs in England*, Liverpool: Liverpool Hope University/ Leuven: HIVA (KU Leuven).

Moth, R. and Lavalette, M. (2019) 'Social policy and welfare movements "from below": the Social Work Action Network (SWAN) in the UK', in U. Klammer, S. Leiber and S. Leitner (eds), *Social Work and the Making of Social Policy*, Bristol: Policy Press, pp 121–36.

Moth, R. and McKeown, M. (2016) 'Realising Sedgwick's vision: theorising strategies of resistance to neoliberal mental health and welfare policy', *Critical and Radical Social Work*, vol 4, no 3, pp 375–90.

Moth, R., Greener, J. and Stoll, P. (2015) 'Crisis and resistance in mental health services in England', *Critical and Radical Social Work*, vol 3, no 1, pp 89–102.

NHS Digital (2017) 'Mental Health Act statistics, annual figures 2016/17', NHS Digital, https://files.digital.nhs.uk/pdf/b/t/ment-heal-act-stat-eng-2016–17-summ-rep.pdf [accessed 30 May 2018].

NHS England (2016) 'Implementing the five year forward view for mental health. Redditch: NHS England', https://www.england.nhs.uk/wp-content/uploads/2016/07/fyfv-mh.pdf [accessed 21 June 2018].

Perkins, R., Meddings, S., Williams, S. and Repper, J. (2018) *Recovery Colleges 10 Years On: ImROC Briefing 15*, Nottingham: ImROC.

Pilgrim, D. and McCranie, A. (2013) *Recovery and Mental Health: A Critical Sociological Account*, Basingstoke: Palgrave Macmillan.

Pilgrim, D. and Ramon, S. (2009) 'English mental health policy under New Labour', *Policy and Politics*, vol 37, no 2, pp 273–88.

Porter, R. (1987) *Mind-Forg'd Manacles: A History of Madness in England from the Restoration to the Regency*, London: Athlone Press.

Ramon, S. (2006) 'British mental health social work and the psychosocial approach in context', in D.B. Double (ed), *Critical Psychiatry*, London: Palgrave Macmillan, pp 133–48.

Razzaque, R. and Stockmann, T. (2016) 'An introduction to peer-supported open dialogue in mental healthcare', *British Journal of Psychiatry Advances*, vol 22, no 5, pp 348–56.

Recovery in the Bin (nd) 'Key principles', https://recoveryinthebin.org/ritbkeyprinciples/

Rogers, A. and Pilgrim, D. (2001) *Mental Health Policy in Britain* (2nd edn), Houndmills: Palgrave.

Rogers, A. and Pilgrim, D. (2014) *A Sociology of Mental Health and Illness* (5th edn), Maidenhead: Open University Press.

Roulstone, A. (2015) 'Personal Independence Payments, welfare reform and the shrinking disability category', *Disability and Society*, vol 30, no 5, pp 673–88.

Scott, M.J. (2018) 'Improving Access to Psychological Therapies (IAPT): the need for radical reform', *Journal of Health Psychology*, vol 23, no 9, pp 1136–47.

Shennan, G. and Unwin, P. (2017) 'The important thing is to keep fighting, and to fight with care, love, respect, and a passion for justice', *Professional Social Work* (October), Birmingham: BASW, pp 28–9.

Simeon, R. (2003), 'Free personal care. policy divergence and social citizenship', in R. Hazell (ed), *The State of the Nations 2003*, Exeter, Imprint Academic.

Tew J. (2005) *Social Perspectives in Mental Health: Developing Social Models to Understand and Work with Mental Distress*, London: Jessica Kingsley.

Tew, J. (2011) *Social Approaches to Mental Distress*, Houndmills: Palgrave Macmillan.

Triggle, N. (2011) 'Prescription charges abolished in Scotland', BBC (1 April), https://www.bbc.co.uk/news/uk-12928485 [accessed 4 August 2018].

Trueman, J. (2013) 'The mirage of mental health law reform', in S. Walker (ed), *Modern Mental Health: Critical Perspectives on Psychiatric Practice*, St Albans: Critical Publishing.

Wacquant, L. (2010) 'Crafting the neoliberal state: workfare, prisonfare, and social insecurity', *Sociological Forum*, vol 25, no 2, pp 197–220.

Walker, C. (2015) 'A dance of destitution – psychology's clash over coercion', *Open Democracy* (16 June). Available at: https://www.opendemocracy.net/ournhs/carl-walker/dance-of-destitution-psychology's-clash-over-coercion [accessed 22 June 2018].

Watts, B. and Fitzpatrick, S. (2018) *Welfare Conditionality*, London: Routledge.

Welsh Government (2015) *Social Services and Well-being (Wales) Act 2014: The Essentials*, Welsh Government. Available at: https://gov.wales/docs/dhss/publications/160127socialservicesacten.pdf

WHO (World Health Organization) (2014) *Social Determinants of Mental Health*, Geneva: WHO.

9

The criminal justice system

Ian Cummins

Introduction

Until 2001, probation officers in England and Wales qualified as social workers. Probation was a social work agency based in the courts and prisons, focusing its work on the rehabilitation of offenders. The changes to probation training were the result of broader moves within criminal justice policy that led to more punitive approaches to offending (Garland, 2001). Social work practice in England and Wales has now been marginalised in the Criminal Justice System (CJS) (Cummins, 2016). In particular, the training and roles of probation officers have changed very dramatically. One of the most significant cultural changes has been the removal of a broader consensus around penal policy that focused on the rehabilitation of offenders and sought to limit the use of imprisonment to the most serious offences. As Simon (2007) notes, progressive political parties have found it difficult to challenge the basic assumptions of the new, punitive approach, which holds that crime is rising and the proper response should be to introduce longer sentences and harsher conditions in prison. The result in England and Wales has been a doubling of the prison population since the early 1990s. The first private prison, HMP Wolds, was opened under the Major Government in 1992. Since then, in addition to the expansion of the use of imprisonment, the private sector has played an increased role in the CJS. As well as running prisons, private companies such as G4S and Serco have won contracts in several areas, for example, the electronic tagging and monitoring of offenders. In political terms, the only influential politician to raise doubts about our addiction to imprisonment has been Kenneth Clarke MP, on his return to the Ministry of Justice in 2010. The appointment of Rory Stewart MP as the minister responsible for prisons in 2018 was another important step. Early in his tenure, Stewart made a number of statements about the need for a rethink on penal policy, emphasising that prisons had to tackle deeply entrenched issues such as staff shortages, violence and drugs if they were to fulfil a rehabilitative function.

The CJS has historically been a key site of social work intervention. Wacquant (2009) argues that the growth of social insecurity and the expansion of the penal state are key features of neoliberalism. These have been accepted by parties of both the Left and the Right. This shift, alongside an increase in inequality, has led to increasing social anxiety and mistrust. One manifestation of these trends is a decline in the belief that the rehabilitation of offenders is a realisable goal of social and penal policy. The expansion of the penal state, the increasing numbers of prisoners, the poor conditions and the over-representation of minority groups make the CJS a key social justice issue. It should therefore be a core social work concern. However, risk and managerialism have side-lined core social work values in the CJS. A wholesale reform of the CJS, including reducing the use of imprisonment and improving conditions in jails, needs to be based on a recognition of the inherent human dignity of offenders (Cummins, 2016).

The role of the CJS

The CJS is a complex, messy and often contradictory system. It includes a huge range of actors and agencies – the police, courts, prisons, politicians, the media, academics, charities and voluntary groups. These often have competing or diametrically opposed goals. The operation of the CJS raises fundamental questions about the relationship between the individual and the state. What should the rights of the suspect in custody be? How should the prison system balance retribution and punishment with the broader aims of rehabilitation. One of the strongest arguments put forward by prison reformers is that the current prison system does little, if anything, to rehabilitate offenders. In England and Wales there are a small number of prisoners who are sentenced to a whole-life tariff, meaning that they will never be released. The rest of the prison population will return to the community one day. The reformist argument is that what happens to people in prison will have a lasting impact on this re-entry into community life. It is important, therefore, that the CJS is transparent, fair and treats people with dignity. The opposing argument is that prison, in particular, should act as a deterrent and that it can do so only if the conditions are harsh. Prisoners, it is argued, have surrendered certain claims to liberty and civic life by virtue of having infringed societal norms. Within this strand, it is often argued that we should focus much more on the impact of offending on victims and families.

Weber (1954) saw the administration of justice as an archetype of rational organisation. There is a clear set of highly defined and prescribed rules that cover all situations. These then produce a predictable set of outcomes. There is a disconnect between this analysis and the day-to-day practice of the CJS. Actors at all levels of the system follow informal, often locally agreed processes – the *rules of the game*. Key actors such as police officers, prosecutors and judges have very significant discretion that they exercise. This discretion arises from the number of rules and their complexity and ambiguity. For example, a police officer attending a disturbance in the street has a range of potential choices for action. These include arrest, but also taking no formal action. An apparently straightforward case, for example, an assault, can be described or categorised in a number of ways. Like all bureaucracies, the CJS would collapse under the weight of its own contradictions if the 'rules' were followed to the letter at all times.

The overall goal of the CJS is to detect and apprehend those suspected of crimes, process those arrested, determine guilt or innocence and then punish those who are found guilty. As outlined below, since the 1970s the focus of punishment has moved from reform and rehabilitation to retribution and incarceration. The liberal view is that punishment must not be so severe as to breach standards and norms. Hence, the banning of 'cruel and inhumane' forms of punishment. The system must also be based on due process, which provides protections for individuals facing prosecution. Martinson's (1974) famous study of penal rehabilitation, *What Works?*, came to the conclusion that nothing did, and that support for the whole notion was flawed. If rehabilitation is not an aim of the CJS, then that means that it must concentrate on the defence of the wider society. Punishment should concentrate, therefore, on retribution and deterrence.

Comparing penal systems

The CJS of any state reflects a range of social, economic, political, historical and cultural factors. Lacey (2008) forcefully argues that it is important to examine these broader influences when discussing penal policy and reform. For example, she argues that liberal market economies, such as the US, have a strong cultural commitment to individualism. This is one of the factors that needs to be examined when discussing the increase in the use of imprisonment across the US. However, within this debate, it is important to recognise that there are significant variations between the 50 states. In similar fashion, Lacey (2008) argues that social democratic countries with a commitment to using welfare state regimes to tackle inequality have lower rates of imprisonment because of this factor. Cavadino and Dignan (2006) developed a typology of the links between political, economic and penal systems. Their ideal types were *neoliberal, conservative corporatist, social democratic* and *oriental corporatist*. There are examples of all these types, apart from oriental corporatist, within Europe and the EU. Rates of imprisonment are discussed in more detail below. Within Europe, the Baltic states and the countries of the former Soviet bloc have the highest rates of imprisonment. It would be expected that these rates would fall as liberal democratic political regimes became more established. Downes and Hansen (2006) outlined a clear correlation between welfare provision and penal policy. Countries with the lowest spending on welfare, such as the UK and the US, have the highest rates of imprisonment. The link between rates of imprisonment and offending is a complex one. However, the use of imprisonment, in the UK and the US, has increased during a period when, as in most liberal democracies, crime rates overall have been falling.

Scandinavian welfare and penal regimes are often seen as exceptional. The Swedish welfare state is usually presented as an ideal type of a welfare state which is well resourced and also politically and socially popular. This model of excellent public services funded by relatively high personal and corporate taxation has come under increasing pressure. Globalisation allows corporations to move capital quickly across the world. This means that the governments of nation-states do not have the power that they once enjoyed. The Scandinavian welfare state – a real-world example of the social democratic ideal type – has come under political pressure from the Right. Anti-immigrant parties have successfully the linked the issues of welfare and immigration – a pattern that is a consistent feature of anti-welfare state discourse. It is important to acknowledge the political and economic pressures on Scandinavian exceptionalism in penal policy. However, the differences between, for example, the prison system in Norway and that in England and Wales are still startling. This is not just about the low rates of imprisonment, but also the physical conditions. Prisoners in Scandinavian penal systems are often working or studying full time. If they are in open prisons, then they can remain in employment. It would take not just a huge investment in English prisons for these conditions to be achieved. It would also require a very significant shift in political and public opinion.

Young people and the CJS

Young offenders present the CJS with a range of ethical and moral dilemmas. The first of these is the age of criminal responsibility. The age of criminal responsibility in England and Wales and in Northern Ireland is ten years old. Under the age of ten, a child cannot be arrested or charged with a crime. In May 2019, the Scottish Parliament introduced legislation to raise the minimum age of criminal responsibility from eight to 12. The age of criminal responsibility varies significantly across Europe. For example, it is 14 in Spain, 18 in France and 12 in Ireland.

In England and Wales, anyone under the age of 18 is defined as a child. Penal systems, on the whole, recognise that children, because they are children, should not be treated in the same way as adults. This argument is based on theories of childhood development but does not mean that children cannot commit the most serious of offences. It is an argument that the state should not only focus on punishment but also recognise welfare issues. For example, the Children and Young Persons Act 1933 stated that the welfare of the child is paramount when any form of court deals with a child.

Post-World War II, the approach to young offenders focused on welfare and treatment. Rising crime rates and a moral panic about youth crime (Hall et al, 2013) saw a swing to more punitive approaches. The 1979 Conservative Manifesto argued that children needed a 'short, sharp, shock', that is exposure to quasi-military-style discipline at attendance centres. The early 1980s saw regular calls at Conservative Party conferences for the reintroduction of physical punishment – birching – of young offenders. These calls were resisted (Gilmour, 1992). Increased crime levels in the 1980s, as well as high-profile cases, for example the murder of James Bulger in 1993 (Morrison, 1998), by two ten-year-old boys, fuelled a much wider concern about youth offending. The CJS became increasingly punitive. New Labour introduced the Crime and Disorder Act 1998, which explicitly stated that 'the principal aim of youth justice is to prevent offending by children and young persons'.

The 1998 Act established the Youth Justice Board (YJB), which has the following aims:

- preventing offending
- reducing reoffending
- increasing victim and public confidence
- ensuring the safe and effective use of custody.

The Police and Criminal Evidence Act 1984

In 1972, Maxwell Confait was murdered in London and his flat was set on fire. This case does not have the profile of some of the other cases of miscarriages of justice, such as those of the Birmingham Six or the Guildford Four that shook the CJS in the 1970s, but it was to have huge ramifications for the legal system. An 18-year-old and two juveniles were convicted of offences related to the crime based on confession evidence that was later found to have been obtained under duress. The case led to the introduction of a new framework for the detention and questioning of individuals in police custody governed by the Police and Criminal Evidence Act (PACE) 1984. Fly-on-the-wall TV documentaries such as '24 Hours in Police Custody' have made the key elements of this legislation, such as the tape recording of interviews, limits on how long people can be detained without charge and the right to legal advice, familiar to the general public.

PACE 1984 recognises three groups who are afforded special protections in custody: all juveniles, and adults with either a learning difficulty or a mental health problem. If a juvenile is interviewed by the police in custody, then an 'Appropriate Adult' (AA) must be present. The AA can be a social worker or family member. The AA role was created to 'facilitate the interview', to ensure that the young person has appropriate breaks and so on. In her research, Pierpoint (2006) identified 'mission creep', with AAs offering welfare advice and support. AAs do not enjoy legal privilege in the same way that a solicitor does, so they may be asked about conversations they have held with the detained person.

The UK's domestic law, alongside international human rights obligations, means that a custodial sentence must be imposed only as a last resort. In the Youth Courts, imprisonment can be used only in cases where the offence is so serious that this is the sole course of action that may be taken. Apart from custodial sentences, Youth Courts have a range of disposals available when sentencing. These include absolute and conditional discharge, reparation orders, youth referral orders and youth rehabilitation orders. A referral order is a welfare-orientated intervention. It requires the young person to attend a Youth Offender Panel, made up of two members of the local community and an advisor from a youth offending team. The young person agrees a contract, which will last between three months and a year. The aim is for the offender to take steps to address their offending behaviour as well as making good the harm that they caused. There is no adult-equivalent sentence. Youth rehabilitation orders are a form of community sentence. The offender must comply with one or more requirements, which could include a curfew, supervision, unpaid work, electronic monitoring or drug treatment.

The Scottish model of youth justice

After the Act of Union in 1707, Scotland retained its distinct legal and penal system. In modern criminal justice, this is perhaps most apparent in the response to young offenders. Since 1971 Scotland has had its own juvenile justice system, based on the principle of the welfare of the child. Children's Hearings are lay tribunals which consider cases involving children who have committed offences. An independent officer, the Children's Reporter, decides which cases appear at these hearings. The Children's Hearing system was established following a review of the juvenile justice system headed by a judge, Lord Kilbrandon. The resulting report included the outline of the key principles that were to underpin a reformed juvenile justice system. At the core of the report is a recognition that young people in trouble with the authorities often come from difficult and disrupted family circumstances and live in deprived communities. The Kilbrandon report argued that in responding to youth offending recognition of the needs of the child must be the primary consideration. The family has a key role in tackling children's problems. Finally, authorities must adopt a preventive and educational approach (Kilbrandon, 1966).

The Children's Hearing system means that in Scotland there is a body separate from the courts with responsibility for making decisions. There are echoes here of Scandinavian Children's Welfare Boards and their welfare approach. 'Safeguarders' were introduced into the Scottish system to deal with situations where conflicts of interest might exist between child and parents.

The system has not been without its critics. Tribunal members are much more likely to come from middle-class and professional backgrounds. In addition, the welfare focus of the system has been attacked for being 'soft on crime'. Policy in this area swings between calls for more punitive approaches – longer sentences for young offenders – and moves to focus on the broader social factors that result in offending. These tensions are evident across the CJS but are particularly apparent in this field.

The penal state

The use of imprisonment has been on an upward trend since the early 1980s. This has been most apparent in the US, and England and Wales is the jurisdiction that has most closely followed the trend. Scholars have used a number of terms to describe this: 'mass incarceration', 'mass imprisonment', 'the prison boom', 'the carceral state' and 'the penal state'. Simon (2014) has compared the expansion of the use of imprisonment to a biblical flood – a flood that he now sees as past its peak. As he notes, the flood is receding, leaving behind the damage it has inflicted and continues to inflict on families, individuals and communities.

It might seem odd, from the current perspective, that in the mid-1970s sociologists and policy makers were predicting the end of the prison as an institution. The question to consider, then, is why rates of imprisonment have increased so dramatically. Simon (2007) outlines the way that, from the mid-1970s onwards, crime and law and order became much more contested political issues. There have always been arguments about the balance between punishment and rehabilitation. However, there was a general consensus that imprisonment should be the last resort. The call for greater use of physical punishment, and particularly the return of the death penalty, was associated with the right wing of the Conservative Party in the UK. Such populist policy was viewed as being on the periphery, but moved much more into the mainstream from the late 1970s onwards. Simon (2007) identifies a mixture of social and political causes. It is important to recognise that the fear of crime, particularly of violent crime, plays a key role here. Simon (2007) argues that there is something of a time lag between changes in the crime rate and changes in broader social and cultural attitudes. Crime rates have been generally falling, but the fear of crime has remained widespread. This fear is in part fuelled by media reports of and focus on the most violent and rarest of crimes, such as serial murder. Penal populism – calls by politicians to ignore the so-called liberal elites, whom they see as having a grip on penal policy – became a key feature of the politics of the New Right in the 1980s. Its main contention was that society had 'gone soft'. The CJS was not on the side of the victim; new laws and a human rights agenda meant the hands of the police were tied in the fight against crime; and conditions in prison were too easy.

The political success of the Reagan and Thatcher Governments was in part due to a strong law and order platform. They argued that their progressive opponents supported policies such as more shorter sentences and community punishments that did not act as deterrents to offenders. Progressive parties feared the political fall-out from being seen as weak on the key issues of law and order. The result was an increase in the use of custody; prosecutors seeking custodial sentences where previously a community penalty would have been imposed; the increasing length of sentences; and the introduction of mandatory and/or indeterminate sentences. Garland (2001) noted that the impact of the penal populism of the 1990s remains long after the politicians who made those decisions have left public life.

Imprisonment is measured by the rate per 100,000 of the population. Since 1999 the overall world prison population has increased from 136 per 100,000 to 144 per 100,000. The US has the highest rate at 716 per 100,000. In a much-quoted statistic the US has just under 5% of the world's population, but 25% of its prison population. The overall average for the US hides huge disparities between individual states. Carson and Golinelli's (2013) analysis shows that the five states with highest levels of imprisonment – Louisiana (1,720), Mississippi (1,370), Alabama (1,234), Oklahoma (1,178) and Texas (1,121) – have rates well above the national average. If they were countries, these states would lead the world in the rates of imprisonment. The impact of imprisonment is not restricted to the individuals involved and it is impossible to overlook the issue of race. There is a significant body of research that demonstrates the wider damage that has been done to the African-American community (Mauer, 2006; Clear, 2009; Drucker, 2011). This damage does not end when individuals are released. Many US states prevent ex-prisoners from voting, accessing social housing or completing educational programmes. Alexander (2012) powerfully argues that the overall effect serves to create a new 'caste' of disenfranchised and marginalised young black men.

Walmsley (2015) notes there are now 10.2 million people who are held in penal institutions across the world, of whom 2.4 million are in prison in the US. The US, Russia (0.68 million) and China (1.64 million) together hold nearly half the world's prisoners. Alongside the expansion in prison numbers, the private sector has had an increasing role in the CJS generally and in prisons in particular. Commercial companies such as G4S have been given lucrative contracts to manage immigration detention centres and the electronic tagging of offenders. Wacquant (2009) shows the ways in which the 'prison industry' has become a key player in local employment. In the US this is particularly the case in rural areas. Prison work provides secure, relatively well-paid jobs with benefits such as health insurance that are not widely available in generally impoverished communities. This creates a vicious circle in which any reductions in the rate of imprisonment will be seen as an economic threat, and this contributes to political pressure at local and national levels.

In the UK, African-Caribbean citizens are imprisoned at a rate of 6.8 per 1,000, as compared to 1.3 per 1,000 for white citizens. Twenty-seven per cent of the UK prison population come from a BME background and over two-thirds of that group are serving sentences of over four years (1990 Trust, 2010). Berman (2012) reports that in June 2011 the ethnicity of 13.4% of the prison population was recorded was Black or Black British. This group comprises 2.7% of the general population. It is estimated that 70% of the French prison population is Muslim; the Muslim proportion in the general population is 8%. As it is illegal to collect figures on ethnic background in France, no official statistics exist. The use of imprisonment is also related to issues of class, poverty and inequality. The overwhelming majority of prisoners come from disadvantaged and impoverished backgrounds.

The CJS is an area that is both common and unknown (Skolnick, 1966). It is common because of the saturation media coverage of crime and law and order. Crime has been a persistently prominent feature of the modern media since its invention. Crime drama abounds on TV and film and these genres are dominated by a series of tropes that are far removed from the day-to-day reality of policing and the courts (Cummins et al, 2014). TV dramas, films and novels are headed by brilliant but jaded detectives tracking down serial killers and rapists, while leaving a trail of havoc and destruction in the detectives' own family and personal lives. The advent of the film-on-the-wall documentary has seen an overlap between fictional and reality TV accounts. TV documentary makers use many of the same techniques – for example, the shot of a detective driving at night through a bleak but beautifully photographed urban landscape. In reality, only a minority of the population have direct contact with the CJS.

Taylor (2003) argues that important social issues are often discussed not in theoretical terms. We use images, stories and myths. This is clearly evident in the area of penal policy where high-profile cases perform a similar function. Wacquant (2009) argues that the US can be viewed as a laboratory and that a nexus of think-tanks and prominent individuals such as Bill Bratton, a former Los Angeles Police Department and New York Police Department commissioner, have facilitated the spread of these penal policies. High-profile crimes – for example, the murder of toddler James Bulger in 1993 – come to be seen as representative of broader social and cultural trends. In the politics of mass incarceration, the use of the Willie Horton case by George Bush (Snr) in the presidential election of 1988 is another example. Horton was convicted of murder in 1974, and committed another murder when he was on weekend release in 1986. Bush used this case to argue that his opponent, Dukakis, was weak on crime. Pfaff (2016) identifies what he terms the 'Horton effect' where one case is used to undermine the argument for all systems of parole or early release. This is clearly not to deny the awful nature of the crimes that Horton committed. It is to emphasise that no system can possibly guarantee that a convicted offender will not commit any further offences on release. Garland (2001) argues that penal populism makes an unrealistic demand of rehabilitative systems. It also uses serious violent offenders, particularly sex offenders, as a proxy for all offenders.

To use Taylor's (2003) notion of myths and images, the increase in the use of imprisonment in the US and the UK has been driven by an often-racialised image of the offender as a young, strong, physically fit male. This is used in part as one of the key arguments for mass incarceration: the need for incapacitation. In the early 1990s the then home secretary, Michael Howard, argued that 'prison works'. He did so on the basis that prison has a deterrent effect, and also that it means that those in custody cannot commit crime. It clearly is the case that offenders can and do commit offences in custody. These are generally not given a high profile because the victims tend to be other offenders. However, the chaos in prisons has seen an increase in assaults on prison officers, alongside examples of offenders dealing drugs and so on. The incapacitation argument is also used by those who see prison conditions as 'soft' or 'too cushy'. One of the biggest changes in the prison population is the age profile of inmates. Longer sentences, stricter systems for parole and restrictions on release mean that the prison population is ageing. Alongside this, the prosecution of historical sexual abuse cases and the development of DNA technologies mean that older offenders, defined as those over 50 years of age, are the biggest growing group in the prison population. This means that prison authorities face a new range of challenges in providing services to deal with the healthcare needs of an ageing population, including, for example, appropriate services to address the physical and mental health needs of prisoners with dementia. The Care Act 2014 means that local authorities have new duties in this area.

Offenders are usually represented as young, physically fit and healthy. However, the reality is somewhat different. Offenders almost overwhelming come from poor and marginalised communities. They therefore have a greater level of healthcare needs than the wider community, including mental and physical health issues (Cummins, 2016). The Trencin Statement (WHO European Office, 2007), which outlines the UN position on the treatment of prisoners, states that 'Prisoners shall have access to the health services available in the country without discrimination on the grounds of their legal situation'. The 2013–14 report from HM Inspector of Prisons in England and Wales paints a very disturbing portrait of the current prison regime. The Chief Inspector reported that there was a 69% rise in suicides in prison in 2013–14, describing it as 'the most unacceptable feature' of a prison system that is experiencing a 'rapid deterioration' in safety standards. The report paints a picture of prisons where bullying, violence (including sexual violence) and intimidation are commonplace. As the Royal College of Nursing (2004) outlines, there is a higher incidence of long-term health conditions and chronic disease. These conditions include coronary heart disease, diabetes, mental health issues, substance misuse and HIV. Those groups in society who face the greatest barriers to or are less likely to access healthcare in the community – young men/sex workers/intravenous drug users – are also much more likely to be incarcerated. The problems outlined above are exacerbated by overcrowding, which is a consistent feature of the wider use of imprisonment.

It was noted above that people from minority communities across the world are over-represented within prison systems. Though women are imprisoned in smaller numbers, there has been a significant rise in the numbers of women in jail. For example, in England and Wales the number of women in prison tripled from 1990 to 2010. There are particular issues related to the imprisonment of women. The Corston Inquiry (2007) was established following a rise in cases of suicide and self-harm among women in prison in England and Wales. Women are much less likely than men to commit violent or other serious offences, meaning that they are more likely to be sentenced to shorter periods in custody. There are also fewer female prisons. Women are thus more likely to be sent to a jail further from their local community. The Inquiry report gives a stark outline of the wider factors in the lives of the women in custody: 37% had attempted suicide at some time in their life; 51% had severe and enduring mental illness; over 50% had been subjected to domestic abuse; and one in three had been sexually abused. These figures are astonishing. A report by the Howard League for Prison Reform (Epstein, 2010) demonstrates that children are the forgotten victims of escalating incarceration.

Finding a way forward

Michel Foucault, one of the most influential scholars of the development of prisons and punishment, wrote *Discipline and Punish* (1977) at a time that, in retrospect, can be viewed as the initial period of mass incarceration. The book begins with a long passage outlining the punishments inflicted on Damiens, who had attempted to assassinate King Louis XV in 1757. The contemporary reader is shocked by the sheer level of brutality inflicted on Damiens *before* he is dismembered. Foucault argued that punishment has to be understood as a regulated cultural practice. The physical nature of the punishment reflects the belief that crime was considered an offence against the monarch. This is not just the case for Damiens, but for all offenders. The symbols and rituals of punishment reflect the value system of the society that produces it. Having outlined the physical punishment inflicted on Damiens in great detail, Foucault contrasts it with the timetable produced by Foucher at a 19th-century Parisian prison. The timetable, almost like a school timetable, sets out what prisoners will be doing at all hours of the day. Other rules of the prison, including, for example, the banning of prisoners talking to each other, meant that the warders exerted a form of total control. The aim of the regime was to force the prisoners to reject their criminal behaviour. For Foucault it represents the core Enlightenment values of rationality. The prison regime is based on ideas about how to bring about change in offenders. There is a shift from physical punishment and a move to modifying behaviour. The focus of punishment is not the body of the offender but their mind. Foucault argues that, from the French Revolution onwards, punishment moves from being a public spectacle to an administrative and bureaucratic process. As the definition of what constituted a crime remained largely unchanged, this shift, Foucault argues, can be explained only by changes in societal values. This does not represent progress but, rather, a shift in the ways that social control and domination are exercised.

There is a danger of assuming that our current systems of punishment, with all their acknowledged faults, still represent progress. We are much more liberal and civilised; we no longer brand, whip or execute offenders – though a return to such punishments might be more popular than we would like to think. However, I would argue that mass incarceration, with its focus on incapacitation, represents another shift. It inevitably leads to overcrowding and the sorts of poor conditions that have been outlined above. In such conditions, constructive rehabilitation becomes almost impossible. The result is that the body of the offender has once again become the site of punishment. There has been a paradigmatic shift. Examples would include the attempt by the then Secretary of State for Justice Chris Grayling to ban the sending of books to prisoners in England and Wales. In the US, the activities and policies of Arizona Sheriff Joe Arpaio, who was given a presidential pardon by President Trump, were widely criticised. Arpaio prided himself on forcing offenders to wear pink underwear and sleep in tents in the baking local heat, as well as boasting of spending more on food for the prison dogs than for the inmates.

The focus in this chapter has been on the rate of imprisonment, which is viewed as a measure of the relative punitive nature of the modern CJS. As well as looking at the rate of imprisonment, it is important to look at the conditions in prisons. The CJS is, or should be, a very important area of concern for social work. This is not just because there is a need for social work in the institutions of prisons. Many who are in prison have had some form of contact with social services; for example, many offenders have experienced periods in public care as children. The Corston Inquiry highlighted the complex needs of women who are in prison. Mental health, the impact of substance misuse and sexual violence, are all areas where social workers have traditionally had an important role in services.

CASE STUDY 9.1: 'WAR ON DRUGS'

Much offending is linked to drug and substance misuse. Alcohol misuse is a factor in much violent offending, including domestic violence and wider public disorder. The policing of the night-time economy is one the most important challenges for police forces. Recreational drug use has become more widespread, but the possession, supply and use of drugs such as ecstasy and cocaine remain illegal. In addition to offending, there are a whole series of personal, social and community harms that are the result of drug and alcohol misuse. The harmful impacts of drug use, however, are greater in poorer and more deprived communities (MacGregor, 2017). In the UK, rates of recorded drug misuse deaths are nine times higher in the most deprived areas than least deprived areas, despite similar consumption rates (Stevens, 2018).

Social work and the CJS are drawn into the response to issues of drug and substance misuse. Social workers and health profession colleagues will be working in services that support people to tackle addiction and other related issues. At the same time, those working in the CJS will be involved in systems that punish those who commit offences related to drug and substance misuse – for example, thefts and shoplifting to fund a drug habit. One of the drivers of the increase in the use of imprisonment outlined above has been the so-called 'war on drugs'. This rhetoric has built up public and political support for a zero-tolerance approach to drug policy, marginalising harm reduction and rehabilitation in favour of more punitive measures (Chatwin, 2018).

The challenge to the 'war on drugs' rhetoric is to argue that substance misuse should be seen as a public health issue. Such an approach is based on the public health principles of education about the potential harms of drug and substance misuse and the establishment of a range of services that can support people to reduce their reliance on or addiction to drugs. Within this approach is an implicit recognition that the 'war on drugs' is unwinnable and does more damage than good to individuals and communities. Policy approaches such as the 'war on drugs' that treat drug use as an individual and moral problem have caused great socioeconomic harm to vulnerable communities, increasing experiences of social isolation, stigmatisation and criminalisation, while failing to reduce drug consumption and deaths from drug misuse (Patten, 2016; Chatwin, 2018). For a longer discussion of addiction and associated issues, see Chapter 13.

Conclusion

As outlined above, the CJS is a complex system that involves a wide range of actors and agencies, including the police, social workers, the courts and charities. The CJS responds to a huge range of crimes and offences, from murder to shoplifting. The reporting of crime has a high media profile. Responses to crime are often a reflection to wider social unease. Crime becomes a site for debates about the nature of society and community relationships. Since the mid-1970s there has been a shift towards more punitive attitudes and policies. When analysing penal regimes, it is important to look at the broader perspectives of social, welfare and education policies. Law and order cannot be viewed in isolation from the wider society. The current crisis in prison systems provides a potential opportunity for reform.

Critical questions

1 What are the links between wider social, welfare and education policies and the CJS?

2 What should the balance be between the rights of offenders, victims and the wider community?

3 Does prison act as a deterrent?

4 Which factors should courts consider when sentencing offenders?

5 What can and should be done to challenge the discrimination that is evident in the CJS?

6 What role should social work and social workers have in the CJS?

Further reading

• British Academy (2014) *A Presumption Against Imprisonment*, retrieved from www.britac.uk
This review argues that too many people are sent to prison, and looks at alternatives.

• Cavadino, M. and Dignan, J. (2006) *Penal Systems: A Comparative Approach*, London: Sage.
This classic text provides an analysis of welfare systems and penal policy.

• Cummins, I. (2016), 'Social work and the penal state', *European Journal of Social Work*, vol 20, no 1, pp 54–63.
This article outlines the expansion of the use of imprisonment and argues that it is a key issue for social work.

• Drug Policy Alliance (2011) *Drug Policy Alliance and Global Commission on Drug Policy June 2011 Media Report*, retrieved from www.drugpolicy.org
This briefing paper outlines alternatives to the war on drugs.

- Martinson, R. (1974) 'What works? Questions and answers about prison reform', *The Public Interest* (Spring), pp 22–54.
  This is a very influential article arguing that prison reform was a failure.

- Simon, J. (2007) *Governing Through Crime: How the War on Crime Transformed American Democracy and Created a Culture of Fear*, Oxford: Oxford University Press.
  The author examines the political impact of law and order policies.

References

1990 Trust (2010) *The Price of Race Inequality: The Black Manifesto*, London: 1990trust.org.uk.

Alexander, M. (2012) *The New Jim Crow: Mass Incarceration In the Age of Colorblindness*, New York: New Press.

Berman, G. (2012) *Prison Population Statistics*, London: House of Commons Library.

Carson, E. and Golinelli, D. (2013) *Prisoners in 2012: Trends in Admissions and Releases 1991–2013*, www.bjs.gov/content/pub/pdf/p12tar9112.pdf

Cavadino, M. and Dignan, J. (2006) *Penal Systems: A Comparative Approach*, London: Sage.

Chatwin, C. (2018) *Towards More Effective Global Drug Policies*, London: Springer.

Clear, T. (2009) *Imprisoning Communities: How Mass Incarceration Makes Disadvantaged Neighborhoods Worse*, New York: Oxford University Press.

Corston, J. (Chair) (2007) *Review of Women with Particular Vulnerabilities in the Criminal Justice System*, London: HMSO.

Cummins, I. (2016) *Mental Health and the Criminal Justice System: A Social Work Perspective*, Northwich: Critical Publishing.

Cummins, I., Foley, M. and King, M. (2014.) '"… and after the break": Police officers' views of TV crime drama', *Policing: A Journal of Policy and Practice*, vol 8, no 2, pp 205–11.

Downes, D. and Hansen, K. (2006) *Welfare and Punishment*, retrieved from www.crimeandsociety.org.uk

Drucker, E. (2011) *A Plagues of Prisons: The Epidemiology of Mass Incarceration in America*, New York: New Press.

Epstein, R. (2010) *Mothers in Prison: The Sentencing of Mothers and the Rights of the Child*, available at www.howardleague.org.uk

Foucault, M. (1977) *Discipline and Punish*, trans A. Sheridan, London: Penguin.

Garland, D. (2001) *The Culture of Control: Crime and Social Order in Contemporary Society*, Oxford: Oxford University Press.

Gilmour, I. (1992) *Dancing with Dogma: Britain under Thatcherism*, London: Simon and Schuster.

Hall, S., Critcher, C., Jefferson, T., Clarke, J. and Roberts, B. (2013) *Policing the Crisis: Mugging, the State and Law and Order*, Basingstoke: Palgrave Macmillan.

Kilbrandon, L. (1966) 'Children in trouble', *The British Journal of Criminology*, pp 112–22. Available at: https://www2.gov.scot/Resource/Doc/47049/0023863.pdf

Lacey, N. (2008) *The Prisoners' Dilemma: Political Economy and Punishment in Contemporary Democracies*, Cambridge: Cambridge University Press.

MacGregor, S. (2017) *The Politics of Drugs: Perceptions, Power and Policies*, London: Springer.

Martinson, R. (1974) 'What works? Questions and answers about prison reform', *The Public Interest* (Spring), pp 22–54.

Mauer, M. (2006) *The Race to Incarcerate*, New York: New Press.

Morrison, B. (1998) *As If*, London: Granta.

Pfaff, J. (2016) *Locked In: The True Causes of Mass Incarceration – And How to Achieve Real Reform*, New York: Basic Books.

Pierpoint, H. (2006) 'Reconstructing the role of the appropriate adult in England and Wales', *Criminology & Criminal Justice*, vol 6, no 2, pp 219–37.

Royal College of Nursing (2004) *Health and Nursing Care in the Criminal Justice Service: RCN Guidance for Nursing Staff*. Available at: www.rcn.org.uk

Simon, J. (2007) *Governing Through Crime: How the War on Crime Transformed American Democracy and Created a Culture of Fear*, Oxford: Oxford University Press.

Simon, J. (2014) *Mass Incarceration on Trial: A Remarkable Court Decision and the Future of Prisons in America*, New York: The New Press.

Skolnick, J. (1966) *Justice Without Trial*, New York: John Wiley and Son.

Stevens, A. (2018) '"Being human" and the "moral sidestep" in drug policy: explaining government inaction on opioid-related deaths in the UK', *Addictive Behaviors*, vol 90, pp 444–50.

Taylor, C. (2003) *Modern Social Imaginaries*, Durham, NC: Duke University Press.

Wacquant, L. (2009) *Punishing the Poor: The Neoliberal Government of Social Insecurity*, Durham, NC: Duke University Press.

Walmsley, R. (2015) *World Prison Population List*, London: Institute for Criminal Policy Research.

Weber, M. (1954) *Max Weber on Law in Economy and Society* (Vol. 6), Cambridge, MA: Harvard University Press.

WHO European Office (2007) *Trencin Statement on Prisons and Mental Health*, Copenhagen: WHO. Available at: www.euro.who.int/Document/E91402.pdf

PART III

Emerging themes and issues

Introduction to Part III

Kate Parkinson

The final part of this book presents contemporary challenges and emerging areas of practice for social workers. Its coverage is by no means exhaustive and there are challenges for social work that are not addressed in this part, such as dementia, a global health and social welfare challenge. The chapters provide an introduction to some of the pressing challenges for social work practice in the UK: insecurity, migration, child sexual abuse and exploitation, addiction and radicalisation.

All of these issues and their associated factors – with the exception of radicalisation and insecurity – have long presented a challenge to social work practitioners. Attitudes and responses to these issues have adapted in response to the changing socio-political and economic landscape in the UK. These changes are addressed in the following chapters.

Radicalisation and insecurity are presented as new, emerging areas for social work practice. The increase in religious radicalisation is a challenge for both the adult and children's social care sectors. For example, encouraging children and young people to become radicalised is now recognised as a safeguarding issue for children, and local authorities have developed relevant policies and procedures for social workers and other professionals in response.

Insecurity relates to poverty and inequality and refers to a situation where individuals and families cannot be certain from one month to the next if they can afford basic human needs, such as food, housing and warmth. This is reflected in the increase in food and fuel poverty and homelessness in the UK since 2010.

The authors of the chapters present critical discussions on the changing practice context in their respective service areas. Their discussions are underpinned by a left-leaning approach, which is congruent with the core values of social work, namely social justice, empowerment and equality. These values are embedded in the International Federation of Social Work's definition of social work:

> Social Work is a practice-based profession and an academic discipline that promotes social change and development, social cohesion and the empowerment and liberation of people. Principles of social justice, human rights, collective responsibility and respect for diversities are central to social work. Underpinned by theories of social work, social sciences, humanities and indigenous knowledge, social work engages people and structures to address life challenges and enhance well-being. The above definition may be amplified at national and/or regional levels. (International Federation of Social Work, 2014)

Indeed, social work is becoming an increasingly global profession and one of the key themes emerging from the chapters is the impact of globalisation on social work practice. Other themes discussed below are austerity and the social work practice environment.

Globalisation

Globalisation has had a profound impact on social work in the UK. Globalisation is defined as:

- The acceptance of a set of economic rules for the entire world designed to maximise profits and productivity by universalising markets and production, and to obtain the support of the state with a view to making the national economy more productive and competitive.
- Technological innovation and organisational change centred on flexibilisation and adaptability.
- The reduction of the welfare state, privatisation of social services flexibalisation of labour relations and weaker trade unions.
- De facto transfer to transnational organisations of the control of national economic policy instruments, such as monetary policy, interest rates and fiscal policy;
- The dissemination of common cultural values, but also the re-emergence of nationalism, cultural conflict and social movements. (Urza, 2000, p 421)

Globalisation has resulted in an increase in numbers of economic migrants, as well as refugees and asylum seekers. This movement of population, while having many benefits, has brought with it some challenges for social workers. For example, social workers are faced with an increased number of cases of female genital mutilation and abuse based in faith and beliefs. They are also tasked with supporting people through a bureaucratic and punitive asylum process.

The introduction of a global definition of social work by the International Federation of Social Workers (2014) has cemented the status of social work as a global profession.

Austerity

The global recession of 2008 and the resulting austerity measures in the UK have also had a profound impact on the working environment for social workers and the experiences of people whom social workers support. Public sector cuts have led to reduced resources and services for social workers to tap into to support people, and an increasingly uncomfortable working environment with heavy caseloads and a focus on bureaucratic, managerial processes. Furthermore, austerity-driven welfare reform and the introduction of Universal Credit have resulted in increased poverty and inequality, as stated in earlier chapters. This has created a climate of insecurity, in which fuel and food poverty and homelessness are on the increase. Insecure working practices such as zero-hours contracts exacerbate a climate of fear, as people are unsure from one month to the next whether they will earn enough money to meet their living costs. As stated in earlier chapters, poverty and inequality are associated with poor mental health, drug and alcohol misuse, domestic abuse and reduced capacity to parent, hence placing additional pressure on social care resources.

The social work practice environment

There is a debate to be had about whether social work in the UK encompasses all elements of the global definition of social work, particularly as practice is increasingly defined by bureaucratic, risk-averse practices underpinned by high thresholds of qualification for services and support, and decisions that are often resource- rather than needs-led.

Indeed, in many cases service responses to the issues presented in this final part are taking place outside of the traditional structures of social work practice, as many social workers and social work academics perceive these very structures to be undermining of social justice and exacerbating the difficulties that individuals face. Furthermore, with limited resources local authorities struggle to meet the needs of their populations. Private and charitable organisations are increasingly filling the service gap, alongside radical social work organisations. Social workers are increasingly becoming disillusioned by what they perceive to be the undermining of their profession and the values of social work and by the injustice of governmental policy that has led to increased poverty and inequality among the people whom they are supporting. The emergence of a radical social work movement has challenged existing social work policy and practice as well as wider governmental policy. It has pioneered research about the link between social work and poverty. Organisations like Social Work Action Network (SWAN) and Social Work Without Borders work to challenge the negative impact of governmental policy and reignite the idea that social work is a profession underpinned by social justice. Furthermore, the British Association of Social Work has engaged social workers in challenging austerity and welfare reform. In 2017 it created the 'Boot Out Austerity' campaign, which involved a 100-mile march by social workers and social work academics from Birmingham to Liverpool to highlight the impact of austerity measures and to encourage members to protest and campaign against government policy.

It is clear from the following five chapters that contemporary social work is increasingly changing. Social workers are faced with emerging areas of practice and are increasingly challenged by a political and economic context which makes it difficult for them to practise in a manner which is congruent with the values of social work. The chapters provide readers with an opportunity to consider these practice challenges for social workers and to reflect on the role of contemporary social work. Each chapter lists some critical questions for readers to consider, and some further reading for those who wish to explore an area of social work in greater depth.

References

IFSW (International Federation of Social Workers) (2014) *Global Definition of Social Work*. Available at: www.ifsw.org/what-is-social-work/global-definition-of-social-work/

Urza, R. (2000) *International Social Science 165*, Blackwell Publishers/UNESCO.

10

Insecurity

Sarah Pollock

Introduction

This chapter will explore the different but interconnecting facets of insecurity in contemporary Britain; how political and ideological decision making has increased insecurity by introducing policies of welfare conditionality; and the impact this has had on those needing support. The chapter ends with a consideration of social work's role in supporting individuals, families and groups to manage living with insecurity. This chapter combines a range of issues not often considered together, for example, housing and welfare policy alongside fuel and food poverty. This is an intentional combination that aims to highlight the impact that policies of conditionality across the spectrum of welfare provision have on individuals and families. Often, those experiencing one of these issues are also experiencing multiple disadvantages as a result of welfare reform.

It is important that we first consider what we mean by insecurity in relation to social welfare. 'Insecurity' is defined by the Oxford Dictionary as 'the state of being open to danger or threat; lack of protection' (Oxford Dictionary online). It is poignant, then, that this term is now used to describe the danger or threat of not having substantial warmth, food, work, money or accommodation. The precarity of living in such insecure circumstances can be linked to the increase in welfare conditionality, defined as the belief that

> Access to certain basic, publicly provided, welfare benefits and services should be dependent on an individual first agreeing to meet particular obligations or patterns of behaviour [...]. Those in favour of welfare conditionality believe that individuals that refuse to behave in a responsible manner [...] or who continue to behave irresponsibly [...] should have their rights to support reduced or removed. (Welfare Conditionality, nd)

In this chapter we will examine the relationship between growing insecurity and welfare conditionality, and the ideological beliefs underpinning the implementation of policies that reinforce this strategy.

Austerity, the Coalition government and the Conservative agenda

Following the global financial crisis of 2008, triggered by the collapse of the American investment bank Lehman Brothers, a number of austerity measures were introduced in the UK. In the run-up to the 2010 general election different ideological positions were presented, with the Labour Party (at that time in government) endorsing further spending on infrastructure in order to increase employment and create a more affluent population with more to spend, thus boosting the economy. In opposition, the Conservative Party predominantly advocated austerity measures, with strict budget cuts in all areas of public spending and notably drastic reductions in funding for the welfare state, in order to reduce national debt. The election result was a hung Parliament, with the Conservative and Liberal Democrat parties entering into a coalition government with a Conservative majority.

Jordan and Drakeford (2012) describe the evolution from the post-war social democratic welfare state to neoliberalism as a continuous and gradual change, whereas the post-2008 measures are characterised as both drastic and radical. This period of austerity, paired with the ideology of welfare conditionality, is the focus of this chapter.

Insecure housing

There are two key policies within the welfare reform plans of the Coalition and Conservative governments that fundamentally challenge the security of people on low incomes: the establishment and roll-out of fixed term tenancies (FTTs) and the introduction of the spare room subsidy, informally referred to as 'bedroom tax'.

The launch of the Right to Buy scheme in 1980 gave those on low incomes who were living in rented accommodation the opportunity to purchase their homes. However, increased government regulation that prevented profits from council house sales being reinvested in building new social housing stock, along with a downturn in the economy, meant that housing was not able to be replaced at the rate it was sold. In fact, the building of social housing has reduced consistently since 1980, with 2017 seeing the fewest such homes built since the establishment of the post-war welfare state (Park, 2018). The growth in the UK population during this time, alongside growing unemployment, has meant that demand for social housing has grown exponentially, and landlords and local authorities have seen increasingly long waiting lists, resulting in the application of a progressively stricter process of prioritisation. The housing and homelessness charity Shelter estimates that 1.15 million families were on waiting lists for council housing across England in 2017, with only 290,000 homes becoming available during that period.[1] The same research indicates that 27% of families had been on waiting lists for over five years. The introduction of points and bidding systems for the allocation of homes means that some people will never be offered a property because there will always be a more vulnerable person or family waiting. This marks an ideological shift away from the promise of security for all that was offered by the post-war welfare state.

The establishment of FTTs under the Localism Act 2012 enabled social landlords to offer short-term rather than lifetime tenancies to those requiring social housing, extending the idea of probationary tenancies that was originally introduced by the Conservative Party in 1990. Tenancies should be for a minimum of five years but in 'exceptional circumstances' could be as short as two years. At the end of the fixed term, the landlord has the power to terminate or extend the contract, based on the tenant's income, employment, under-occupancy and behaviour. The Housing and Planning Act 2016 extends FTTs so as to make them mandatory for all new local authority tenants, with a maximum agreement of ten years to ensure consistency for young school-age children.

This shift towards short-term tenancies highlights an ideological division, encapsulated by Watts and Fitzpatrick (2018), who describe the Conservative strategy as focused on those most in need, rather than on a universal provision, promoting the notion that not everyone can be helped. Using fixed-term agreements is intended to prevent the learned dependence which they believe can develop as a result of providing long-term support. In comparison, long-term housing offers security and stability to those with the lowest incomes, allowing such families the opportunity to build stable communities.

In their research with both tenants and landlords Watts and Fitzpatrick found that tenants felt anxious about the temporary nature of their contracts, describing a 'feeling of insecurity', and of being 'always on edge' and on a 'ticking clock that could end in losing their home' (Watts and Fitzpatrick, 2018, p 2) even when they were some time away from the renewal date. The researchers identified that those with existing vulnerabilities, for example people with young children, poor health and/or disabilities, or older people, were significantly more likely to feel anxious. Landlords were divided in their feelings about FTTs, depending on their political allegiance; 'interventionists' exercised more monitoring of tenants, expecting high levels of engagement in exchange for contracts, and 'utility maximisers' saw the potential profits to be made from FTTs. Social landlords with a focus on place-making felt that FTTs were unethical and didn't encourage families to build communities. The fate of tenants resting on the political persuasion of their landlord further increases insecurity, alongside the inclusion of behaviour as factor when renewal is being considered.

Since 2011, government housing policy has encouraged the construction of 'affordable housing', which is meant to be targeted at those who otherwise could not afford to rent. These schemes have been funded in part by developers mixing 'affordable' properties into regular new-build developments, offering the possibility of families developing a sense of security and community. However, the definition of 'affordable homes' can mean rents as high as 80% of the market rate, meaning that they are not 'affordable' for those on very low incomes or dependent on benefits.

Park (2018) uses the tragic fire at Grenfell Tower in 2017 to illustrate the dangers of neoliberal housing policy. Grenfell Tower was a high-rise tower block of mostly social housing in the Royal Borough of Kensington and Chelsea, one of the richest areas in England. On 14 June 2017 a fire started in the tower, thought to have been caused by a fridge-freezer in a fourth floor flat. The fire spread quickly due to the type of cladding used on the building. Tenants of Grenfell Tower had repeatedly raised concerns about multiple health and safety issues in the building with their landlords, but had seen little action on their complaints. The fire caused the deaths of 72 people and had life-changing consequences for many more. Park (2018) states that 'privatisation and deregulation almost certainly played a significant role in the fire'.

On top of the insecurity and conditionality introduced by the use of FTTs, and the poor condition of some social housing, the Welfare Reform Act 2012 introduced further measures to control tenancies. The spare room subsidy, informally referred to as the 'bedroom tax', deducts money from a person's Housing Benefit on the basis of the number of 'spare rooms' they have in their property, deducting 14% for one such room and 25% for two. A number of exemptions were made to this policy, including rooms used by members of the armed forces or students if they are expected to return to their previous home. However, children of different sexes are expected to share until they are ten years old, with children of the same sex having to share until their 16th birthday.

In 2017, following two Supreme Court rulings, further exemptions were made to the spare room subsidy: dependent adults or children with a disability who required a carer overnight and adult couples who are unable to share a room for health reasons no longer have their benefits restricted.

The introduction of this legislation meant that many people who had lived in their council or social housing for their whole lives were suddenly expected to manage with reduced financial support towards their rental costs or to downsize into alternative accommodation. The shortage of social housing and the high cost of private sector rents has meant that many people are unable to relocate, resulting in a considerable impact on their finances. Many foodbank users cite the 'bedroom tax' as a reason for their referral (Loopstra et al, 2018).

The introduction of the 'bedroom tax', alongside new tenancy agreements often being offered on a fixed-term basis, means that some families are having to choose between a home that is unaffordable or moving to a home that may be only temporary. This combination of insecurity and conditionality is causing increased anxiety for those who are most vulnerable, as demonstrated by Watts and Fitzpatrick's (2018) research.

Welfare benefits

In addition to the challenges facing social housing tenants, the Welfare Reform Act 2012 also implemented a new framework to regulate benefits, including the introduction of sanctions that are described by Slater (2012, p 2) as 'the most punitive welfare sanctions ever proposed by a British government'.

The changes to benefits came in the form of Universal Credit, which is a combined benefit that replaces child, housing and employment-related financial support, as proposed in the 2010 White Paper *Universal Credit: Welfare that Works* (DWP, 2010). The Coalition government believed that a single, individualised benefit would make the welfare system easier for claimants to navigate. However, for many recipients there were delays in the transition to Universal Credit, which had significant financial implications.

In addition to the changes in the distribution of welfare, the Welfare Reform Act 2012 also introduced a Mandatory Work Activity Scheme, whereby some claimants are obliged to complete work experience placements and expected to provide evidence of their attendance at training, appointments and interviews, job applications and other activity. Failure to complete the requirements leads to strict sanctions and the loss of the unemployment-related component of their benefit for three months for a first breach and six months for a second, with a maximum three-year penalty period.

The scheme is based on the ideological assumption that sanctions will motivate people back into employment, and is underpinned by the behaviourist belief that unemployment is a result of lack of motivation or choice, rather than a lack of opportunity or appropriate employment options. The employment minister at the time, Conservative MP Chris Grayling, stated: 'People need to be aware that for those who are fit enough to work it is simply not an option to sit on benefits and do nothing' (DWP, 2012). This is in direct contrast with the post-war context, where the wealth of employment opportunities led to near-full employment, and has clear links to the definition of welfare conditionality at the beginning of the chapter. The introduction of sanctions and mandatory work activity under the Welfare Reform Act was not the first attempt to introduce workfare into the benefits system, as these themes were evident in the previous Jobseekers' Allowance and even earlier. However, it does signify a significant increase in regulation and penalty.

Fletcher (2015) draws comparisons between the severity of the sanctions system and the pre-war labour camps of the 1930s, where young unemployed males were encouraged to participate in work camps and subjected to long, hard manual labour without pay. The author identifies multiple similarities between the two systems, including the economic position of austerity, behavioural explanations for worklessness, lack of new skills learned during the work activities and the use of advisor discretion. This final point is evidenced by the testimonies of many current benefit claimants, who describe their advisors as applying unnecessarily harsh sanctions when their reasons for not completing work activity were valid (Fletcher, 2015). Similar to social housing tenants feeling at the mercy of their landlords, benefits claimants appear to be at the mercy of Job Centre advisors, further exacerbating the sense of insecurity for those that are both living in social housing and claiming benefits.

Although the commitment of both the Coalition and the Conservative governments continues to the perspective that sanctions and cuts to benefits will increase motivation and spur the unemployed back to work, Dwyer et al (2018) indicate that there is little national or international evidence that sanctions schemes are successful in increasing long-term employment. They state that 'Analysis has found that welfare conditionality, and particularly the threat or experience of a benefit sanction within the social security system, is routinely ineffective in facilitating people's entry into, or progression within, the paid labour market over time' (p 2).

In addition, Dwyer and colleagues identify that personalised support was most helpful to those seeking employment, and that the sanctions actually acted as a deterrent, resulting in some disengaging from the system altogether, triggering financial and health difficulties.

Grady (2017) points to the irony of the neoliberal workfare system, identifying that only 26% of people who completed work activity schemes secured employment following completion, and 60% failed to complete. This indicates that benefits claimants and low earners gain relatively little from the scheme, whereas business owners who accommodate work activity schemes receive consistent free labour, benefitting from it immensely. Grady asserts that the increase in free labour from these schemes has driven down wages for those on low incomes, meaning that when and if those undertaking the activity do secure employment, their salaries will be low, due to the existence of the schemes they have completed.

Alongside the punitive and conditional benefits system, adding to the insecurity of the unemployed and those on the lowest income is the increase in the use of zero-hours contracts. These contracts mean that employees are paid only for the hours they work, and these hours are changeable depending on the employer's needs, making it difficult for employees to plan their finances, childcare and benefits claims. In addition, in their research with care workers employed on zero-hours contracts, Ravalier et al (2018) found that workers felt a more significant power imbalance between themselves and their employers, compared to fixed-hours employees, and as a result were less likely to complain about poor treatment or, notably, poor care towards service users. Employees described a fear of reprimand in the form of being offered fewer work hours the following week if they complained.

Zero-hours contracts are not new, and can be utilised successfully by some groups. For example, they enable students to negotiate hours around their studies. They are, however, more prevalent among low-income households, and particularly affect women (Ravalier et al, 2018).

So far we have explored the impact of welfare conditionality on the increasing insecurity of both tenure and finances, particularly for those in vulnerable groups. Living in insecure and/or unsuitable housing and having an unpredictable and low income has significant effects on people's mental health and emotional wellbeing. In addition, such families are forced to attempt to make up for the shortfall in finances. The next two sections describe ways in which people are restricting their fuel usage and food intake in order to manage their circumstances.

Fuel poverty

Middlemiss defines fuel poverty, stating that 'a household is fuel poor when it is unable to afford the level of energy services required to allow its members to live a decent life' (Middlemiss, 2017, p 425). Living in fuel poverty can mean a family living in just one room of their home, due to their inability to pay to heat the whole house, not using the heating at all, wearing additional clothing or using unsafe portable heating devices as an alternative to the fixed system, all of which can have a detrimental effect on their lives.

As described in the previous section, the changes in welfare benefits have had a significant negative impact on household incomes, and Boardman (2012) suggests that the reorganisation of the benefits system has played 'a major part in destabilising household incomes', often meaning that people are unable to pay their fuel bills. Figures indicate a 24% reduction in fuel consumption between 2005 and 2011, with prices doubling during the same period (Middlemiss and Gillard, 2015). Those most likely to experience fuel poverty are unemployed, disabled, unwell, retired or on low incomes (Sherriff, 2016). Put simply, they are usually in an already vulnerable group. They are also more likely to live in energy-inefficient homes, meaning that their fuel costs are higher than an average household would experience.

In 2010 the Marmot Review of Health Inequalities (Marmot Review Team, 2011) acknowledged fuel poverty as a growing problem, particularly for those already vulnerable to other insecurities. The review outlined the impact of fuel poverty as increasing existing inequalities between the affluent and those on low incomes, including the exacerbation of existing health conditions, causing new health conditions (particularly respiratory illnesses) and mental health difficulties such as stress, depression and anxiety. Moreover, the review indicated that children living in fuel poverty were less likely to achieve the required developmental progress at school, thus contributing to cycles of inequality.

Boardman (2012) proposes that, in order to challenge fuel poverty, structural inequalities must be addressed. These include fuel prices, household income and dwellings inefficiencies, for example poorly insulated walls and single-glazed windows. Government responses, however, have chosen to focus only on energy-efficiency measures (Middlemiss, 2017), rather than challenging the privatised energy suppliers or addressing household incomes, which, as described above, have fallen as a result of cuts to benefits and the growth of insecure working environments. Middlemiss (2017) asserts that 'a focus on energy efficiency rather ignores the lived experience of fuel poverty'.

The introduction of a new definition of fuel poverty – 'low income – high cost' – has seen support with fuel costs through schemes such as Warm Front, which target only the most vulnerable. Ideologically, this targeted distribution of support fits with the Conservative position that there are limited resources and these must be allocated to the most deserving. This reasoning platforms the notion that it isn't possible to support everyone, and that eliminating fuel poverty is neither possible or desirable. The new definition replaces the guideline that a household spending more than 10% of its income on energy bills places it in fuel poverty. The result of this shift is that half the previous number of households are now deemed to be experiencing fuel poverty.

Middlemiss (2017) describes that 'the new politics of fuel poverty follows the austerity maxim that money must be spent cost-effectively, and that by extension it is impossible to help everyone in need; instead money must be spent on the most deserving' (p 433).

It is evident, in considering the nature of fuel poverty, that there is a correlation with those experiencing insecurity in different aspects of their lives: those identified by Sherriff (2016) as most likely to be in fuel poverty are also those most likely to be affected by benefits changes and to be living in insecure housing. In addition, this group are also most likely to be accessing foodbanks, and Loopstra et al (2018) specifically identify benefits sanctions as linked to foodbank usage, as is explored in the next section.

Food poverty

Dowler and O'Connor (2012, p 45) define food poverty as 'the inability to acquire or eat an adequate quality or sufficient quantity of food in socially acceptable ways, or the uncertainty of being able to do so'. This is the definition accepted by researchers in this field, who also share an understanding that most data collected about foodbank use and food poverty more generally is based on under-estimates. Several factors influence food poverty figures, including the stigma connected to accessing food from foodbanks (described by Purdham et al (2016) as 'emotional cost'), lack of local resources and the conditional nature of referrals to food distribution organisations such as the Trussell Trust (Pollock, 2018) – meaning that there is likely to be a 'hidden hungry' population (Loopstra et al, 2018). Despite acknowledgement that available data are not accurate, recorded foodbank figures estimate that over half a million households are dependent on food aid, with three million individuals at risk of malnutrition in the UK (Garthwaite et al, 2015; Purdham et al, 2016), indicating a consistent increase in access since 2010.

Loopstra and Lalor (2017) report that lone parents and their children are the largest group of foodbank users, with single males being the largest household type. Interestingly, single males are not perceived as a vulnerable group in any other aspect of welfare discussed in this chapter. Their presence as the main group accessing foodbanks could be explained by their lack of receipt of support in other areas. The researchers also found a high prevalence of those with disabilities or supporting large families accessing food aid.

The impact of food poverty means that a household's food choices are restricted, particularly since fresh food costs have risen as incomes have fallen. As a result, low-income families have reduced their fresh fruit and vegetable intake and now rely more on processed, fatty foods. Correspondingly, there has been a national increase in obesity, diabetes and other diet-related ill-health. For children, malnutrition can mean slower development and lower educational outcomes, which, when paired with the negative implications of fuel poverty documented above, can have a significant long-term impact as they grow into adulthood.

Increasing evidence points to a correlation between the welfare reforms introduced by the UK government from 2010 onwards and the increase in food poverty:

- Loopstra et al (2018) describe that between 2011 and 2013 'a rapid rise in the number of people being sanctioned was concurrent with a large increase in the distribution of emergency food parcels' (p 438).
- The Trussell Trust (2018) indicates that 'sanctions are a key reason why people receive foodbank referrals'.
- Purdham et al (2016) describe benefit delays and benefit changes as responsible for 48% of foodbank referrals and identify a larger growth in foodbanks in areas of high unemployment, where more households rely on benefits.

The state response to food poverty has shifted since 2010; the Coalition government initially praised the work of The Trussell Trust, the largest food distribution organisation in the UK, perceiving it to be a good example of the 'Big Society'. The Big Society was a government initiative introduced by Conservative Prime Minister David Cameron in 2010. It was aimed at encouraging communities to support each other, and subsequently cushioning the impact of reducing local authority support. The creation and expansion of the Trussell Trust appeared to fit this ideology. As Trussell has become more established, its remit has broadened and the organisation has become increasingly critical of the poor government response to growing food poverty. Rather than accepting responsibility for this surge in the need for food aid, the government and its MPs have sought to blame those in receipt of support, implying that their lack of will and poor budgeting and cooking skills are the cause of their situation (Wells and Caraher, 2014). There have also been public attempts by MPs to discredit the need for food aid, suggesting that the growth in the use of foodbanks is due to their increased presence rather than to increased need, and referencing users' ownership of mobile phones as 'proof' of their access to finances for luxury items (Loopstra and Lalor, 2017). Access to a mobile phone is often essential for those on low incomes in order to complete the workfare requirements of arranging interviews, attending appointments and contacting benefits agencies.

Livingstone (2015, p 193) proposes that 'a neoliberal discourse of food aid under the current government is one of subordination, alienation and dispossession'. This ideological positioning of foodbank users as undeserving due to personal failings is challenged by Garthwaite et al (2015), who interviewed recipients of food aid. This research found participants to be highly competent in budgeting and cooking, and well aware of the poor nutritional content of the food they consumed but unable to afford alternatives. This lack of choice often left those with food intolerances or health conditions unwell as a result of consuming food that they knew would exacerbate their illness.

Unfortunately, the increasingly organised charitable response to food poverty via organisations such as the Trussell Trust can, for some individuals, also reinforce the insecurity of their food provision. The requirement to be referred by a professional, and restrictions on the quantity and type of food distributed, mean that some households are not able to access foodbanks. The Trussell Trust began providing food aid local to its base in Salisbury in 2000. It operates a franchise system which has since grown exponentially, starting to publish results in 2014, and publishing an online blog since 2015. It distributed over 1.3 million food parcels in the 12-month period from April 2017. Overwhelmingly, the response from those in need is positive. However, Livingstone (2015, p 190) warns of the 'commercialisation of basic food through charities, the franchising of the disenfranchised and impoverished'. The author's suggestion reflects that of international literature, which warns against a large-scale charitable response to food poverty, as this enables government to eschew its responsibilities to the population (Poppendieck, 1999).

Social work and insecurity

Alongside the difficulties that neoliberal welfare reform poses to the security of those in need, particularly those in vulnerable groups, the support available from local authority social work has also been restricted. As described in Chapter 6, the introduction of the NHSCCA 1990 brought eligibility criteria and 'needs led' assessment, with 'care-coordinators' commissioning support for those deemed deserving. In 2014 the Care Act overhauled adult social care policies, revoking much of the existing legislation and introducing a new 'strengths based' approach to working with individuals. This system prioritises focusing on individual wellbeing and access to both a person's own assets and those of their connections and wider community. The challenge of the Care Act is its introduction during a period of austerity, where both local authority budgets and community resources have been severely reduced and morale is low.

The critical social work paradigm offers some hope here, acknowledging that structural oppression is at the heart of inequality. The approaches collectively known as critical social work advocate a redistribution of capital, starting with direct work in and with communities and alongside those experiencing insecure living environments in order to challenge the systems that perpetuate their circumstances.

Poverty-aware social work is in its infancy in the UK but has seen success in Israel and is gaining increasing prominence. Krumer-Nevo (2016) developed a Poverty Aware Paradigm (PAP) that enables social workers and other professionals to reflect on their own positions and challenge traditional methods of engaging with service users. The paradigm includes three interrelated facets that encourage practitioners to explore three questions.

- Ontological: What is poverty? What does it include and what does it look like in our context?
- Epistemological: What do we consider knowledge? What do I need to know in order to support this person, and who is best placed to share that knowledge with me?
- Axiological: What is my ethical position? Where should I be positioned both practically and ideologically as a practitioner?

Working with service users in this way facilitates social workers to consider themes such as human rights, advocacy and empowerment, and providing practical and financial help through their work. Using professional knowledge and the power associated with professional roles to work alongside people experiencing poverty can enable the establishment of a secure household. For example, paying a person's rent arrears and supporting them to apply for benefits can provide much-needed emotional and practical support to make sure the correct funding is in place. This also relieves the need to fund public transport and the anxiety of facing an emotional situation alone. Rather than perceiving this as disempowering, the PAP would view it as offering genuine, humane support during a time of crisis. In addition, paying for childcare for a short period can enable someone to return to work, while the upfront cost of nursery or wrap-around childcare to cover before and after school may otherwise prevent this.

CASE STUDY 10.1: POVERTY-AWARE PRACTICE IN ACTION

Rachel is a 32-year-old single parent of two children, Rosie (5 years) and Oliver (7 years). They live in a two-bedroom terraced house that Rachel rents privately. Rachel is a qualified nurse, but when her marriage ended 18 months ago she quit her job as a paediatric nurse at a local hospital, as a lack of childcare meant that she was unable to do the shift work that her job required.

Rachel has been on the waiting list for a council property for the last 18 months, but the housing association that manages the local authority housing stock has a bidding system and she doesn't have access to a computer or the internet, so when the properties go 'online' at midnight she is unable to bid and misses out on suitable properties. She is getting into increasing debt because of the high cost of the rent and is now at risk of eviction.

Rosie has just started in the reception class at a local school, but she has not been allocated a place at the same school as her brother and, as Rachel has no local support or transport, she has had to alternate which child she drops off at school first each day. Consequently, each child has been late 50% of the time. The teachers

---

of both children have raised concerns with Rachel about this and have noticed that the children often look tired and their uniforms are dirty when they arrive at school. Rachel explains that they often have to walk for long distances in bad weather, and she can't afford to run her washing machine every day.

On top of the teachers' concerns, the Job Centre has sanctioned Rachel, cutting her Jobseekers' Allowance by a significant amount, as she has been late to appointments and has not completed the required number of hours applying for jobs. The appointments were made for 10am, and Rachel wasn't able to drop both children at their respective schools and walk to the centre on time. When she rang to rearrange the appointments, she was told this wasn't possible.

Rachel attends a foodbank at a local community centre and breaks down while telling one of the volunteers about the challenges she is facing. The volunteer is worried about her and puts her in touch with the local authority.

Traditional social work responses

Traditional social work practice may consider this example and identify the many different agencies that need to be contacted; children's services, teachers, landlords, housing associations, the Job Centre and probably many more localised support services. They could work with Rachel to contact the different organisations and access the support they offer individually; each service having their own eligibility criteria and assessment documents. But, as Rachel is clearly distressed, and struggling with the amount of challenges she is already facing, she is unlikely to manage this, on top of the existing struggles of getting through the day. The expectation that she will attend more appointments, and the guilt of not being able to, impacts on Rachel's self-esteem further, and she may withdraw from engaging with professionals.

Poverty-aware practice responses

A poverty-aware response considers the material support that Rachel needs. Rachel is loaned a laptop with a dongle to connect to the internet so that she is able to bid for properties that meet her needs, and the social worker provides a statement to boost her priority with the housing association. Providing transport and childcare to ensure that the children are both taken to and collected from their respective schools allows Rachel to focus on finding a job that suits the hours she is able to work, and, once she has secured employment, providing childcare ensures that she is able to maintain her position.

Paying off Rachel's rising debt, helping her move into her new accommodation and providing a new washing machine, mean that she can now go to work and that her children can go to school, well presented and on time, and socialise with other children in the after-school childcare. Once the family are settled, Rachel and the social worker can work out a plan to pay back the money to the local authority in

> small amounts each month. Through working closely together, the social worker and Rachel develop a strong and trusting relationship; Rachel feels supported and is confident that she will contact social services for support if she needs it in future.

It is important to note that poverty-aware practice is not widespread in the UK and is currently emerging from Israeli social work. However, this example demonstrates how providing immediate material support can achieve long-term success where traditional social work may fail to do so.

Conclusion

This chapter has explored the political decision to implement austerity measures, and the relationship between the introduction of welfare conditionality that followed and the insecurity of those dependent on the welfare system. It has explored how changes to housing and welfare benefits policies in the UK have led to an increase in the rights of those already in positions of power, such as landlords and employers, while tenants and employees on low or no incomes have seen a reduction in their rights, via short-term tenancies, benefits sanctions and zero-hours contracts. The impact of these changes is evidenced by the increase in inequality between the richest and poorest in society, with both food and fuel poverty affecting more households as a result. These inequalities form the context within which social workers and associated professionals conduct their practice, with the implementation of new legislation during a period of austerity diluting its impact. The emergence and growth of critically informed approaches such as the PAP offers some hope for the future by instilling a rights-based approach to welfare support in practitioners. The chapter has outlined how direct work with families and individuals living in poverty, including the provision of practical and financial aid, can contribute to the redistribution of resources and capital to those in need. It is hoped that this exploration of insecurity has demonstrated the complexity of the combined impact of policies that implement welfare conditionality, with households often experiencing multiple disadvantages as a result.

Critical questions

1 Think about a person experiencing the type of insecurity described in this chapter. Work through the questions that the Poverty Aware Paradigm asks of practitioners.

2 How do you think the poverty-aware approach differs from the current UK welfare system?

3 What do you think you could do as a professional to use this approach?

4 How do you feel about welfare conditionality? Are there benefits to this approach?

5 How does welfare conditionality relate to the values and ethics of social workers and other caring professions?

6 How do you think different political ideological perspectives would respond to PAP? Why?

Further reading

These texts have been selected in order to direct readers to more focused material about insecurity.

• Standing, G. (2011) *The Precariat: The New Dangerous Class*, London: Bloomsbury.
 Guy Standing's key text explores the emergence of a new class, referred to as the 'precariat' specifically because of the insecure status of those within it. The author presents an argument for more equitable distribution of wealth and the capital that accompanies it, in order to enable those living within the 'precariat' class to re-establish stability in their living conditions.

• Cummins, I. (2018) *Poverty, Inequality and Social Work*, Bristol: Policy Press.
 Cummins' text continues Standing's theme but relates issues such as poverty and insecurity to the existing theory and to social work practice, exploring the challenges of this context for social workers.

• Garthwaite, K. (2016) *Hunger Pains*, Bristol: Policy Press.
 Garthwaite is a key academic in the growing field of food poverty and insecurity and her book tracks her research into foodbanks in England, relaying relatable and emotive insights into the lives of those working in and using them.

• Krumer-Nevo, M. (2016) 'Poverty-aware social work: a paradigm for social work practice with people in poverty', *British Journal of Social Work*, vol 46, pp 1793–808.
 Krumer-Nevo is an Israeli academic who specialises in social work practice with those living in poverty. This influential and important peer-reviewed article proposes a new paradigm for practice in this area, which has the potential to influence international practice.

References

Boardman, B. (2012) 'Fuel poverty synthesis: lessons learnt, actions needed', *Energy Policy*, vol 49, pp 143–8.

DWP (Department for Work and Pensions) (2010) *Universal Credit: Welfare that Works*, London: HMSO.

DWP (2012) 'Mandatory work activity scheme extended', www.gov.uk/government/news/mandatory-work-activity-scheme-extended

Dowler, E.A. and O'Connor, D. (2012) 'Rights-based approaches to addressing food poverty and food insecurity in Ireland and the UK', *Social Science and Medicine*, vol 74, no 1, pp 44–51.

Dwyer, P., Scullion, L. and Wright, S. (2018) *Work and Pensions Committee Inquiry; Benefits Sanctions*, Written Evidence. Welfare Conditionality. Available at: www.welfareconditionality.ac.uk/wp-content/uploads/2018/06/WelCond_evidence_benefit_sanctions_May2018.pdf

Fletcher, D. (2015) *Workfare – a Blast from the Past? Contemporary Work Conditionality for the Unemployed in Historical Perspective*, Sheffield: Sheffield Hallam University.

Garthwaite, K., Collins, P.J. and Bambra, C. (2015) 'Food for thought: an ethnographic study of negotiating ill health and food insecurity in a UK foodbank', *Social Science and Medicine*, vol 132, pp 38–44.

Grady, J. (2017) 'The state, employment, and regulation: making work not pay', *Employee Relations*, vol 39, no 3, pp 274–90.

Jordan, B. and Drakeford, M. (2012) *Social Work and Social Policy Under Austerity*, Basingstoke: Palgrave Macmillan.

Krumer-Nevo, M. (2016) 'Poverty-aware social work: a paradigm for social work practice with people in poverty', *British Journal of Social Work*, vol 46, pp 1793–808.

Livingstone, N. (2015) 'The hunger games: food poverty and politics in the UK', *Capital and Class*, vol 39, no 2, pp 188–95.

Loopstra, R. and Lalor, D. (2017) *Financial Insecurity, Food Insecurity and Disability*, The Trussell Trust, University of Oxford, ESRC, Kings College London.

Loopstra, R., Fledderjohann, J., Reeves, A. and Stuckler, D. (2018) 'Impact of welfare benefit sanctioning on food insecurity: a dynamic cross-area study of foodbank usage in the UK', *Journal of Social Policy*, vol 47, no 3, pp 437–57.

Marmot Review Team (2011) *The Health Impacts of Cold Homes and Fuel Poverty*, London: Friends of the Earth and Marmot Review Team.

Middlemiss, L. (2017) 'A critical analysis of the new politics of fuel poverty in England', *Critical Social Policy*, vol 37, no 3, pp 425–43.

Middlemiss, L. and Gillard, R. (2015) 'Fuel poverty from the bottom-up: characterising household energy vulnerability through the lived experience of the fuel poor', *Energy Research and Social Science*, vol 6, pp 146–54.

Park, J. (2018) 'Social housing in an increasingly politicised landscape', *Counterpoint*, vol 254, pp 136–41.

Pollock, S. (2018) 'Foodbanks, austerity and critical social work', in S. Webb (ed) *The Routledge Handbook of Critical Social Work*, London: Routledge, pp 349–60.

Poppendieck, J. (1999) *Sweet Charity? Emergency Food and the End of Entitlement*, New Caledonia, US: Penguin.

Purdham, K., Garratt, E.A. and Esmail, A. (2016) 'Hungry? Food insecurity, social stigma and embarrassment in the UK', *Sociology*, vol 50, no 6, pp 1072–88.

Ravalier, J., Morton, R., Russell, L. and Fidalgo, A. R. (2018) 'Zero-hour contracts and stress in UK domiciliary care workers', *Health and Social Care in the Community*, vol 27, pp 1–8.

Sherriff, G. (2016) *'I was Frightened to Put the Heating On.' Evaluating the Changes4warmth Approach to Cold Homes and Mental Health*, University of Salford, Chesshire Lehmann Fund and Beat the Cold.

Slater, T. (2012) 'The myth of "Broken Britain": welfare reform and the production of ignorance', *Antipode*, vol 45, pp 1–22.

Trussell Trust (2018) Foodbank statistics for previous financial years with regional breakdown, https://www.trusselltrust.org/news-and-blog/latest-stats/end-year-stats/

Watts, B. and Fitzpatrick, S. (2018) *Fixed Term Tenancies: Revealing Divergent Views on the Purpose of Social Housing*, Edinburgh: Heriot Watt University, I: Sphere, Housing Quality Network and Welfare Conditionality.

Welfare Conditionality (nd) www.welfareconditionality.ac.uk [accessed 1 October 2018].

Wells, R. and Caraher, M. (2014) 'UK print media coverage of the food bank phenomenon: from food welfare to food charity?', *British Food Journal*, vol 116, no 9, pp 1426–45.

11

Migration and asylum

Philip Brown

Introduction

For centuries people, or migrants, have moved across the world to improve their life chances, to seek refuge, or due to consequences arising out of some kind of disaster. The causes of this past movement continue to reflect the reasons why people migrate today, albeit the UK, among other countries, has an ever-nuanced classification of 'migrants' which includes asylum seekers, refugees, family-joiners, third-country nationals, high-skilled migrants, guest workers and so on. Such classifications matter, and those who fall within particular groups are subject to particular, and potentially fluid, forms of immigration status which, in turn, impact on the support they can access from the state (Jordan and Brown, 2006). This chapter will provide an overview of how migration legislation and policy have been shaped in the context of the UK. It will also look at how political responses to migration and related policy frameworks have shaped the development of social welfare services, and the ways in which migrants can access these. It will do so by focusing specifically on those people who have migrated to the UK and are subject to particular vulnerabilities, namely asylum seekers and refugees. By drawing on the UK government's management of asylum the chapter moves on to explore the interaction of policies aimed at asylum seekers in the UK and how they 'fit' with the role of the social worker.

Definition difficulties

The discipline of 'refugee studies' is dominated by debates over definitions which attempt to classify various forced or involuntary migrants depending upon a variety of legal and political categories. These categories have practical significance, as each label affords certain international responsibilities and 'identities' to the holder (Boyle et al, 1998). Making the distinction is inevitably intertwined with how such individuals are treated in international and domestic law and policy. In popular terms, all such forced or involuntary migrants are referred to as 'refugees', but in legal terms this is actually quite a narrow category reflecting only those who can demonstrate a compatibility with the definition of a refugee outlined in the 1951 United Nations (UN) Convention Relating to the Status of Refugees. In Article One of the Convention a refugee is defined as an individual who:

owing to well-founded fear of being persecuted for reasons of race, religion, nationality, membership of a particular social group or political opinion, is outside the country of his nationality and is unable or, owing to such fear, is unwilling to avail himself of the protection of that country; or who, not having a nationality and being outside the country of his former habitual residence as a result of such events, is unable or, owing to such fear, is unwilling to return to it. (1951 UN Convention Relating to the Status of Refugees)[1]

Some commentators have doubted the relevance of this Convention in the present day, while others have commented upon those whom it excludes, such as those fleeing from gender-related persecution (Kumin, 2001) and yet others have questioned its ability to include populations displaced, through conflict, within the borders of their own country (Crisp, 1999). Regardless, the Convention still operates as a framework from which a large number of refugees can be 'identified' and provided with the appropriate protection. Castles et al (2003) argue that it must be noted that the vast majority of forced or involuntary migrants move for reasons not recognised by this definition. Therefore, although the United Nations High Commissioner for Refugees (UNHCR) notes that the numbers of refugees in the world accounts for approximately 25.4 million people, the number of people who are forcibly displaced is around 68.5 million (UNHCR, 2018). Unfortunately, as a result, reasonably reliable data is accessible on only two kinds of forced migrant, one being those refugees who are compatible with the definition above, the other being 'asylum seekers'. However, further complexity is generated when researchers such as Castles et al (2003, p 5) claim that in 'many complex emergencies ... many displaced people belong to more than one category'. Similarly, Silove et al (2000) argue that this is the case for asylum seekers arriving in developed countries, who can be seen as both political migrants and simultaneously economic migrants. Khan expands this notion and highlights the tensions associated with poverty and politics:

[B]y suggesting that there are 'genuine' people that are forced out of their homes by persecution and war, on the one hand, and those who simply seek a better life, on the other, the simplistic and unhelpful dichotomy between the asylum-seeker and an economic migrant ... is perpetuated ... It has been noted that leading migration scholars have argued that asylum-seekers and economic migrants arise out of the same situation of societal transformations and crisis linked to war, poverty, and nation-state formation ... In this context, to question whether people leave out of desperation or aspiration is irrelevant. They seek to escape from social, economic and/or political insecurity to a more secure future. (Khan, 2000, p 121)

Asylum seekers are those people who travel to countries that are not their own in search of protection (asylum), but whose claim for refugee status has not yet been decided. For the vast majority of states, the definition provided in the Refugee Convention provides them with a guideline as to which asylum claimants should be recognised as refugees (granted asylum), and which fall outside the definition.

UK policy: historical context

Migration arising from persecution has shaped the way in which all immigration legislation has developed in the UK. As ancient as the tradition of seeking refuge is, it is still relatively new in its present legal form. Until an international framework was shaped by the Refugee Convention, individual states accepted refugees for a number of reasons such as: a way of asserting sovereignty; wider obligations to the principles of humanism (Schuster, 2002); in response to specific emergencies; or on an ad hoc basis (Delahunty, 1996). Originally the church or temple played a major role in providing sanctuary to the persecuted, but with the decline in the power of the church this was eventually superseded by the modern-day concept of 'territorial asylum' (Schuster, 2002). The term 'territorial asylum' refers to the act of an individual claiming asylum in a state/nation that is not their own. In order for territorial asylum to be successfully operationalised two major prerequisites had to be in place: recognition of 'distinct political jurisdictions' and of the 'parity of power' between the countries involved (Schuster, 2003, p 66). However, those countries, such as Britain, that granted asylum to those who were seen as political 'criminals' (guilty of treason) were continually open to hostility from the countries of origin of such 'criminals'. The practice of territorial asylum therefore may be said to serve two strategically political purposes: those of undermining the sovereignty of the prosecuting state and of asserting the sovereignty of the receiving state (Schuster, 2002). This has been said to be the major motivation for introducing and applying the practice of asylum in Britain by the 18th century.

It was in the wake of the French Revolution that Britain saw a particular increase in political refugees arriving at ports. However, the security fears that were said to be posed by these French 'subversives' prompted their exclusion and the legislation of the Aliens Act 1793, which remained in force until 1826. Up to the introduction of this Act, refugees entering Britain were welcomed, for the most part, and were largely seen as ideological equals. However, because of the ideological 'threat' that the French exiles were seen to pose they were increasingly viewed as 'dangerous'. According to Schuster (2002), the 'threat' that was presented to Britain by the French exiles and the need to maintain safety and security for the citizens of Britain appeared to outweigh the possibility that a deserting individual might need protection from foreign states.

Until the late 19th century the entry and settlement of migrants into Britain was relatively unrestricted by practice or legislation. At this time, the height of the British Empire, hundreds of thousands of native Britons were leaving each year, seeking opportunity and wealth in the British colonies and in the US. Coupled with the demands on labour of industrial growth this large-scale emigration required a constant need for the domestic labour force to be replenished, and there was little opposition to the idea that this could be achieved by granting refuge to those who sought it (Schuster, 2003). In Britain during the 1800s, Foot (1965) claims such economic need for continued industrial prosperity could be 'cloaked in the woolly idealism of Victorian liberalism. British politicians of both parties, particularly the Liberals, regarded themselves as champions of the right of political asylum' (Foot, 1965, p 84). However, during the last years of the 19th century and the opening years of the 20th century domestic reaction to migration was changing, as were public opinion and wider political events.

Immigration into Britain during the opening decade of the 20th century continued to grow, with large numbers of Irish immigrants, increasing numbers of Italians and a substantial German population present, mainly in the London area (Holmes, 1991). Holmes (1991) claims that it was a small minority of the German population, those seen as 'Gypsies', which appeared to generate the most hostility from 'native' people. Missionaries, the social welfare actors of the time, sought to convert the 'heathen', and politicians attempted to circumscribe their freedom of movement by introducing restrictive housing legislation (Holmes, 1991). The arrival of Gypsies from Russian Poland instigated a fierce immigration debate, with Sir Howard Vincent, Conservative MP for Sheffield Central, asking in 1906, 'How are we to get rid of these wretched people?'

In 1905 the Aliens Act was enacted, targeting a variety of 'undesirable aliens' who could be refused entry to Britain (Holmes, 1991). Although there was no specific mention of refugees in this Act, it did specify that leave to land in Britain should not be refused to those who were seeking entry 'to avoid persecution or punishment on religious or political grounds or for an offence of a political character or persecution involving a danger of imprisonment or danger to life or limb, on account of religious belief' (Aliens Act 1905, section 1(3)). This distinction highlighted an extremely significant aspect of asylum within Britain that has continued into present times. In providing a framework for discriminating between immigrants it highlighted the discretionary powers available to the immigration officers and confirmed the granting of asylum as an act of benevolence.

> Since asylum has always been an *ex gratia* act, that is, granted at the discretion of the Home Office, it is susceptible to the whims of the holder of that office and the government of the day. Shifts in public opinion towards refugees can quickly result in new legislation and influence the implementation of asylum policy. (Schuster, 2003, p 83)

Policy changes and the World Wars

Fear of war with Germany instigated the next legislative change in the UK as the government became increasingly concerned about the 'threat' that such 'enemy aliens' were viewed as posing. The Aliens Restriction Act 1914 placed controls over the registration, movement and deportation of all individuals classified as aliens. The Aliens Act 1919 introduced charges for sedition and industrial unrest by aliens and instigated a policy of internment. Later, it was economic need and labour shortage in Britain that prompted the government to offer refuge to Polish servicemen who had fought against Germany during the Second World War. There were an unprecedented number of displaced individuals dispersed throughout Europe, posing significant political issues for Britain and the other countries of Europe. With memories of Nazism and the Holocaust still reverberating throughout Europe and the world there was an international determination to create a framework whereby human beings would never be expected to endure state persecution and global inaction again. As a result, the United Nations High Commission for Refugees (UNHCR) was created in 1950, designed to be of a humanitarian nature, non-political and to concentrate on the needs of the displaced. The organisation was given a three-year task to assist in the resettlement of those still displaced throughout Europe as a result of the events of the Second World War.

While the UNHCR attended to the one million displaced, the demand for labour in the UK continued to be a reliable indicator for migration movements into the UK. During the 1950s Black workers from the Caribbean and Asians from the Indian sub-continent journeyed to Britain to occupy posts which it was proving hard to fill from the native population. These new arrivals did not meet any restrictions on their entry, as the British Nationality Act 1948 allowed free entry into Britain and rights of abode for all Commonwealth citizens. However, wary of public opinion on immigration and increased violent, racially motivated attacks, the Home Office commissioned a Working Party on Coloured People seeking Employment in the UK. It was formed, according to Dummett (2001, p 93), to 'examine the possibilities of preventing any further increase in "coloured people" seeking employment in the UK'. As Lord Home (later Sir Alec Douglas Home) wrote in 1955, when Secretary of State for Commonwealth Relations:

> On the one hand it would presumably be politically impossible to legislate for a colour bar and any legislation would have to be non-discriminatory in form. On the other hand we do not wish to keep out immigrants of good type from the old Dominions. I understand that, in the view of the Home Office, immigration officers could, without giving rise to trouble or publicity, exercise such a measure of discrimination as we think desirable. (Cited in Dummett and Nichol, 1990, p 180)

Further legislative developments meant that in 1962 the Commonwealth Immigrants Act initiated an entry system for Commonwealth workers based on the acquisition of vouchers available from the British authorities. By restricting the number of vouchers available for the unskilled, the Act successfully reduced the number of immigrants from the Caribbean and the Indian sub-continent arriving in Britain. Dummett (2001) proposes that, from this moment on, immigration and race became synonymous and inextricably entangled in the public mind, albeit such adverse perceptions were not new. Visram (2002) traces a line back to the 18th century, when Black and Asian migrants were treated unfavourably by employers and wider society. In the 1960s there was a clear distinction drawn between the perceived characteristics of immigrants, who were becoming seen as undesirable, and those of refugees, who were welcomed. However, Schuster claims that the reception of these various migrants was underpinned by a perception of their ethnicity: 'Immigrants were black and came from former colonies and the commonwealth (regardless of their motives for leaving), while refugees were white and came from communist regimes (regardless of their motives for leaving)' (Schuster, 2003, p 138).

Refugees, predominantly from Soviet-bloc countries, continued to be admitted to Britain with relative ease (Kushner and Knox, 1999). The refugee migration to Britain of African–Asians in 1968 changed things. These refugees (although they were Commonwealth citizens), who were fleeing the policies of Africanisation in Kenya and Uganda, threatened the UK government's perceived control, up to that time, of a relatively small number of refugees entering the country. The incoming Labour government, in response to the perceived large numbers of people likely to flee the East African countries, passed the Commonwealth Immigrants Act 1968. This Act denied admission to those Commonwealth citizens who could not demonstrate a close ancestral link to the UK. In an attempt to help Asian citizens of the UK and colonies who were living in the East African countries to enter the UK, a reorganised system of vouchers permitting entry was made available. Individuals could apply for vouchers to enter the UK, with the limit on numbers set initially at 1,500, and increased to 3,000 in 1971. Those individuals who entered Britain with a voucher were able to live and work in Britain. Those who came without a voucher were 'shuttlecocked', meaning that they were put back on the planes on which they had arrived and returned to their country of embarkation. However, the reason for departure from those countries meant that they were not accepted there, and so they had to stay on the plane for their onward journeys elsewhere, and eventually back to Britain. At that stage, they would be again put back on the plane, to repeat the whole process, for three or four times, effectively becoming 'refugees in orbit' (Schuster, 2002, p 138).

Further immigration-related legislation was enacted in 1971 and in 1977. In 1977 the government, responding to reports of increased racist attacks in various parts of Britain, tightened immigration control further. Dummett asserts that the enactment of immigration legislation during the 1960s and 1970s meant that both the Conservative and the Labour governments were convinced of two things:

> First, that the propaganda of the past three decades had ensured that there were votes to be gained by being tough on immigration, and votes to be lost by being soft on it. And, secondly, that the public mind had been thoroughly imbued with the belief that the admission of a single person whom there was any means of keeping out was an unparalleled disaster. (Dummett, 2001, p 124)

According to Schuster (2003), the most significant piece of immigration legislation passed in the 1980s was the Carriers' Liability Act 1987. This Act imposed a fine of £1,000 per head on air or shipping lines for each passenger arriving without papers fully in order. This meant that ticket clerks for airline and shipping companies effectively became 'unofficial immigration officers', restricting passage to those without valid passports or visas and attempting to protect the financial interests of their respective companies.

Influence of political agenda

There has been an apparent political and economic need since the close of the 19th century to begin to classify, label and separate the motives of migrants. Migrants can now be viewed as tourists, students, high-skilled workers, agricultural workers, refugees, asylum seekers, work permit holders, undocumented workers and so on. Historically, transnational migration has not always fitted these modern-day categories. Indeed, motives for movement were rarely questioned in the 19th century and early decades of the 20th century (Schuster, 2003). While present-day governments arguably see the benefit of certain migrants and actively rely on them for high-skilled workers and agricultural labour, other migrants – such as undocumented workers, refugees and asylum seekers – are viewed as an economic burden and threat to community cohesion.

In the 21st century most countries 'control' migration in some way and stipulate certain requirements of prospective migrants, whether the migration be economic, for tourism, for education or for asylum. The granting of legal access to enter a country is thus heavily dependent upon a combination of factors such as: the nature of the migration, the state of the domestic economy, the domestic reaction to immigration and the number of prospective migrants likely to be involved. Mechanisms to control the entry of migrants have existed for decades. Such common features as passports, the American 'green card' visa, holiday visas, work permits and student visas have all helped countries to control the number of people entering and to monitor their motives for doing so. Immigration has risen in prominence on the international political agenda and within the public gaze. The US approach to immigrants, particularly students from 'Islamic' countries, has become more restrictive (Akram and Johnson, 2002). Castles has argued that in some European countries, such as Austria, Denmark and the Netherlands, 'refugees have been branded as a sinister transnational threat to national security' (Castles, 2003) and support for, and the prominence of, the immigration policies of the far Right has grown (Castles, 2003, p 16).

Jordan and Düvell (2003) have argued that it is the process of globalisation since the 1980s that may have resulted in both the encouragement of certain forms of migration and the restriction of others to suit the needs of 'powerful' economies. For instance, the desire for states to compete in a global market has meant that 'first world' countries actively seek to attract high-skilled workers from overseas to fill their labour demand and contribute to the host economy via production, services and taxes. As well as these high-skilled immigrants living in the communities of the UK, other migrants are attracted by the opportunities that a growing economy presents. As such, employment becomes available in low-income, unskilled sectors, particularly the service industry, and is filled by a significant proportion of immigrant workers who live in various communities throughout the UK. Migrants entering under such intentions are encouraged by the authorities and portrayed as beneficial both to the UK economy and the social and cultural identity of the country.

At the same time, Jordan and Düvell (2003) have argued that because irregular migrants and asylum seekers are increasingly portrayed as threats to the labour market, public spending and social and racial harmony, restrictive entry mechanisms and restrictive support procedures aimed at such 'undeserving' migrants have been legitimised and increased. Such a widely accepted portrayal of refugees and asylum seekers has added to the 'demonisation' and, according to Robinson et al (2003, p 11), the 'depersonalised' nature of asylum seekers. Asylum seekers, as a result of the restrictions, are required to use more innovative techniques in order to reach and enter destination countries, and a number of informal and professional smugglers and trafficking operators have reacted to fill such a service demand. Over the last two decades there has been a proliferation in the numbers of people adopting inventive and desperate strategies to leave their countries of origin, largely characterised by the so-called migrant crisis of 2015 (see Crawley et al, 2016).

In the UK at the beginning of the 1990s, a decade that saw three further Acts of asylum and immigration reform, asylum seekers began to experience a change in popular perceptions. During the recession in 1990–91 all manner of 'benefit fraud' and 'cheats' were targeted in order to cut down on public spending. The government concluded that, because only a small percentage of all asylum claimants were actually being granted asylum, the large numbers that were being refused were 'cheating' the benefit system and were a 'drain' on resources. Similarly, in order to maintain 'good race relations' the threat that 'bogus' asylum seekers posed of destabilising the labour market and social harmony meant that their numbers had to be controlled. Asylum seekers therefore began to be treated with suspicion, their motives for coming to the UK were increasingly scrutinised and if they were unsuccessful in their asylum claims they were labelled as 'frauds' and 'cheats'. This happened against the backdrop of a reportedly more restrictive interpretation of the definition of the UN's Refugee Convention (Silove et al, 1997). Castles et al (2003) suggest that this was occurring not only in the UK, and that there were similar developments in immigration policy in other countries within the EU.

> The increased incidence of racist violence and the growth of anti-immigrant extreme-right movements led some policy makers to see immigration as a threat to public order and social cohesion, and national governments took measures to strengthen border controls. (Castles et al, 2003, p 3)

The control of such 'threats' became a major focus for the UK government during the 1990s, thus legitimising the increasingly restrictive immigration measures (Schuster, 2003). The Asylum and Immigration Act 1993 was aimed, once again, at the so-called 'pull factors' which attracted refugees and 'economic migrants' to the UK. This policy portrayed the UK as irresistible to prospective migrants and therefore the 'opportunities' that were presented to asylum seekers, such as benefits, had to be restricted. The Act limited access to housing, increased the carriers' liability fine to £2,000 and implemented a ruling whereby asylum seekers who had travelled to the UK via a 'safe third country' could be returned to that country. The next significant piece of legislation was in 1999 and, according to Sales (2002, p 463), 'created a new social category of "asylum seeker", separating them both in policy and in popular discourse from recognised refugees'. The 1999 Act ended the direct local authority benefit provision that had stood for a number of years and introduced a centralised agency called the National Asylum Support Service[2] (NASS). Up to this point, despite the increasing control exercised at the border, those seeking asylum had been able to draw on a wide range of social welfare support, including social workers, to help them. However, with the 1999 Act this all changed. The drive behind the creation of NASS was the claim that the 'burden' of asylum seekers that was borne predominantly by the local authorities of London and the South-East should be shared by local authorities throughout the UK. The government concluded that the South-East was disproportionately supporting more asylum seekers than other areas of the UK and that asylum seekers should be 'accommodated in areas where there is a greater supply of suitable and cheaper accommodation' (Home Affairs Committee, 2018). Ten regional consortia were contracted to provide services on behalf of NASS and asylum seekers were dispersed to areas which had relatively little experience of accommodating and supporting them. The organisations (a mixture of local authorities, private landlords and refugee community organisations) attached to the regional consortia would liaise with NASS in order to fulfil the support entitlements of asylum applicants.

During the 2000s the UK government continued to focus on reducing the flow of asylum seekers into the UK. In 2002 asylum seekers lost the right to work, as it was considered a pull factor. Further legislation was passed with the Nationality, Immigration and Asylum Act 2002 and the Immigration and Asylum (Treatment of Claimants) Act 2004. The civil disturbances in a handful of northern mill towns in the UK in 2001 and the events of 11 September 2001 also broadened the focus of this legislation in an attempt to address public concerns around extremism and integration. Subsequent legislation (the Immigration, Asylum and Nationality Act 2006 and the Immigration Acts 2014 and 2016) has sought to further reduce the so-called pull factors (which are imagined to encourage people to come to the UK and seek asylum), expedite the asylum process, further bureaucratise the asylum and related support processes and refine the processes which are in place to ensure that people leave the UK once their claim for asylum is judged unfounded.

Throughout these legislative changes the policy towards the dispersal, support and entitlements of asylum seekers has continued since its radical overhaul in 1999. At its inception the implementation of a bespoke social welfare support system, and in particular the dispersal programme, brought a number of criticisms which focused on its possible detrimental effects on asylum seekers and refugee communities (Medical Foundation for the Care of Victims of Torture, 1999; Institute of Race Relations, 2000; Oxfam, 2000). The Medical Foundation for the Care of Victims of Torture (1999) emphasised that areas intending to provide support for asylum seekers would need to have support networks, a secure and well-resourced environment, as well as established organisations to provide advice and support to refugees. The Institute of Race Relations argued that the change in policy and the lack of experience of the consortia responsible for delivering a dispersed programme of support was thought to show a 'disturbing lack of consideration for the welfare of the already vulnerable … [leaving asylum seekers] … isolated, socially excluded and vulnerable to racist attack' (Institute of Race Relations, 2000, p 4). Robinson et al (2003), in their retrospective review of dispersal within the UK, presented an implementation of the dispersal policy during these formative years that was characterised by a lack of planning and research into its operation. Ultimately, the dispersal areas were often ill-prepared, in some cases unwilling, and lacking in experience to accommodate asylum seekers. Although it is argued that the policy of dispersal has not been a failure (see Rutter, 2015), the sudden commencement of a policy which impacted on thousands of potentially vulnerable people by relocating them, with no choice, to ill-prepared professionals, towns, cities and communities was a challenge for a number of years after its implementation. From 1999 and for the two decades since, the role of the social welfare professional in the lives of asylum seekers has been not only about supporting them as individuals with regard to their dislocation and settlement in the UK, but also about mitigating and ameliorating the effects of a highly conditional and restrictive asylum system. As the Refugee Convention is largely silent on the position of those people applying for refugee status, it is the European Convention on Human Rights (ECHR), by way of the Human Rights Act 1998, that has been used to safeguard the rights of asylum seekers.

Challenges have been brought against the UK government's asylum policy and processes with respect to the right to subsistence support, the timely provision thereof and detention. While the Human Rights Act 1998 cannot support a claim for asylum per se, as the European Court of Human Rights continues to maintain that the guarantees of Article 6 of the ECHR do not apply to asylum decisions, it does offer additional protections, predominantly in relation to removals. Even if an asylum seeker does not qualify for refugee status the Human Rights Act enables the courts to prohibit removal where an asylum seeker's return to their home country would otherwise result in a 'real risk' of ill-treatment, contrary to Article 3, or a 'flagrant breach' of any other Convention right.

An up-to-date, at the time of writing, description of the process that asylum seekers have to go through to claim asylum when in the UK can be found in Hirst and Atto (2018). The essence of the changes in the way that support and accommodation are provided to asylum seekers since 1999 has largely remained in place over subsequent 20 years. However, instead of local authorities playing a key role in the provision of support, the role of private providers has increased, with all asylum support in the UK being delivered by three private companies: Serco, G4S and Clearsprings Group. Asylum seekers continue to have no recourse to public funds, but those who can demonstrate that they are destitute can receive a basic support package (known as Section 98), either for the duration of the asylum claim or until their application for an enhanced support package (known as Section 95) is approved. Section 98 support consists of accommodation (in the form of reception centres), three meals a day, bedding and toiletries. There is no financial support available to those on Section 98 support, and anything above the basic provision can be only provided by friends, non-governmental organisations and charities. Those who are deemed eligible to receive the enhanced Section 95 support can benefit from housing and a monetary allowance of £37.75 per family member per week (Asylum Information Database, 2018). There is a small increase of £3 a week for a pregnant women or a parent with a child between the ages of one and three years, and a parent with a child under five years of age receives an additional £5. The accommodation is arranged by one of the three private providers and people usually experience no-choice dispersal and are accommodated in dwellings mostly within the private rented sector. The continuation of Section 95 support is conditional on particular behaviours and the recipient's ongoing destitute position. If an individual retains Section 95 support this ends at the point of conclusion of their asylum claim: 28 days after a successful claim is made, or 21 days after appeal rights have been exhausted or have expired. Those with Section 95 support have access to education for their children, primary and secondary healthcare, and legal aid if they cannot afford to pay their own legal costs. Where people cannot access support from the Home Office they may sometimes be able to access support from social services or the local authority. These include adult asylum seekers requiring care and support, asylum-seeking families with children under 18 years of age or refused asylum-seeking families with children under 18 years.

CASE STUDY 11.1: CHARITABLE RESPONSES TO THE NEEDS OF ASYLUM SEEKERS I: THE BOAZ TRUST

The Boaz Trust is a charity working to relieve the suffering of destitute asylum seekers in Greater Manchester and was founded in 2004 in response to the growing problem of destitution among asylum seekers. Boaz has a small number of houses and a network of local host families accommodating over 50 asylum seekers and five refugees in Greater Manchester. They also run a winter night shelter which rotates around local churches. The Boaz Night Shelter at Manchester Universities' Catholic Chaplaincy was established in October 2016, sharing its ministry with six other churches in Greater Manchester, in order to provide a place where destitute asylum seekers can stay every night of the week from October to April. The Chaplaincy hosts a group of up to 12 destitute asylum seekers every Saturday night, providing a meal, sleeping accommodation and breakfast. Forty-five volunteers, most of them university students, assist at the Chaplaincy. There are four teams of two volunteers every weekend: hospitality to set up the sleeping and dining space, kitchen, sleepover and breakfast. There is also a team of weekly laundry volunteers.

Source: Adapted from Manchester Universities' Catholic Chaplaincy, www.muscc. org/refugee-night-shelter.html

CASE STUDY 11.2: CHARITABLE RESPONSES TO THE NEEDS OF ASYLUM SEEKERS II: LEEDS ASYLUM SEEKER SUPPORT NETWORK

Leeds Asylum Seeker Support Network (LASSN) ran the Befriending Project, which provided an opportunity for isolated asylum seekers and refugees to forge a relationship with a supportive adult for a period of 6 to 12 months. Volunteer befrienders were matched with clients for regular visits. The aim was to familiarise people with Leeds, help them to integrate into the local community and gain access to other services, and help to alleviate the emotional stress caused by past trauma and the asylum process. LASSN also ran the Grace Hosting Project, which aimed to support the many refugees and asylum seekers who experience homelessness at some point during their asylum claim. Grace Hosting volunteers provided a hot meal and a bed for the night to people who have nowhere else to turn.

Source: Adapted from Social Care Institute for Excellence, https://www.scie.org. uk/publications/guides/guide37-Good-practice-in-social-care-with-refugees-and-asylum-seekers/practiceexamples.asp

Conclusion

In the UK the statutory role of social workers in supporting asylum seekers has been subject to increasing restrictions since 1999. Social workers and those involved in ensuring the welfare of asylum seekers have become increasingly intertwined in the ongoing dilemma of care versus control (Sales and Hek, 2004; Brown and Horrocks, 2009). Such a position places demands and strains on the ethical principles adopted by social welfare actors and puts pressure on their working environment (see Robinson, 2014). However, far from blindly implementing a conditional asylum system and the subsequent 'hostile environment' (Lewis et al, 2017), social welfare actors, in spite of the difficulties, have been artful in their practice and continue to mobilise an ethically astute value base. Across the landscape of immigration control, professionals who offer welfare support to asylum seekers have a range of important roles to play. Asylum seekers who have been granted support have many of the same entitlements to social support that UK citizens have, and social workers play a crucial role in helping individuals to access the additional support that they require in order to meet their needs. These rights and entitlements are not always known about and the complexity of the asylum system and related support process has created a significant amount of uncertainty and misinformation which has impacted on the wellbeing of individuals awaiting a decision on their asylum claim (HEAR, 2016). Social workers also play a vital role in the support of unaccompanied minors, in that they can help to ameliorate the dislocation and social disintegration caused by their migration and the asylum process (Kohli, 2007). Social workers can help work with the Red Cross to trace family members, facilitate a supportive environment to learn English and cultivate new relationships, and help to source many of the mundane artefacts such as phone cards, games and clothes which ease a life in transition. Asylum seekers who are not granted status are restricted from social welfare services, and non-governmental organisations and charities have increasingly become the only source of support for this marginalised population. The City of Sanctuary movement in the UK (see https://cityofsanctuary.org) has developed to fill the void created by the way that the asylum system is managed. Although it cannot be claimed to be a product of social work per se, in its values and mission the City of Sanctuary movement shares the values of the social work profession. Finally, a central role adopted by social welfare professionals in the environment of increasing restrictions around immigration has been, and should continue to be, resistance and knowledge exchange. Such professionals have a duty to exercise their rights-based practice so as to shed a light on the often chaotic, destructive, conditional and painful impacts of immigration control. Organisations such as Social Work Without Borders (see www.socialworkerswithoutborders.org) and the No Recourse to Public Funds Network (see www.nrpfnetwork.org.uk/Pages/Home.aspx) are prime examples of ways in which those concerned with the impact of immigration control are pushing against an overarching narrative of control and restriction. Although the official roles available to social work have been increasingly curtailed from the late 1990s, with the changes brought in as part of the 1999 Act and the introduction of public sector austerity measures, there are still spaces and places to exercise sound and ethical practice and to make both large-scale and small changes to policy, communities and people.

Critical questions

1 In an increasingly organised and controlling asylum system what can social workers do to deploy their responsibilities to engage in rights-based practice?

2 In light of the way that the asylum system is currently organised, in what sectors, roles and jobs can social workers be most effective in supporting asylum seekers?

3 To what extent is having an awareness of issues at the global level important to ensure effective social work practice at a local level?

4 At what point does care turn into control?

Further reading

• Hayes, D. and Humphries, B. (eds) (2004) *Social Work, Immigration and Asylum*, London: Jessica Kingsley.

Although this book has been around for a few years it remains an important text in exploring the role social workers have had in the support of migrants, refugees and asylum seekers in the UK.

• Kohli, R.K.S. (2007) *Social Work with Unaccompanied Asylum Seeking Children*, Basingstoke: Palgrave Macmillan.

When working with asylum seekers it is with children that social workers will tend to spend most of their time. This text provides practitioners with a rounded picture of some of the issues arising with children who are unaccompanied through the process.

• Robinson, K. (2014) 'Voices from the front line: social work with refugees and asylum seekers in Australia and the UK', *The British Journal of Social Work*, vol 44, no 6, pp 1602–20. This article takes a comparative approach to exploring the experience of practitioners working across two countries. It draws on the narratives of a large number of practitioners to identify the challenges faced by those on the front line, and will be particularly useful when read in conjunction with Hayes and Humphries (2004).

• Rutter, J. (2015) *Moving Up and Getting On: Migration, Integration and Social Cohesion in the UK*, Bristol: Policy Press.

This book provides a wonderful overview of the immigration system in the UK and how it has developed over the years. Although the focus is on migration and integration broadly, it is crucial that readers can appreciate how asylum seeking fits into the wider polity of migration control.

References

Akram, S.M. and Johnson, K.R. (2002) 'Race, civil rights, and immigration law after September 11, 2001: the targeting of Arabs and Muslims', *Boston University of Law. Working Paper Series, Public Law and Legal Theory*, Working Paper 03-01.

Asylum Information Database (2018) Country report: United Kingdom, www.asylumineurope.org/reports/country/united-kingdom

Boyle, P., Halfacree, K. and Robinson, V. (1998) *Exploring Contemporary Migration*, Harlow: Longman.

Brown, P. and Horrocks, C. (2009) 'Making sense? The support of dispersed asylum seekers', *International Journal of Migration, Health and Social Care*, vol 5, no 2, pp 22–34.

Castles, S., Crawley, H. and Loughna, S. (2003) *States of Conflict: Causes and Patterns of Forced Migration to the EU and Policy Responses*, London: Institute of Public Policy Research.

Crawley, H., Duvell, F., Sigona, N., McMahon, S. and Jones, K. (2016) *Unpacking a Rapidly Changing Scenario: Migration Flows, Routes and Trajectories Across the Mediterranean*, www.medmig.info/research-brief-01-unpacking-a-rapidly-changing-scenario/

Crisp, J. (1999) 'Who has counted the refugees? UNHCR and the politics of numbers', *New Issues in Refugee Research, Working Paper No. 12*, UNHCR.

Delahunty, R. (1996) *The Refugee Convention in the Twenty-First Century*, Oxford: Refugee Studies Centre.

Dummett, M. (2001) *On Immigration and Refugees*, London: Routledge.

Dummett, A. and Nichol, A. (1990) *Subjects, Citizens, Aliens and Others*, London: Butterworths.

Foot, P. (1965) *Immigration and Race in British Politics*, Harmondsworth: Penguin.

HEAR (2016) *A Guide to the Rights and Entitlements of Disabled Asylum Seekers, Refugees and Refused Applicants in the UK*, http://reap.org.uk/wp-content/uploads/2016/09/Rights-and-entitlements-of-disabled-asylum-seekers-refugees-and-refused-applicants.pdf

Hirst, C. and Atto, N. (2018) 'Global migration: consequences and responses. United Kingdom – country report', University of Cambridge, www.diva-portal.org/smash/get/diva2:1248430/FULLTEXT01.pdf

Holmes, C. (1991) *A Tolerant Country? Immigrants, Refugees and Minorities in Britain*, London: Faber and Faber.

Home Affairs Committee (2018) *Asylum Accommodation: Replacing COMPASS*, December, https://publications.parliament.uk/pa/cm201719/cmselect/cmhaff/1758/175807.htm

Institute of Race Relations (2000) *The Dispersal of Xenophobia*, http://s3-eu-west2.amazonaws.com/wpmedia.outlandish.com/irr/2018/04/04143749/dispersal_xenophobia.pdf

Jordan, B. and Düvell, F. (2003) *Migration: The Boundaries of Equality and Justice*, Cambridge: Polity.

Jordan, B. and Brown, P. (2006) 'The Sangatte work-visa holders: a "natural experiment" in immigration policy', *Parliamentary Affairs*, vol 59, no 3, pp 509–21.

Khan, P. (2000) 'Asylum-seekers in the UK: implications for social service involvement', *Social Work and Social Sciences Review*, vol 8, no 2, pp 116–29.

Kohli, R.K.S. (2007) *Social Work with Unaccompanied Asylum Seeking Children*, Basingstoke: Palgrave Macmillan.

Kumin, J. (2001) 'Gender: persecution in the spotlight', *Refugees*, vol 2, no 123, pp 12–13.

Kushner, T. and Knox, K. (1999) *Refugees in an Age of Genocide: Global, National and Local Perspectives during the Twentieth Century*, London: Frank Cass.

Lewis H., Waite L. and Hodkinson S. (2017) '"Hostile" UK immigration policy and asylum seekers' susceptibility to forced labour', in F. Vecchio and A. Gerard (eds), *Entrapping Asylum Seekers: Transnational Crime, Crime Control and Security*, London: Palgrave Macmillan, pp 187–215.

Medical Foundation for the Care of Victims of Torture (1999) *Comments of the Medical Foundation on the White Paper Entitled: Fairer, Faster and Firmer: A Modern Approach to Immigration and Asylum*. Previously available at: www.torturecare. org.uk/archivebrf/brief01.rtf

Oxfam (2000) *'Token Gestures': The Effects of the Voucher Scheme on Asylum Seekers and Organisations in the UK*, London: Oxfam.

Robinson, K. (2014) 'Voices from the front line: social work with refugees and asylum seekers in Australia and the UK', *The British Journal of Social Work*, vol 44, no 6, pp 1602–20.

Robinson, V., Andersson, R. and Musterd, S. (2003) *Spreading the 'Burden': A Review of Policies to Disperse Asylum Seekers and Refugees*, Bristol: Policy Press.

Rutter, J. (2015) *Moving Up and Getting On: Migration, Integration and Social Cohesion in the UK*, Bristol: Policy Press.

Sales, R. (2002) 'The deserving and the undeserving? Refugees, asylum seekers and welfare in Britain', *Critical Social Policy*, vol 22, no 3, pp 456–78.

Sales, R. and Hek, R. (2004) 'Dilemmas of care and control: the work of an asylum team in a London borough', in D. Hayes and B. Humphries (eds), *Social Work, Immigration and Asylum*, London: Jessica Kingsley, pp 59–76.

Schuster, L. (2002) 'Asylum and the lessons of history', *Race and Class*, vol 44, no 2, pp 40–56.

Schuster, L. (2003) *The Use and Abuse of Political Asylum in Britain and Germany*, London: Frank Cass.

Silove, D., Steel, Z. and Watters, C. (2000) 'Policies of deterrence and the mental health of asylum seekers', *Journal of the American Medical Association*, vol 284, no 5, pp 604–11.

UNHCR (2018) Figures at a glance, www.unhcr.org/uk/figures-at-a-glance.html

Visram, R. (2002) *Asians in Britain*, London: Pluto Press.

12

Child sexual abuse and exploitation

Donna Peach

Introduction

The sexual abuse and exploitation of children has endured, and continues, on what is arguably an unimaginable scale, with the World Health Organization (WHO and ISPCAN, 2006) estimating that worldwide 223 million children experience child sexual abuse (CSA). The multiple terms used to define the sexual abuse and exploitation of children are intertwined with the political interest and newly acquired or rediscovered attention that precipitates public attention on such abuse (Brown and Barrett, 2013). In the UK, the difference in terminology, and the justification for the legal and social abhorrence, or tolerance, of the sexual abuse of children has largely been dependent on the familial or commercial relationship between the adult and the child. Thus, a child who is abused by a member or close friend of their family is currently considered to have been subject to CSA, whereas a child subject to abuse by someone beyond their family is now constructed as being exploited. This chapter explores the various terms that construct what is deemed a sexual offence against a child and critiques the problematic nature of this binary model. In doing so, it will explore the definition of childhood and the broad range of ages that different countries use in legislating on the ability to consent to sexual activity.

Given the prolific nature of childhood sexual abuse and exploitation, many of you may have experienced this type of trauma or may know someone who has. You are not alone. We are all human, and too many of us are not sheltered from the impact of abuse. Therefore, I would like to affirm the importance of good self-care and of seeking support when you deem it necessary. Knowing when to seek support is a key function in maintaining our wellbeing and ensuring the quality of our practice. With that said, this chapter interrogates the policies that intertwine with social work practice, to construct what is deemed to constitute CSA and exploitation and how we respond (or not) to it.

International legislative context

Across the world, the age at which a person can legally consent to sexual activity ranges from 11 years of age in Nigeria and 12 years in the Philippines to 20 years in South Korea and 21 years in Bahrain. Across Europe ages range from 14 years in Germany, Portugal and Italy to 15 years in Sweden, Denmark and France, 16 years in the UK, 17 years in Cyprus and Ireland and 18 years in Malta, Turkey and the Vatican. In addition, some countries have what they term a 'close in age' examination, which is a law that allows a person who is below the age of consent to have lawful sexual contact with an older partner. For example, a 'close in age' exemption might include a four-year age difference between two young people. Some countries do not have a legally defined age of consent but insist that those engaging in sexual activity must be married to each other. One example here is Pakistan, where the minimum age for marriage is 16 years for women and 18 years for men. However, in Qatar, although all sexual activity outside marriage is unlawful there is no limit on the age at which people can marry, though marriage requires parental consent.

In the UK, the legal responsibilities of the state to protect children are embedded in domestic law; importantly, the UK has also ratified international treaties that promote the rights and safety of children against being exploited by UK citizens across the globe. The enactment of extraterritorial legislation was supported by Baroness Lucy Faithfull, and permits UK courts to hold UK citizens accountable for crimes they commit abroad. This legalisation is embedded in the Sexual Offences Act 2003. However, the use of this legislation to enforce extraterritorial agreements aimed to limit what is commonly referred to as 'child sexual exploitation tourism' has been extremely rare. The 1989 UN Convention on the Rights of the CHILD (UNCRC) sets out 54 articles that form a comprehensive human rights treaty for children and was ratified by the UK in 1991. Article 34 of the UNCRC asserts that governments have a duty to protect children from sexual abuse and exploitation. The United Nations further developed the specificity of the above assertion in the compilation of a 17-article 'Operation Protocol' on the sale of children, child prostitution and child pornography which was agreed by the UK in September 2000. It is important to have a clear legislative structure, but without the political will to robustly resource its application it is unlikely to meet the purpose for which it was created.

Within the UK there are limits to our understanding of the extent of the sexual abuse and exploitation of children. The Office for National Statistics (ONS) maintains statistics for sexual offences victims aged from 16 to 59 years in the UK. Notably, a report from Her Majesty's Inspectorate of Constabulary showed under-recording by 26% (HMIC, 2014). However, statistics on sexual offences against children are not collated. The Crime Survey for England and Wales by ONS records crimes experienced by children aged 10–15 years, but not sexual offences or 'trafficking'. However, figures suggest that sexual violence and abuse against children represent a major public health and social welfare problem within UK society and the ONS estimates that it affects 16% of children under 16 years of age. That figure suggests that we should have concerns about approximately two million children in the UK experiencing sexual abuse.

Defining the 'child'

In the UK different pieces of legislation construct the 'child' in accordance with their chronological age, which can arguably create both confusion and space for subjective opinion. Broadly, two key pieces of legislation, the Children Act 1989 and the Modern Slavery Act 2015, position children as people who are under 18 years of age. Currently in the UK the age at which a person can legally consent to sexual activity is 16 years, and this has been the age in England and Wales for young people engaged in a heterosexual relationships since 1885. A decade prior to that, in 1875, the age of consent was raised from 12 years to 13 years after concerns were raised about the prolific 'prostitution' of children (Brown and Barrett, 2013). Against this backdrop, it is important to recognise that the UK criminalised sexual relationships between men until the passing of the Sexual Offences Act 1967, which decriminalised sex between men aged 21 years or over. (Notably, other areas of discrimination also continued, as a ban on gay men and lesbian women serving in the armed forces remained in place until 2000.) The age of consent for men in a same-sex relationship was lowered to 18 years in 1994, and lowered again to 16 years in 2001 to create equality.

Despite these progressive steps, simultaneously Section 28 of the Local Government Act 1988 prohibited local authorities from promoting homosexuality and same-sex relationships. Section 28 was finally repealed in 2003, which meant that schools were able to openly offer support to their lesbian, gay and bisexual students. Notably, as our social consciousness of sexual identity continues to evolve we can challenge perceived and constructed norms. However, the pathway to sustainable progressive change is always a test of endurance. For example, at present the social and legislative constructions of the rights for people who identify as transgender are enveloped in codes of practice related to the Equality Act 2010, while remaining subject to intense interrogation both politically and within research (Elischberger et al, 2018).

As stated above, the age of consent to sexual activity for all young people in the UK is now 16 years; this means that anyone aged under 16 years cannot legally consent to their participation in sexual activity. Section 74 of the Sexual Offences Act 2003 defines consent as 'if he agrees by choice, and has the freedom and capacity to make that choice'.

The Crown Prosecution Service suggests that prosecutors should consider the following:

- whether a complainant had the capacity (that is, the age and understanding) to make a choice about whether or not to take part in the sexual activity at the time in question;
- whether he or she was in a position to make that choice freely and was not constrained in any way. Assuming that the complainant had both the freedom and capacity to consent, the crucial question is whether the complainant agreed to the activity by choice.

The above description depicts the degree of subjectivity required to determine whether a person has/had the capacity to make a choice; it includes the undefined concept of 'age and understanding'. More specifically, the Sexual Offences Act 2003 makes age-based distinctions for rape and other offences against children between those who are under 13 years of age, those under 16 years of age and those under 18 years of age. Sections 5 to 8 of the Sexual Offences Act 2003, detailed below, identify what legally constitutes a crime against a child or vulnerable person:

- rape of a child under 13;
- assault by penetration of a child under 13;
- sexual assault of a child under 13;
- inciting or causing a person to engage in sexual activity with a child under 13;
- child sexual offences involving children under 16;
- children under 18 having sexual relations with persons in a position of trust;
- children under 18 involved with family members over 18;
- persons with a mental disorder impeding choice;
- persons with a mental disorder who are induced, threatened or deceived;
- persons with a mental disorder who have sexual relations with care workers.

For more than a century the age of consent to sexual activity in the UK has been 16 years. Despite that, the dominant focus of our current legislation is specifically on children under the age of 13 years. Arguably, this suggests an inherent view of early adolescent biological sexual maturity and/or a perception of the child as sexually available to adults that is reminiscent of the beliefs that underpinned the 1875 legislative construct of the age of consent. Notably, where the Sexual Offences Act 2003 defines the child as under 18 years of age, it is when the adult is defined as a family member or someone in a position of trust. That distinction implies an additional responsibility on the part of adults whom a child should be able to trust as including and beyond members of their family.

Incest

If a child is sexually abused by a member of their family it is deemed to be an incestuous relationship. Research with an evolutionary focus suggests that the emergence of social norms and laws that prohibit close familial relationships was due to the detrimental genetic effects of 'inbreeding' (Kresanov et al, 2018). In Britain it has long been an offence for immediate family members, over the age of 16 years, to have sexual intercourse with someone they know to be a sibling, half-sibling, grandchild, parent or grandparent. However, there has not been a matter in the British courts to test the human rights of consenting 'adults' who are legally prohibited from having a sexual relationship due to their familial relationship (Roffee, 2014).

Our current substantive legislation is the Sexual Offences Act 2003, which extends familial child relationships to include aunts, uncles, cousins, step-parents, step-siblings, foster parents and adoptive parents. This Act also encompasses a broader range of offences that incorporate any sexual activity with a child, or incitement of a child to engage with sexual activity. The inclusion of non-biological relationships and of sexual activities that do not involve intercourse represents a change in social attitudes to reach beyond the prevention of genetic incompatibility. However, despite the expanded definition of familial CSA, Anne Longfield, Children's Commissioner for England, produced a critical assessment in 2015 which estimates that we are failing to identify seven out of eight child victims. Longfield (Children's Commissioner, 2015) asserts that the high commitment from practitioners to safeguarding these children is challenged by multiple barriers which include:

- an onus on disclosure from a child;
- practitioners' fear that in exploring their concerns they could inadvertently be perceived as 'leading' the victim;
- meeting the significant legal criminal burden of proof;
- misconstruing aspects of a child's behaviour.

In 2017 the Children's Commissioner followed up her concerns about the lack of response to children experiencing familial CSA with a focus on the length of criminal investigations of the one in eight cases that are identified. Longfield (Children's Commissioner, 2017) reports that CSA-related cases take longer to investigate than all other crimes. She reports that investigations of incestuous crimes will take more than three times longer to complete than those of other violent crimes. Despite the concerns raised by the Children's Commissioner, it is notable that we are not having a national conversation about the strategies needed to better identify the child victims who are hidden from public view. That is a grave concern, especially when research based on clinical analysis reflects the often-complex trauma experienced by child victims, across all social classes, who have been victims of sexual abuse by family members (Rachman and Klett, 2015).

The invisibility of victims from public view is not new. Historically, on a wave of feminism in the 1970s, we saw the emergence of women talking and writing about their previously hidden incestuous abuse. However, the power differentials inherent in our misogynistic and patriarchal society ensure that women's and children's narratives are not sustained. Their contributions are temporal, often arriving with an upsurge of momentum, like the recent 'Me Too' movement. Despite these fluctuations in public consciousness, as social workers we need to consistently recognise that a child's experience of sexual activity is inherently bound to the overt power that adults have over them (Brown and Barrett, 2013).

Despite the temporality of public attention, the voices of survivors are there, waiting to be (re)discovered. In 1987 a survivor, Jacqueline Spring (1987; pseudonym), published a book titled *Cry Hard and Swim* about her experience of incest. More recently, survivors of child sexual exploitation in the UK have been publishing their accounts of abuse. Titles include but are not limited to, *Violated* by

Sarah Wilson (2015); *I Never Gave My Consent: A Schoolgirl's Life Inside the Telford Sex Ring* by Holly Archer (2016) and *Just a Child* by Sammy Woodhouse (2018). Furthermore, survivor-led charities such as Voicing-CSA (https://voicingcsa.uk/), of which I am an ambassador, hold regular public meetings across the country to help share and support the voices of victims and survivors. These meetings provide opportunities for you to attend in person and listen to the testimony of those with lived experience. They also provide a live stream from each meeting and upload videos on their website. In my view, there is no limit on the amount of information to be discovered, and learning to be gained, from talking with and listening to survivors.

Child sexual abuse or child sexual exploitation?

The relationship between legislation, social policies and social work practice in relation to the sexual abuse and exploitation of children is both complex and multifaceted. It has endured in largely unexamined ways for decades, making it difficult to unravel an ever-evolving concept that manifests itself in multiple ways. To illuminate our understanding of this phenomenon, this chapter next directs its focus on the contemporary issue of child sexual exploitation (CSE) to examine how this type of abuse is constructed within political discourse and legislative structures. It demonstrates how the definition of CSE originated via the work of Ann Coffey MP to replace legislative use of the term 'child prostitution' and has contributed to our understanding of CSE as a concept and how CSE is constructed as different from CSA. There are multiple sources of definitions which can in itself become confusing; you may find resources such as the NSPCC website valuable in this regard (https://learning.nspcc.org.uk).

It is important to examine the descriptions of CSA and CSE. I argue that all criminal sexual activity towards children should be viewed as abusive and that it is unhelpful, if not harmful, to distinguish between CSA and CSE. This section critiques how the purported difference between the two could influence practice and our propensity to blame victims. Definitions are important, as they provide the basis of the agreement on what constitutes a phenomenon, so that when we talk about it we know we are each talking about the same thing. In relation to CSE and CSA, legal definitions are also important to support both the police and the judiciary to critically examine whether a behaviour constitutes a crime. However, less attention is given to interrogating the factors that led to the development of CSE as a concept, and its subsequent adoption into practice and the political definitions which seep, largely unexamined, into everyday discourse.

The rise of the term 'child sexual exploitation' is firmly anchored within a complex socio-political landscape which developed as scandals involving large-scale abuse of children and the failure of public services in England to protect and respond came to public attention. Three English towns in particular, namely, Rochdale, Oxford and Rotherham, were subject to intense public scrutiny, while other cities and towns have, to date, avoided the same widespread interrogation. In particular, the media coverage of the northern towns of Rochdale and Rotherham had a particularly high profile. That public exposure led to political representations, press reports, independent investigations and, in the case of Rochdale, a televised dramatisation, titled *Three Girls*, which starred the actress Maxine Peake. More recently, in 2018, Telford and Wrekin Council agreed to commission an inquiry into concerns that children in their borough were subjected to CSE and were potentially failed by the services that were meant to protect them. Thus, the issue of how we prevent and respond to child sexual abuse and exploitation remains current. However, although some councils are inevitably responding to similar concerns away from public view, there are concerns that other local authorities do not recognise the issue as prevalent in their area.

Prior to the term 'child sexual exploitation' coming into common usage, the language used in British legislation to describe the commercially driven sexual abuse of children was 'child prostitution'. That terminology was challenged by Ann Coffey MP in response to the construction of victimhood inherent in the CSE scandals. Coffey engaged with young people in order to understand their experiences of sexual victimisation and this led to the publication of two reports, *Real Voices* (2014), and the follow-up report, *Real Voices: Are they being heard?* (2017). In addition to promoting the importance of including young people in any cultural change, Coffey also sought to have the term 'child prostitution' removed from 16 pieces of legislation, arguing that the term implied that children were complicit in their abuse. When addressing the Public Bill Committee, who were considering the Serious Crime Bill [Lords], Coffey argued that the use of language was crucially important to the subsequent response to a victim of sexual exploitation.[1]

> The use of language in this regard is interesting. We are conflicted in our attitudes towards children. For example, a 14-year-old girl who is the subject of sexual exploitation can be described as a child and as a young person, but the way we describe her influences the way we respond to her. If she is described as a child, we immediately have a sympathetic response, because it indicates to us her relationship to adults. If she is described as a young person, our response is more ambivalent, because she is seen as a mini-adult – in some way as having some equality with adults. The language used is a key factor. (*Hansard*, 2014–2015)

As the public and the politicians began to make sense of this apparently new 'phenomenon', researchers started to explore definitions of what constitutes CSE (Hallett, 2017). Although there remains debate about its definition, several bodies have supported the concept of how CSE differs from CSA. CSE is commonly viewed as a form of CSA, and other researchers have aimed to further define types or modes of CSE, including that perpetrated by gangs (Beckett et al, 2012), by peers (Firmin, 2015), by commercial means (Dodsworth, 2014) and via technology (Ringrose et al, 2012).

The distinction between the child sexual abuse and exploitation still occurs, although some victims and survivors report experiencing abuse from perpetrators both familial and otherwise. I argue that one of the consequences of that defined variation is the multifaceted construction of 'victimhood', which is often reliant on the criminal definition of the behaviour of the perpetrator. Thus, the identity of victims becomes synonymous with the defined criminal activity of the perpetrator, such that they and their experiences are identified as abused, exploited, groomed and trafficked. Although the commercial sexual exploitation of children has been documented for more than a century (Brown and Barrett, 2013), our lack of sustained public awareness and interrogation means that many victims do not report their abuse for many decades, often after the abuse has ended. Indeed, in modern times some victims of CSE report that during their abuse they did not perceive themselves as victims, in part because they had been convinced by the perpetrators that they were willingly complicit in the sexual activities they engaged in. We are therefore limited in the extent to which we understand the harm suffered and the long-term impact of the abuse experienced by victims of abuse and exploitation. Furthermore, the time period in which they experienced the abuse could have a different construction of the terminology that was used to define it, as compared to that at the time when it came under the public gaze.

Abuse or a moral panic?

Notably, some researchers argue that society's response to the concerns of the purposeful geographical movement (trafficking) of children for the alleged purpose of sexual abuse is a form of moral panic (Cree et al, 2014). Cree et al (2014) suggest that there is value in understanding current concerns by perceiving them within a broader historical context. This chapter has offered some historical contextualisation, which could suggest that 'moral panic' is reflective of the temporal public attention given to what can be described as enduring, but frequently unexamined, large-scale sexual abuse of children. More recently, Smith and Woodiwiss (2016) argued that social workers contribute to the construction of children engaged in sexual activity as victims. They suggest that there is value in separating how we determine what behaviour is wrong, and what harm or not is caused. I agree that it is important to understand and define the scope of sexual development and activity, but that this needs to be in conjunction with the knowledge of those adults who individually and collectively intend to sexually victimise children.

Following public scandals of a failure of some English towns to protect hundreds of girls from sexual exploitation, in 2014 the government appointed Dame Louise Casey to investigate 'the case of Rotherham'. Casey's report (Casey, 2015) was highly critical of social work agencies, claiming that they were in denial about the extent of the public's concern. Her findings were accepted by Prime Minister David Cameron, who proceeded to challenge the role of social workers, suggesting that they could be subject to criminal charges if they failed to protect children from sexual abuse by assuming they had given consent to sexual activity prior to their 16th birthday (Crossley and Leigh, 2017). Simultaneously, numerous public statements and documents raised concerns about the failure to identify and meet the needs of children who had been sexually abused and exploited (Peach et al, 2015).

Amid these competing narratives, social workers have to learn to navigate the multifaceted demands associated with CSA and CSE, and this also entails interrogating the relationship between political construction and research evidence. Notably, these are not necessarily independent of each other. As you read this chapter, you may experience a reliance on the words of the author or of other academic researchers whose assertions you feel a need to accept. It is commonplace for us to ascribe power to those who have knowledge that we are yet to learn. As you write your assignments and further your understanding of various topics it is important to understand that when any academic (myself included) writes something we are actually constructing knowledge based on what we know. The concepts in this chapter are presented and explored on the basis of my current understanding of what I have read, researched and learned from others who have experienced child sexual abuse and exploitation. However, that is not and will never be the whole story. Learning is a continuous process and, as you read my analysis, you may query what aspect of my discussion you think is more valuable or more concrete than those of others. The development of your own critical analysis is crucial to the development of your skills as a social worker. Unlike social researchers and policy makers, social workers are tasked with the application of theory and are responsible for and witness to its effect on the lives of others. Given that knowledge is always evolving, we are required to manage uncertainty and to use our foundational ethics and values to bridge the gaps left by legislation, policy and theory.

The geographical movement of children for the purpose of commercial sexual abuse (commonly termed 'trafficking')

Additionally, CSE is positioned as a form of child 'trafficking' (Sangster et al, 2018). The movement of children for the purpose of their exploitation is a major concern across the world, with approximately 4.5 million children estimated to be victims of commercial sexual exploitation and forced labour. The UK's Modern Slavery Act 2015 was enacted in response to crimes of human trafficking and slavery. It defines slavery as 'knowingly holding a person in slavery or servitude or knowingly requiring a person to perform forced or compulsory labour'. The movement of children (or adults) as part of criminal exploitation is often termed 'domestic trafficking' and can be difficult to identify. Researchers Brayley and Cockbain (2014) have created a model to assist in identifying the features of domestic trafficking. However, it remains problematic to have a blanket definition for an activity that is varied and often hidden, albeit in plain sight.

The UK is a party to ILO Convention No. 182 and the Palermo Protocol and – specifically in relation to trafficking – accordingly holds the view that a child is anyone below the age of 18 years. The Palermo Protocol is also relevant to the incidence of trafficking that is transnational and involves organised criminal groups; its definition of trafficking is now widely agreed and used outside these parameters.

Box 12.1: Defining human trafficking: the Palermo Protocol

- Article 3(a) defines 'trafficking in persons' as 'the recruitment, transportation, transfer, harbouring or receipt of persons, by means of the threat or use of force or other forms of coercion, of abduction, or fraud, of deception, of the abuse of power or of a position of vulnerability or of the giving or receiving of payments or benefits to achieve the consent of a person having control over another person, for the purpose of exploitation. Exploitation shall include, at a minimum, the exploitation of the prostitution of others or other forms of sexual exploitation, forced labour or services, slavery or practices similar to slavery, servitude or the removal of organs.'
- Article 3(b) explains that 'consent' – for example, to take up work in prostitution – is irrelevant where any of the means set forth in Article 3(a) have been used.
- Article 3(c) explains that 'the recruitment, transportation, transfer, harbouring or receipt of a child for the purpose of exploitation' is considered to be trafficking even if none of the means set forth in Article 3(a) have been used.

The UK is at a formative stage in understanding the extent to which children are 'trafficked' into, out of and within the UK. As part of its commitment to the Council of Europe Convention on Action Against Trafficking in Human Beings (2005), the UK government has established a process for counting people who may have been trafficked, known as the national referral mechanism (NRM). In 2016 NRM began to include minors trafficked internally as part of criminal drug enterprise extending out from London, commonly termed 'County Lines', which includes young people domestically trafficked for labour and sexual exploitation. As these newly formed constructive terminologies begin to take shape in the form of categorisation and policy, it is vital to maintain a focus on victims and the resources available to those who are victimised and to their families.

Parents of children who have been enslaved and transported to another geographical area can be left not knowing if their children are alive or dead, producing what Samuels (2015) describes as 'haunting uncertainties'. Oram et al (2015) suggest that 'Childhood abuse doesn't just affect the mind – it affects the body too, severe mental illness in trafficked people is associated with longer admissions and high levels of abuse before and after trafficking. Evidence is needed on the effectiveness of interventions to promote recovery for this vulnerable group.' Children who feel perpetually in danger grow to develop a heightened stress response; this, in turn, can heighten their emotions, make it difficult to sleep, lower immune function and, over time, increase the risk of a number of physical illnesses. Adult survivors of child abuse can be at increased risk of chronic pain and fibromyalgia, gynaecological problems, irritable bowel syndrome, diabetes, arthritis, headaches, cardiovascular disease and chronic fatigue syndrome (Oram et al, 2015).

In their study of the health of 207 women and adolescents who had been 'trafficked', Zimmerman et al (2011) found that almost every corporeal system was affected by the impact of the abuse. More than half (60%) experienced sexual health needs and 17% reported having terminated at least one pregnancy. In a later study of 107 women who had been 'trafficked', Lederer and Wetzel (2014) found complex health needs, with some participants reporting that they had been sexually abused up to 50 times a day. A fifth of these participants reported that they had had multiple pregnancies and 71.2% asserted that at least one of their pregnancies had occurred during their exploitation. It is not a moral panic to bear witness to these crimes and their effects. To respond so as to reduce the incidence of criminality and to meet the long-term needs of those affected requires a strategic and well-resourced national, regional and locally integrated plan. Arguably, it is our moral duty to do so.

Conclusion

The construction of what constitutes CSA and CSE is complex. Although having a legally defined age of consent can assist, the myriad of historical factors that construct legislation contributes to increasing that complexity. Situating the UK within a global context helps to reflect on the concept of adolescence and serves to raise questions about how adolescents negotiate relationships amid changing discourses, social media communication and social expectations. This chapter has demonstrated that political interest and public reporting facilitate which topics are publicly scrutinised and which are not. The existence of scandal attracts public attention, which can assist greater interrogation of a topic, but the method of any intervention and subsequent knowledge also contribute to how the topic is defined and understood. The argument of Smith and Woodiwiss (2016) that some children under 16 years of age may willingly engage in (albeit not legally consented) sexual activity without being traumatised or identifying as victims remains an important point for deliberation. However, that should not be at the expense of the millions of children who are traumatised by their sexually abusive experiences.

The role of social workers to act as protective agents is complicated and not sufficiently served by legislation, funding, research or theory. Social workers need to have a good understanding of the complexity of CSA and CSE, but this can raise more questions than answers. At times of 'moral panic' (Cree et al, 2014) social work intervention can be placed under increased public scrutiny, and research knowledge that aims to understand the phenomenon is often constructed after those concerns have been raised. As a profession, there are multiple areas where we are practising with the best knowledge available. The inevitable gaps in that knowledge are filled by the core values that underpin the best of relational social work. Therefore, what we know, how we know it and when we know it will influence how we make sense of any subject. Whether you are a student, social worker, practitioner or academic, it is always important to remain critically reflective of how we understand the world and its influence upon us. To retain a level of interrogation requires us to ascertain what viewpoints we value and on what basis we make those determinations. For social work students and practitioners, critical reflection is a skill that extends beyond higher educational learning, as our professional standards and values require us to contextualise our behaviour, our interactions and those of others. This level of self-understanding is of particular importance when we examine issues pertaining to childhood trauma. Finally, survivors of CSA are some of the bravest and most insightful people I have ever met. I am grateful for all the learning they so willingly share.

Critical questions

Look up relevant research papers and review the descriptions and definitions of CSA and CSE that they present. Reflect on the following questions:

1 How do the definitions compare/differ in their construction of perpetrators and victims? Consider how they are generalised and what other assumptions underpin how they are identified.

2 Consider the relationship between the construction of the perpetrator and how that defines the victim, and vice versa. How are these useful, and what limitations do they bring to your understanding of each person/group?

3 How helpful or not are the definitions if an individual has been both a victim and a perpetrator?

Further reading

• Children's Commissioner (2015) *Protecting Children from Harm: A Critical Assessment of Child Sexual Abuse in the Family Network in England and Priorities for Action*, London: Children's Commissioner for England.
The Children's Commissioner for England provides a useful report on assessment of CSA in the family. I encourage you to read it so as to ensure that you contextualise the incidence of sexual abuse of children in England and our response (or lack of response) to that issue.

• Woodhouse, S. (2018) *Just A Child: Britain's Biggest Child Abuse Scandal Exposed*, London: Blink Publishing.

Sammy Woodhouse is a survivor of CSE from Rotherham who dropped her right to anonymity in order to actively campaign for changes in the law. Most recently, her post-abuse experiences have led to a call for a Bill to remove the parental rights of the fathers of children conceived through rape; to make provision for an inquiry into the handling by family courts of domestic abuse and violence against women and girls in Child Arrangement cases; and for connected purposes. You can read more about that via this link: https://hansard.parliament.uk/commons/2019–04–10/debates/52CE1E25–3F43–4786–8701–603C9DCECFF2/ParentalRights(Rapists)AndFamilyCourts

• Hallett, S. (2017) *Making Sense of Child Sexual Exploitation: Exchange, Abuse and Young People*, Policy Press: Bristol.

Sophie Hallett is an emerging voice in the topic of CSE. Although the focus of her work is, at this time, limited to what I would argue is a narrow contemporary view of CSE, in this text she presents a useful initial guide.

• Cree, V.E., Clapton, G. and Smith, M. (2014) 'The presentation of child trafficking in the UK: an old and new moral panic?', *British Journal of Social Work*, vol 44, pp 418–33, http://doi.org/10.1093/bjsw/bcs120

If you are interested in matters related to 'moral panic', Viv Cree and colleagues have published multiple papers which address this subject. This one above provides a critical historical focus on how society responds to the exploitation of children.

• Peach, D. and Allen, D. (2015) *Needs Analysis Report following the Sexual Exploitation of Children in Rotherham*, University of Salford, https://moderngov.rotherham.gov.uk/documents/s103693/APPROVED%20FINAL%20RMBC%20CSE%20Needs%20Analysis%20report%20-%20Salford.pdf

The CSE needs analysis undertaken in Rotherham in the aftermath of the Jay Report reflects the experiences of individuals, families, organisations and communities. It is a reminder of the pervasive impact that CSE can have on a whole community and the further impact of the moral panic and blame that can arise as a result.

References

Beckett, H., Brodie, I., Factor, F., Melrose, M., Pearce, J., Pitts, J. et al (2012) *Research into Gang-associated Sexual Exploitation and Sexual Violence: Interim Report*, Luton: University of Bedfordshire.

Brayley, H. and Cockbain, E. (2014) 'British children can be trafficked too: towards an inclusive definition of internal child sex trafficking', *Child Abuse Reviews*, vol 23, pp 171–84.

Brown, A. and Barrett, D. (2013) *Knowledge of Evil Child Prostitution and Child Sexual Abuse in Twentieth-century England*, Cullompton: Willan Publishing.

Casey, L. (2015) *Report of Inspection of Rotherham Metropolitan Borough Council*, London: Department of Communities and Local Government.

Children's Commissioner (2015) *Protecting Children from Harm: A Critical Assessment of Child Sexual Abuse in the Family Network in England and Priorities for Action*, London: Children's Commissioner for England.

Children's Commissioner (2017) *Investigating Child Abuse: The Length of Criminal Investigations*, London: Children's Commissioner for England.

Coffey, A. (2014) *Real Voices: Child Sexual Exploitation in Greater Manchester: An Independent Report by Ann Coffey MP, October 2014*, Manchester: Greater Manchester Police.

Coffey, A. (2017) *Real Voices: Are They Being Heard? Child Sexual Exploitation in Greater Manchester: A Follow up Report from Ann Coffey, MP, March 2017*, Manchester: Greater Manchester Police.

Cree, V.E., Clapton, G. and Smith, M. (2014) 'The presentation of child trafficking in the UK: An old and new moral panic?', *British Journal of Social Work*, vol 44, pp 418–33, http://doi.org/10.1093/bjsw/bcs120

Crossley, S. and Leigh, J. (2017) 'The "troubled" case of Rotherham', *Critical and Radical Social Work*, vol 5, no 1, pp 23–40, http://doi.org/10.1332/20498 6016X14798319535531

Dodsworth, J. (2014) 'Sexual exploitation, selling and swapping sex: victimhood and agency', *Child Abuse Review*, vol 23, no 3, pp 185–99.

Elischberger, H., Glazier, B., Hill, J. and Verduzco-Baker, J. (2018) 'Attitudes toward and beliefs about transgender youth: a cross-cultural comparison between the United States and India', *Sex Roles*, vol 78, no 1, pp 142–60.

Firmin, C.E. (2015) 'Peer on peer abuse: safeguarding implications of contextualising abuse between young people within social fields', Professional Doctorate Thesis, University of Bedfordshire.

Hallett, S. (2017) *Making Sense of Child Sexual Exploitation: Exchange, Abuse and Young People*, Bristol: Policy Press.

Hansard, Session 2014-2015, Serious Crime Bill, Public Bill Committee debate, 4th sitting, 15 January, col 90, https://publications.parliament.uk/pa/cm201415/cmpublic/seriouscrime/150115/pm/150115s01.htm

HMIC (Her Majesty's Inspectorate of Constabulary) (2014) *Crime-recording: Making the Victim Count: The Final Report of an Inspection of Crime Data Integrity in Police Forces in England and Wales*. Available at: www.justiceinspectorates.gov.uk/hmicfrs/wp-content/uploads/crime-recording-making-the-victim-count.pdf

Kresanov, P., Kotler, J., Seto, M., Lieberman, D., Santtila, P. and Antfolk, J. (2018) 'Intergenerational incest aversion: self-reported sexual arousal and disgust to hypothetical sexual contact with family members', *Evolution and Human Behavior*, vol 39, no 6, pp 664–74.

Lederer, L. and Wetzel, C. (2014) 'The health consequences of sex trafficking and their implications for identifying victims in healthcare facilities', *Annals of Health Law*, vol 23, no 1, pp 61–91.

Oram, S., Khondoker, M., Abas, M., Broadbent, M. and Howard, L.M. (2015) 'Characteristics of trafficked adults and children with severe mental illness: a historical cohort study', *The Lancet Psychiatry*, vol 2, no 12, pp 1084–91.

Peach, D., Allen, D. and Brown, P. (2015) *Needs Analysis Report Following the Sexual Exploitation of Children in Rotherham, for Rotherham Metropolitan Borough Council*, https://moderngov.rotherham.gov.uk/documents/s103693/APPROVED%20 FINAL%20RMBC%20CSE%20Needs%20Analysis%20report%20-%20Salford. pdf

Rachman, A.W. and Klett, S.A. (2015) *Analysis of the Incest Trauma: Retrieval, Recovery, Renewal*, London: Karnac Books.

Ringrose, J., Gill, R., Livingstone, S. and Harvey, L. (2012) *A Qualitative Study of Children, Young People and 'Sexting': A Report Prepared for the NSPCC*, London: NSPCC.

Roffee, J.A. (2014) 'No consensus on incest? Criminalisation and compatibility with the European Convention on Human Rights', *Human Rights Law Review*, vol 14, no 3, pp 541–72.

Samuels, A. (2015) 'Narratives of uncertainty: The affective force of child-trafficking rumors in postdisaster Aceh', *American Anthropologist*, vol 117, no 2, pp 229–41.

Sangster, A.M., Crowley, M. and McGrandles, A. (2018) 'Identifying child sexual exploitation', *Community Practitioner*, vol 91, no 5, pp 44–6.

Smith, M. and Woodiwiss, J. (2016) 'Sexuality, innocence and agency in narratives of childhood sexual abuse: implications for social work', *British Journal of Social Work*, vol 46, no 8, pp 2173–89, http://doi.org/10.1093/bjsw/bcw160

Spring, J. (1987) *Cry Hard and Swim: The Story of an Incest Survivor*, London: Virago Press.

WHO (World Health Organization) and ISPCAN (International Society for Prevention of Child Abuse and Neglect) (2006) *Preventing Child Maltreatment: A Guide to Taking Action and Generating Evidence*, Geneva: World Health Organization Press.

Zimmerman, C., Hossain, M. and Watts, C. (2011) 'Human trafficking and health: a conceptual model to inform policy, intervention and research', *Social Science and Medicine*, vol 73, no 2, pp 327–35, http://doi.org/10.1016/j. socscimed.2011.05.028

13

Addiction

Chris Yianni

Introduction

How should we approach the problem of addiction? I make no apologies for using the term 'problem' because social workers will inevitably deal with people who have developed problems due to addiction. In seeking to understand the power inherent in political rhetoric and how this might influence attitude, this chapter will explore one of the main sites of debate when tackling the above question. This debate largely centres on the bifurcation between zero-tolerance and harm-reduction approaches.

What is addiction?

> Addiction is a chronic condition involving a repeated powerful motivation to engage in a rewarding behaviour, acquired as a result of engaging in that behaviour, that has significant potential for unintended harm. Someone is addicted to something to the extent that they experience this repeated powerful motivation. (West and Brown, 2013, pp 15–18)

The term 'rewarding behaviour' offers insight into the reasons why people begin to engage in a particular behaviour. The rewards can be in the form of the pursuit of a pleasant feeling or the masking of an unpleasant feeling. A problematic addiction can impact on the life of the person addicted to the extent they start to neglect themselves, their responsibilities and the significant people in their life. Therefore we can see the need for social workers to consider not only the addicted person but also those who are around that person.

There are many activities that one can become addicted to, such as gambling, eating/not eating and even seemingly healthy pursuits such as exercise. For the purposes of this chapter I will focus on drug and substance use, including the use of alcohol. The problem of addiction and how to address it is a phenomenon that is bound with political values rather than political allegiances; therefore it crosses party-political boundaries. This chapter will consider the political development of zero-tolerance and harm-reduction, with a focus on values.

Values

All of us have a relationship with drugs and alcohol. Some of us use substances, some drink alcohol and some do both. Equally, many people do not use drugs and/or alcohol and they will have their reasons for this. These reasons define the basis of our relationship with use and non-use and are mostly driven by the values we wish to abide by. It is true that, for some, non-use is an imperative driven by necessity such as a desire or need to give up, a religious belief or even a legal requirement. Nonetheless, our relationship with drug and alcohol use is something derived from our experiences and values.

For Bell (2018, p 4), 'values are those elements of life that one believes should be cherished, preserved, promoted or respected'. Social workers are no exception to this, and the fact that they will have to work with those who are identified as problematic users means that they will have to consider their own relationship with drugs and alcohol and put their own values into context when undertaking such work. Our values can be derived from a variety of sources, including the media, friends and family and cultural and religious influences. A social worker may have to identify the overriding issue that needs to be promoted when dealing with problematic substance use. A dilemma can arise when having to decide if this is then congruent with maintaining respect for others as well as maintaining the rights of others to choose a particular course of action.

Choice

Choice is a site of much debate when discussing pathways into and the maintenance of addictive behaviour. West and Brown (2013) offer the term Rational Informed Stable Choice (RISC), which considers the life of, for example, a person addicted to heroin. They may have a chaotic life-style characterised by homelessness and ill-health, but the idea of giving up heroin and the subsequent life options open to them is less attractive than continued use. In this way, we can see that not all drug and alcohol users want to give up their use because positive alternatives are not identifiable options for them. If the option was that by giving up you would gain access to a comfortable house, a stable and happy family unit and a healthy income, then most would choose this. Clearly, this is not a viable option for many of those addicted to drugs and alcohol, and so the phenomenon of choice is rendered redundant. Indeed, West and Brown (2013, p 44) state that if the user's 'emotional state or life circumstances as an ex-drug user are bleak and unhappy, it would be quite rational to choose to remain a user'.

Although some would argue that the choice to use was made in the first instance (the aforementioned rewarding behaviour), there are certainly those who have not been in a position to make rational choices at the outset. Consider the patient who is prescribed a particular drug and, through a process whereby the doctor continues to renew the prescription, becomes dependent on, and ultimately addicted to, the medication.

> **CASE STUDY 13.1: WHAT IS A CHOICE? JIMMY (AGE 23)**
>
> Jimmy had been arrested and bailed to a probation hostel, due to stealing to feed his heroin addiction. In a key-work session he disclosed that he came from a large family with six siblings. His mother and father were largely absent from his and his siblings' lives, choosing instead to spend most of their time in the pub drinking and procuring/using drugs. The only person who actually cared for Jimmy was one of his older sisters, who ensured that he was fed, clothed and safe. When Jimmy was 11 years old this sister introduced him to intravenous heroin use. She told him that this was a good thing and would always make him feel good. In much the same way that many people are reliant on parents and carers for guidance and their development, Jimmy was reliant on his sister. In this way, he became addicted to heroin use.

This case study provides an example of how one can be initiated into drug use and begs the question 'Did Jimmy have any choice but to start to use heroin at 11 years old?' Indeed, one of the risk factors that Heanue and Lawton (2012) indicate one should look for when assessing the potential for harm to children, or the potential for them to use drugs in a mimetic way, is whether others in the house use drugs. McKeganey's (2014) assessment of gateways into drug use speaks of family influence and relationships and how these are linked to the initiation of adolescents into drug use.

Zero tolerance and harm reduction

Having set out the parameters of the terms 'addiction', 'values' and 'choice', it would be useful to do the same for zero tolerance and harm reduction.

Zero-tolerance approaches are based on abstinence, the ultimate goal being to eradicate the use of drugs and, for those addicted to alcohol, to stop drinking. In terms of policy, one of the vehicles utilised to pursue a zero-tolerance approach is legislation and the judicial system. A zero-tolerance approach can see drug users, as well as dealers/producers, arrested and charged with offences relating to drugs. The ideology behind this is that all illegal drug use is bad and should not be tolerated. Within the parameters of a zero-tolerance approach, people are encouraged to maintain a drug-/alcohol-free life and not use at all.

For those who are addicted to alcohol, a zero-tolerance approach would require them to completely abstain from alcohol use. Even though use might be within the parameters of the law – and, indeed, for some people, quite acceptable and unproblematic – the individual would have to consider alcohol to be something that had to be avoided.

The premise behind a harm–reduction approach is that there has to be some degree of toleration towards use. Indeed, Arnull's (2014, p 69) discussion includes a sub-heading: 'Harm reduction: toleration by another name?'. Harm-reduction policies will see the accommodation of drug use within a framework that seeks to minimise the concomitant risks. Accepting that for some people complete abstinence is a difficult goal to reach, or within a RISC framework an undesired goal, harm-reduction approaches can blur the boundaries between the normalisation of substance use and the dominant societal mores that would view such normalisation as problematic.

The Global Commission on Drug Policy (2017, p 19) points to harm-reduction approaches for those activities that are not illegal and cites examples such as the use of 'nicotine patches, light beer, condoms, seat belts and protective gear in sports'. This demonstrates further the view that the risks of those activities that can be positioned as risky can be mitigated by a moderation in, rather than a cessation of, behaviour.

A simple comparison between the two approaches is highlighted by the use of opiate substitution prescriptions. A user who is addicted to heroin might be offered regular doses of methadone in order to steer them away from illegal drug use. This prescription could be in the form of a reduction programme whereby the dosage is titrated down over a set period until the user's dependence is reduced to the point of no longer needing drugs. This would facilitate total abstinence within a zero-tolerance framework and it would be expected that the user would avoid opiates thereafter.

A harm-reduction approach would acknowledge that the user was not ready/able to give up opiates completely and would see the prescription of methadone in the form of a maintenance programme. The user would continue to receive the same dosage for a prolonged period in order for them to avoid the need to use illegal drugs. Both of these approaches seek to minimise the harm to users; however, the harm-reduction approach accepts that opiate use is a continuing necessity for some people.

McKeganey (2011) writes of the differing attitudes to methadone prescription and, highlighting the controversial nature of the opposing views, shows that for some it is viewed as a life saver and for others as a life sentence. For some, methadone is key to enabling users to achieve some form of stability in their lives, yet for others it compounds their addiction, making their lives worse. These views highlighted by McKeganey show that the complexities in seemingly straightforward approaches make them in fact far from straightforward. Therefore, it would be surprising if the debate around zero tolerance and harm reduction was anything but problematic. Indeed, Keene (2010) points to the variety of views offered by different academics discussing zero tolerance and harm reduction. Each offers their own view of the best approach based on the advantages therein and points to flaws within the opposing approach.

Use of language

Opposing views are so entrenched that the language used in discussing the landscape of drug and alcohol use can further cement preconceptions. When considering the use of language with student social workers I advocate for the abandonment of terms such as 'abuse' and 'misuse' and ask them to consider terms such as 'substance use problems'. Similarly, I argue that terms such as 'addict' and 'alcoholic' should be eschewed in an attempt to minimise the effects of labelling. Allan (2014) points to the problem of labelling and the fact that this can stigmatise and exclude people from gaining social capital. It can negatively impact on a person's life to the extent that further drug/alcohol use is the only positive outlook remaining, which again raises the issue of RISC.

Interestingly, the issue of language is not one that is wholeheartedly embraced by all, and this is evidenced by the fact that academics and professionals produce books around the subject whose titles use terms such as 'misuse' and 'abuse', alongside others that use terms such as 'drug use'.

CASE STUDY 13.2: IMPACT OF LANGUAGE

The effect of distinctions such as this is highlighted by Kelly and Westerhoff (2010), who, in a randomised study, presented mental health professionals with identical case studies in which a subject was due to appear in court. In one, the subject was referred to as a substance abuser and in the other they were referred to as having a substance use disorder. The professionals who read about a substance abuser were shown to be more likely to deem the subject personally culpable for their actions and subsequent situation. They believed that in this case more punitive measures should be taken.

With this in mind, it is easy to see the dilemma faced by policy makers who are charged with the duty of somehow controlling the substance/alcohol use problem.

What do policies need to control?

In order to answer this question it is necessary to understand what is the problem with addiction. There are many views as to what harms addictive behaviours cause, and they range from personal harms, through harms to family and friends, to wider societal harms. Those views that emphasise societal harms being a result of addictive behaviours will see people with drug and/or alcohol problems as failing in their duty as citizens and responsible for many of the ills of society, including such issues as declining moral standards and criminal behaviour. The need to implement policies that address this is thus apparent, and issues such as scapegoating and punishment become topics for discussion.

Harm to others is a consideration that policy makers turn their attention to when attempting to tackle the problem of addiction. This somewhat side-lines the argument that drug/alcohol use is a personal issue and should be a matter for personalised treatment. Framing the issue as a societal problem has enabled the rhetoric of the 'war on drugs' to flourish (despite evidence of its failings, highlighted by the Global Commission on Drug Policy (2011)), and policies that seek to criminalise behaviour are used by successive administrations globally to show they are taking a tough stance. Punishments ranging from mandatory treatment programmes to the death penalty are used for people who transgress the law in terms of drug production, trafficking and use. Here we see a situation in which zero-tolerance approaches can thrive, in that advocating for the eradication of use shows consistency with this tough stance.

An issue for policy makers is that framing addiction as a penal matter minimises the view that it can be viewed as a health matter, as evidenced by Case Study 13.2. Arnull's (2014) discussion regarding the implementation of UK drug and alcohol policy shows that one of the main considerations in the 1990s was the penal/health divide. Other considerations included harm-minimisation and abstinence models (consistent with harm reduction and zero tolerance) and the divide between social and medical models. The split between penal and health, and social and medical, indicated a need for partnership working in which practitioners from a variety of professional backgrounds would need to offer perspectives that should provide holistic approaches that take all key issues into consideration.

Partnership working

Galvani (2012) offers a comprehensive assessment of supporting those with alcohol and drug problems and she discusses partnership working extensively. Highlighting issues such as parenting, domestic abuse, mental distress and disabilities shows that, no matter what area of practice they are in, social workers will inevitably work with individuals with substance use problems. Alongside this is the need to consider work with younger people, older people and those from minority ethnic communities.

Galvani (2015, p 5) confirms that social workers 'work daily with diversity... [but]... they are not expected to be an expert in every social and health care issue that impacts upon people's lives'. This clearly shows the need for some form of collaboration between professionals when addressing the variety of individuals and families affected by alcohol and drug problems. Public Health England (2015, p 4) asserts that doctors working in addiction services need to:

> liaise with a wide range of clinical non-substance-misuse services, to support their assessment and care for their patients with substance misuse disorders and physical and mental health problems, particularly those with complex needs, those at high risk of harm and those who utilise high levels of community and healthcare resources.

Their guidance continues to highlight the necessary link between services such as social care, criminal justice, housing, medical care, psychiatric care, employment and children and families work.

The term 'partnership working' can be applied to professionals and has become increasingly used, replacing 'multi-disciplinary working and inter-professional practice'. Partnership provides the opportunity to appreciate the importance of working in collaboration with not only other professionals but also service users themselves, as well as carers and significant others, reflecting the advice given by Public Health England.

Harm reduction: how far can we go?

The evidence that harm-reduction strategies are successful is compelling. Public Health England (2017) point to the effectiveness of needle exchange programmes in reducing rates of HIV and hepatitis. They also cite opioid substitution treatment (typically methadone) as being instrumental in crime reduction. It is of little surprise, then, that harm reduction has been the single most influential idea to impact on the substance use field in the last 30 years (McKeganey, 2014). The UK has successfully utilised the aforementioned treatments and programmes, together with other methods such as advice on safe injecting and even prescribing heroin.

However, there is a harm-reduction method that has been successfully implemented in countries including Germany, the Netherlands, Australia and Canada that is a step too far for the UK. Safe injecting centres, also known as drug consumption rooms, are places where drug users can go to inject street drugs under some form of medical supervision. This creates an environment in which the possibility of overdose and infection is reduced and, according to its advocates, saves lives. Furthermore, the use of safe injecting centres has seen a reduction in drug use/administration in the open community (streets, parks and so on) and the concomitant risks therein. Despite evidence of the reduction in harm to both individuals and the community, the UK Home Office has rejected proposals to implement such centres (Zampini, 2014).

The main counter-argument to safe injecting centres is that they facilitate and, by association, condone illegal activity. Commentators such as Liddle (2013) branded a plan to open a safe injecting centre in Brighton as 'liberal claptrap' and asserted that to do so would be to collude with drug addicts. In the face of populist opposition such as that shown by Liddle, to endorse a controversial initiative such as this could be politically damaging for any politician. Consequently, it has been too much of a gamble for successive governments to take the step of sanctioning the approach. It appears that a zero-tolerance approach is more attractive to a high proportion of the electorate.

Zero tolerance: politically expedient

Zero tolerance is a term that has been associated for a long time with the control of crime and is deployed in an effort to combat a range of criminal activity. Zero tolerance indicates a robust and resolute approach, signifying strength. The language of zero tolerance is not confined to one political ideology; indeed, in the early 1990s New Labour prime minister in waiting Tony Blair advocated a tough stance on crime by stating the need to be 'tough on crime and tough on the causes of crime'. This type of posturing has not changed, and the present Conservative government talks of tougher sentencing guidelines and stricter prison regimes.

For politicians to adopt such stances is an indication they are not afraid that they might turn the electorate away; rather, it is an indication that stances advocating a zero-tolerance approach are vote winners and, indeed, politically expedient. Newburn and Jones (2007, p 223) assert that the term 'zero tolerance' has 'been used primarily as a rhetorical device, used to signal uncompromising and authoritative action by the State and its agencies, against an external and *internal* enemy' (emphasis added). It is this framing of fellow citizens as the 'enemy' that targets the emotions of people who may be all too ready to accept the need to scapegoat others for perceived problems in society.

Drug users, and those addicted to alcohol in particular, fit the profile of those who can be blamed for societal problems; therefore zero-tolerance policing when dealing with these people can be seen as a popular move in some quarters. In spite of this, Newburn and Jones (2007) explain that the popularity of the term 'zero tolerance' (at times favoured by both the Left and the Right) has lost some of its lustre; however, the sentiment is still clear in the approaches taken to deal with the problem of addiction and the problems associated with drug and alcohol use.

Where local authorities such as Brighton have had the appetite to offer safe injecting centres there is still opposition from UK central government, some of the rationale for such opposition being the requirement for those running such centres to accept some element of illegal activity, namely procuring and using street drugs. This opposition is despite the evidence that safe injecting centres do offer positive results in reducing harm to society as well as to individuals. One explanation for this is revealed by the frustrations of Caroline Lucas MP, who, while advocating for the safe injecting centre in Brighton, argues that drugs policy is implemented on the basis of very little evidence. This cements further the notion that, for many, drug policy is value driven and crosses party-political boundaries. Brownstein (2016, p 598) adds to this by suggesting that 'drug policy should be based on scientific evidence, but historically values and assumptions have mattered as much as science'.

Decriminalisation is not legalisation

One of the arguments against safe injecting centres highlighted above is that of accepting/condoning illegal activity. This raises the question of decriminalisation of drug use/possession. There is a distinct difference between decriminalisation and legalisation, in that the former moves from imposing criminal sanctions such as arrest and imprisonment to imposing civil sanctions such as a fine or a warning, in much the same way as minor motoring offences are dealt with. This is different to legalisation; decriminalisation does not legalise illicit drugs and drug use.

The 20th century saw a process whereby framing drug use as a social problem saw increasing use of legislation to criminalise certain drugs and certain behaviours related to drugs. Once such legislation is entrenched, it becomes difficult to overturn it by a process of decriminalisation. Around the turn of the 20th century the criminalisation of drugs was a popular theme, but 100 years later the decriminalisation agenda became prominent among those who were pushing for drug policy reform (Brownstein, 2016).

Political, moral and economic drivers saw the criminalisation agenda gather momentum throughout the 20th century, and this was at the expense of the health and welfare of vulnerable individuals (Goode, 2012). To decriminalise the possession and use of certain drugs could offer individuals greater scope to be open about the health and welfare problems related to drugs, and in turn afford greater opportunities for help. This help is less readily accessed because users can be reluctant to come forward, due to the nature of the stigma that comes with a criminal record. In being seen to be breaking the law, one is transgressing the accepted norms and mores of society and the process of stigmatisation can be engendered. Stigmatisation is linked to social exclusion, and the resultant poor outcomes for people would naturally follow, due to the lack of life opportunities created by exclusion.

The idea of decriminalisation is not to rewrite the policy of criminalisation but to modify it in order to decriminalise certain behaviours. By using policy that regulates and manages drug involvement, minimising harm and not making outlaws of everyone involved in drugs (Brownstein, 2016), the process of stigmatisation can be addressed. Framing responses to the problem of addiction so as to address the social issues that people face can facilitate a process whereby realistic responses offer ways to address problems without the need for punitive measures.

> From a social problem perspective, the notion of drugs as a problem is a social construction, as are the public policy responses to drugs, drug use and drug involvement. There are both negative and positive consequences for individual health and wellbeing from using or being involved with drugs. (Brownstein, 2016, p 609)

Social issues such as family relationships and employment can benefit from the replacement of punitive measures with responses geared towards treatment and/or rehabilitation. To replace the aforementioned political, moral and economic drivers towards drug policy with measures reflecting a genuine concern for the welfare of vulnerable individuals would facilitate a landscape in which more positive outcomes would ensue, as evidenced by the harm-reduction agenda.

Conclusion

The bifurcation between harm reduction and zero tolerance is closely linked to the debate regarding decriminalisation. Those advocating for greater use of harm-reduction techniques view this as offering viable treatment options.

However, those who advocate for the use of zero-tolerance approaches view many harm-reduction methods as facilitating illegal activity and gratifying people's addictions. Their tenet is that an approach that seeks to eradicate illicit drug use and problematic drinking is the only viable way to combat the problem of addiction.

The values people hold, and the resultant views, are so diverse that even the arguments for the use of evidence-based practice are dismissed by some. Policies and approaches can change over time, but some approaches present too much of a leap of faith to be embraced by policy makers, particularly in the UK. Needle exchange services have operated for many years and their effectiveness in reducing harms is undoubted. However, even these services have been criticised in the past, not least by those who argue from the point of view of nimbyism. It would follow, then, if needle exchange programmes are not welcome in some neighbourhoods, that safe injecting centres would be equally if not more vehemently opposed.

Decriminalisation of certain drugs and certain activities is a debate that again crosses value boundaries, and for each argument in favour there appears to be a counter view. What remains is the *problem of addiction*, and social workers are among those at the forefront of services who deal with the problem. In discharging their duties, social workers will need to address their own value bases and react accordingly when working with people who may have problems with activities that, for the social worker, are either alien to them or part of their own everyday activities.

Ultimately, the matter of RISC gives social workers an insight into the viability of successful interventions with those with addictions. If problems such as stigmatisation leading to exclusion contribute to a bleak outlook for people, then services and the policies driving them need to seek to address this by shifting attitudes from the punitive to the therapeutic.

Critical questions

1 You are a social worker supervising a service user who has a bail condition that he should not drink alcohol. You base your relationship with him on openness and honesty. He saw you entering a pub one evening and he is now quizzing you about your own alcohol use, saying that it is not right that you drink alcohol when he cannot. How would you respond to this?

2 Now that he is an adult, to what extent does Jimmy, in case study 13.1, have a choice regarding his continuing addiction to heroin?

3 In preparing for a debate regarding the opening of a safe injecting centre in your neighbourhood, list the arguments that might be offered by those in favour and those that might be offered by those against. In doing this, consider how you would feel if a safe injecting centre were to be opened next to your home.

4 The debate around decriminalisation focuses on illicit drugs; thus, the issue of alcohol is largely side-lined. It has often been mooted that if alcohol were invented today it would be made illegal. Why are there no moves to criminalise the use of alcohol in the UK?

Further reading

For the most up-to-date issues and debates around the addictions landscape, one should access both reports and journal articles outlining research and policy developments in the field. The references list provides examples of such writing. The following texts offer discussion and a variety of viewpoints that will provide a solid grounding in the subject.

- Kolind, T., Thom, B. and Hunt, G. (eds) (2017) *The Sage Handbook of Drug and Alcohol Studies*, London: Sage.
  A comprehensive exploration of issues in the field.

- McKeganey, N. (2014) *A–Z of Substance Misuse and Drug Addiction*, Basingstoke: Palgrave Macmillan.
  For significant terms and related issues.

- Arnull, E. (2014) *Understanding Substance Use: Policy and Practice*, Northwich: Critical Publishing.
  For policy and practice as it relates to drugs and alcohol, including a consideration of values.

- Allan, G. (2014) *Working with Substance Users: A Guide to Effective Interventions*, Basingstoke: Palgrave Macmillan.
  Explores practice issues when working with those with drug and alcohol problems.

References

Allan, G. (2014) *Working With Substance Users: A Guide to Effective Interventions*, Basingstoke: Palgrave Macmillan.

Arnull, E. (2014) *Understanding Substance Use: Policy and Practice*, Northwich: Critical Publishing.

Bell, J. (2018) 'Values and ethics', in J. Lishman, C. Yuill, J. Branna and A. Gibson (eds) *Social Work: An Introduction (2nd Edition)*, London: Sage.

Brownstein, H. (2016) 'The decriminalisation of drugs', in T. Kolind, B. Thom and G. Hunt (eds) *The Sage Handbook of Drug and Alcohol Studies*, London: Sage.

Galvani, S. (2012) *Supporting People with Alcohol and Drug Problems: Making a Difference*, Bristol: Policy Press.

Galvani, S. (2015) *Alcohol and Other Drug Use: The Roles and Capabilities of Social Workers*, Manchester: Manchester Metropolitan University.

Global Commission on Drug Policy (2011) *War on Drugs*, www.globalcommissionondrugs.org/wp-content/uploads/2017/10/GCDP_WaronDrugs_EN.pdf

Global Commission on Drug Policy (2017) *The World Drug Perception Problem: Countering Prejudices about People Who Use Drugs*, www.globalcommissionondrugs. org/reports/changing-perceptions/

Goode, E. (2012) *Drugs in American Society*, Boston, MA: McGraw Hill.

Heanue, K. and Lawton, C. (2012) *Working with Substance Users*, Maidenhead: Open University Press.

Keene, J. (2010) *Understanding Drug Misuse: Models of Care and Control*, Basingstoke: Palgrave Macmillan.

Kelly, J.F. and Westerhoff, C.M. (2010) 'Does it matter how we refer to individuals with substance-related conditions? A randomized study of two commonly used terms', *International Journal of Drug Policy*, vol 12, pp 202–7.

Liddle, R. (2013) 'Get Brighton to A&E – it's overdosing on liberal claptrap', *The Sunday Times*, 21 April.

McKeganey, N. (2011) *Controversies in Drugs Policy and Practice*, Basingstoke: Palgrave Macmillan.

McKeganey, N. (2014) *A–Z of Substance Misuse and Drug Addiction*, Basingstoke: Palgrave Macmillan.

Newburn, T. and Jones, T. (2007) 'Symbolizing crime control: reflections on zero tolerance', *Theoretical Criminology*, vol 11, no 2, pp 221–43.

Public Health England (2015) *Role of Addiction Specialist Doctors in Drug and Alcohol Services: A Resource for Commissioners, Providers and Clinicians*, https://assets. publishing.service.gov.uk/government/uploads/system/uploads/attachment_ data/file/669487/the-role-of-addiction-specialist-doctors.pdf

Public Health England (2017) *An Evidence Review of the Outcomes that can be Expected of Drug Misuse Treatment in England*, https://assets.publishing.service. gov.uk/government/uploads/system/uploads/attachment_data/file/586111/ PHE_Evidence_review_of_drug_treatment_outcomes.pdf

West, R. and Brown, J. (2013) *Theory of Addiction (2nd Edition)*, Chichester: Wiley Blackwell.

Zampini, G.F. (2014) 'Governance versus Government: drug consumption rooms in Australia and the UK', *International Journal of Drug Policy*, vol 25, pp 978–84.

14

Radicalisation

Ian Cummins

Introduction

In the context of politics, the term 'radical' has been applied to a wide range of figures. Both Jeremy Corbyn and Nigel Farage could be considered radical, in the sense that each is campaigning for a society based on a different set of political and economic relationships and values. However, in politics radicalism has come to be associated with the adoption of revolutionary tactics and approaches. Radicals can come from across the political spectrum. Historically, 'radical' is a term that has been most closely associated with progressive politics. The tactics that radicals adopt do not have to be violent; for example, being a conscientious objector and refusing conscription in the First World War was a radical act. The suffragettes were radical in both their aims and their methods (Purvis, 1995). In the current political climate 'radicalisation' is the term used for the processes by which individuals become involved in political groups that are committed to the overhaul of political and social structures (Kundnani, 2012). There is an implicit assumption that such radical approaches include a rejection of parliamentary democracy as a means of bringing about lasting and fundamental change. Since the 9/11 terrorist attacks in the US, radicalisation has largely been associated with terrorism inspired by radical interpretations of Islamic religious texts (Kundnani, 2012). There is not the space here to discuss in depth the use of violence as a political weapon.

Radical critiques of parliamentary democracy argue that it is based on a sham of equality, in which one person, one vote serves as a cover that hides the real power and inequalities that exist in society. In this perspective, it is impossible for the gradualism of liberal political democracy to produce fundamental change. In addition, such perspectives would argue that the violence that has its root cause in capitalism is hidden or ignored. When exploring these issues, it is important to recognise that it is perfectly possible to be a radical and to totally reject violence and terrorism. In addition, an understanding of the political context is required in order to understand the use of the term 'terrorist'. Famously, Nelson Mandela was tried, and imprisoned for 20 years, on charges of treason and labelled a terrorist by the apartheid regime of South Africa and its supporters (Joffe, 2013), while to the wider world he was fighting for freedom and social justice. Those who become involved in political violence are often dismissed as madmen, and so on. One impact of this is that the political ideas or disputes that are the root of the cause for which they choose to fight are ignored. This is not a defence of political violence, but recognition that it does not occur in a vacuum.

In the 1970s radical political groups such as the Red Army Faction (also known as the Baader Meinhof Group or Gang) in West Germany and the Red Brigades (Brigate Rosse) in Italy carried out a series of politically motivated kidnappings, robberies and murders. These groups had their roots in the radical student politics of the late 1960s (Becker, 2014) and were inspired by anti-imperialism and anti-colonialism. The founder of the Red Brigades was Renato Curcio, who set up a radical study group at the University of Trento in 1967. The group studied Marx, Mao and Che Guevara. In November 1970 the Red Brigades carried out the firebombing of various factories and warehouses in Milan, and in 1978 they kidnapped and murdered former Italian prime minister Aldo Moro. The Red Brigades, along with the Red Army Faction, rejected what they saw as the cosy hypocrisy of the post-war consumer society. In West Germany the Red Army Faction also sought to highlight what they saw as attempts to avoid any examination of the involvement of their parents' generation in the development of Nazism (Laqueur, 2017). The acts of violence were not simply random. In Italy the Brigate Rosse argued that the response of the state – increased surveillance, restriction on liberty and greater powers for the police – would demonstrate the fundamental hypocrisy of bourgeois liberal democracy (Bull, 2015). This would in turn create greater support for radical political approaches among the working class and trade union movements. This proved to be wildly optimistic and naive. The arrest and imprisonment of many of the Red Brigades' leaders and ordinary members from the mid-1970s onwards led to the collapse of the organisation.

Post-9/11

The terrorist attacks of 11 September 2001 were clearly one of the most significant events of the past 50 years. The geopolitical ramifications included the instigation of the so-called War on Terror, the US invasion of Afghanistan and, ultimately, the invasion of Iraq and the overthrow of Iraqi President Saddam Hussein. The events of 9/11 and the response of Western governments were a key factor in the development of narratives of radicalisation, which came to be associated almost exclusively with jihadism. On 9 September 2001 four passenger airliners were hijacked by 19 al-Qaeda terrorists. Two planes – American Airlines (AA) flight 11 and United Airlines (UA) flight 175 – were crashed into the North and South towers, respectively, of the World Trade Center complex in Lower Manhattan, New York. In under two hours, both 110-storey towers collapsed. The images of the planes flying into the towers, people jumping from the buildings and individuals in the streets covered in dust and debris have become among the most iconic of the modern era. A third plane, AA flight 77, was crashed into the Pentagon, near Washington, DC and a fourth plane, UA flight 93, was initially flown towards Washington, DC, but crashed into a field in Pennsylvania after its passengers overpowered the hijackers. All 64 passengers, the crew and the hijackers on board AA flight 77 were killed, along with 125 people in the building. In all, 2,996 people died in the attacks and over 6,000 were injured. It is estimated that the attacks caused over $10 billion worth of damage (Dwyer and Flynn, 2005). In addition to the deaths at the time, there have been a series of deaths due to 9/11-related cancers and respiratory diseases caused by contact with dust and debris. One of the most widely viewed images was of Marcy Borders, a 28-year-old Bank of America employee. She was pictured fleeing from the North tower of the World Trade Center covered from head to toe in debris. She became a 9/11 celebrity: the 'Dust Lady'. She subsequently experienced mental and physical health problems and died of stomach cancer in 2015 (Pilkington, 2015).

As noted above, the attacks were carried out by members of the al-Qaeda group. In 1979 the Soviet Union had invaded Afghanistan. Osama bin Laden, a member of a wealthy Saudi family, travelled to Afghanistan to support the guerrilla fighters (the mujahideen) fighting against the Soviet occupation. The invasion of Afghanistan was a disaster for the Soviet Union and played a role in its collapse. In 1996 bin Laden issued his first fatwā, calling for US soldiers to leave Saudi Arabia – location of the holiest sites in Islam. In a second fatwā, issued in 1998, bin Laden outlined his objections to US foreign policy with respect to Israel, as well as the continued presence of US troops in Saudi Arabia after the Gulf War. Bin Laden used religious texts to justify attacks on the US and the West more generally (Burke, 2007). US president George W. Bush declared a 'war on terror' in a speech to Congress on 16 September 2001, a few days after the 9/11 attacks, in which he stated that 'Our enemy is a radical network of terrorists and every government that supports them'. The War on Terror saw the establishment of the Guantanamo Bay detention camp at a US naval base in Cuba. Inmates have been detained there indefinitely without trial and there have been reports of torture. The camp regime is viewed by many, including Amnesty International, as a major breach of international human rights (Amnesty International, 2012). Supporters of the regime and the use of techniques such as waterboarding argue that these are justified because terrorism requires the suspension of the normal rules of the game.

Since 9/11, there have been a series of attacks committed by groups or individuals linked to or inspired by Al-Qaeda, such as the 2002 Bali bombings in Indonesia; the 2004 Madrid train bombings in Spain;, the 7 July 2005 London bombings in the UK, perpetrated by four UK-born terrorists; the 2012 Toulouse and Montauban shootings in France, committed by Mohammed Merah. The nature of these attacks and more recent ones such as those in Nice in 2016 and at London Bridge in 2017 shows that there is a loose grouping of radical groups which have taken their ideological inspiration from Al-Qaeda.

Radicalisation is not a process that is limited to the radical Left. As we shall explore in more detail below, the authorities are increasingly concerned by the neo-fascist Right. During the EU Referendum campaign in the UK in 2016,

Jo Cox, the MP for Batley and Spen, was stabbed and shot by Thomas Mair, who had links with British and US neo-Nazi groups (Winter, 2016).

Radicalisation

Governmental and broader policy responses to radicalisation are based on a mixture of approaches. There has clearly been a significant investment in the development of security and other law-and-order approaches. These include tighter security and increased security checks at airports, and also a greater presence of armed police. For example, following the Manchester Arena bombing in 2017 armed police patrolled the centre of the city. These moves are designed both to prevent further attacks and also to reassure citizens. The security services and the police have also invested heavily in technology to identify and track potential terrorists. One of the impacts of these changes is that they target whole communities. As Kundnani (2012) outlines, the response to terrorist attacks has been to increase surveillance on Muslim groups and neighbourhoods. This repeats a pattern from the 1970s and 1980s, when Irish nationalist and Catholic communities in mainland Britain were regarded with suspicion and hostility because of the IRA's bombing campaign.

The remainder of this chapter will focus on social policy rather than criminal justice responses to radicalisation. It will also consider the potential implications for social work of policies such as the Prevent Strategy. Throughout government policy documents, radicalisation is presented or regarded as a process. Thus, it is argued that the role of anti-radicalisation policies should be to identify those who are 'at risk' of being recruited and to engage them in more constructive, alternative activities that will prevent them from being recruited. These approaches are very similar to anti-gang and CSE policies, in that they are based on a need to prevent vulnerable individuals from being drawn into exploitative situations or circumstances. One of the criticisms of this approach is that it minimises or disregards political ideology. Radicalisation, in this model, does not allow for the individual choices that those who commit political violence make. This is not in any way to defend such acts. It is simply to acknowledge that terrorists, like other individuals, exercise agency and make choices.

In 2005 the EU produced a *Strategy for Combating Radicalisation and Recruitment*. It had three key aims:

- to disrupt the activities of individuals and networks that draw people into terrorism;
- to ensure that mainstream opinion prevails over extremism;
- to promote security, justice, democracy and opportunities for all.

It should be noted that the standard response to radicalisation has focused on young men at risk of becoming involved in politically motivated violence. Sites of radicalisation have included community groups, places of worship and also prisons. There are many examples of people who have committed terrorist acts who adopted radical views while serving custodial sentences. With its continuing development, social media has also become a much more powerful factor. Thomas Mair, for example, was something of a recluse but was able to access neo-Nazi propaganda very easily online. The fact that individuals can do this means that their views are never challenged; social media acts as an echo chamber. Extremist groups such as Islamic State have been particularly successful in posting videos that serve as recruiting officers. The political situation in the Middle East is a potent factor here. The occupation of the West Bank and Gaza by Israel, the invasion and chaos that were created in Iraq, the civil wars in Syria, Yemen and Chechnya have all been factors in the radicalisation of individuals. One aspect of globalisation is that conflicts such as these have potentially much wider implications and effects. These include the displacement of huge numbers of people and the creation of refugees. The refugee crisis has been exploited by neo-fascist groups.

A number of models of radicalisation have been developed using insights from the psychological and social sciences (Kundnani, 2012). Sociological approaches have focused on such factors as poverty and discrimination, the argument here being that the marginalisation of communities makes individuals within them more open to radical political ideas. One aspect of the ideologies of Al-Qaeda and Islamic State is the way that they link the experiences of Muslim communities across the world. In this model, marginalisation is experienced and therefore has to be addressed on a number of levels:

- *micro*: individuals experience discrimination and racism;
- *meso*: the group or community experience marginalisation and stigmatisation;
- *macro*: the influence of government policy and also of global political events.

The majority of the literature that examines radicalisation has focused on Islamic terrorism. As noted above, following the assassination of Jo Cox MP there has been an increased interest in and focus on neo-fascist groups. Her killer, Thomas Mair, was not the first neo-Nazi to be convicted of political murder. David Copeland was jailed in 1999 for a 13-day nail bombing campaign in London that left three people dead and 139 injured. He placed bombs at a gay pub in Soho and attacked Black communities in Brick Lane and Brixton (Chakraborti, 2017). In the US, prior to 9/11 the deadliest terrorist attack had been carried out by the far Right. Timothy McVeigh, a US army veteran inspired by *The Turner Diaries*, detonated a truck full of explosives outside the Alfred P. Murrah Federal building in Oklahoma City, Oklahoma. Two events involving the FBI's actions against separatists added fuel to Timothy McVeigh's hatred of government institutions. In the first, in the summer of 1992 white separatist Randy Weaver was engaged in a standoff with government agents at his cabin in Ruby Ridge, Idaho. The siege resulted in the death of Weaver's son and wife. In the second, in April 1993, federal agents surrounded the Texas compound of a religious cult called the Branch Davidians to arrest their leader, David Koresh. On 19 April McVeigh watched on television as the FBI stormed the compound, causing a firestorm that killed dozens of Branch Davidians, including children. The explosion resulted in 168 deaths and another several hundred casualties. *The Turner Diaries*, an anti-government polemic written by a neo-Nazi William Pierce, includes a bombing of a federal building. McVeigh's actions were in part driven by paranoid ideas about a government plot to repeal the second amendment of the US constitution – the right to bear arms. McVeigh was executed in 2001 (Michel and Herbeck, 2015).

As already noted, there are several different models of the process of radicalisation that attempt to explain the social and psychological processes that combine and lead to an individual or group of individuals being prepared to undertake violent acts in the furtherance of a political cause. There is, of course, a long and noble tradition of nonviolent radical protest and dissent, the US civil rights movement of the 1950s and 1960s being a prime example. These movements make a clear statement that they will not adopt violent methods.

Borum (2011) outlines four factors in radicalisation. The first is what he terms 'context'. Radical politics obviously takes place in a specific political and economic context. Individuals are sympathetic to a particular cause or supportive of a marginalised group; for example, the Israel/Palestine conflict is seen as one of the biggest drivers of the recruitment for radical Islamic terrorism. The perceived injustice is then framed, in this model, as being overlooked or ignored in comparison to other geopolitical issues. Borum (2011) terms this second stage 'comparison'. In the third stage of this model the political injustice is framed as being the responsibility of a policy, person or nation. Borum (2011) terms this process 'attribution'. The stages of comparison and attribution can be viewed as indoctrination – they are not processes that take place in isolation. They involve the exposure of individuals to information – perhaps, more accurately, propaganda – about the causes. Finally, the party or nation-state that is seen as responsible for the aggression or perceived injustice is seen as a legitimate target. Borum (2011) terms this fourth stage 'reaction'. Terrorism does not make any distinction between military or security and civilian targets: all are regarded as legitimate. There are two elements to this. The first is that the aggressor does not distinguish between civilian and military targets. The second is the impact of such violence, if it is aimed at civilian targets such as train stations or large public events such as a pop concert. Terrorists know that, realistically, it is impossible for the authorities to provide complete protection. In December 2016 a terrorist drove a truck into crowds at the Christmas markets in Berlin, killing 12 people and injuring over 50. Unless the police have information that enables them to intervene beforehand, such attacks are difficult to prevent.

The models of radicalisation that are discussed here see the individual moving from the world of liberal parliamentary democracy, of campaigns and lobbying elected representatives, to a world where violence is seen as a legitimate tactic. Moghaddam (2005) produced a seven-step staircase model in which there is a perceived deprivation and feelings of discontent and frustration. The feelings of unfair treatment become displaced into aggression. These increasing feelings of aggression lead to a tendency to sympathise with the violent and extremist ideology of terrorist groups. Some sympathisers eventually join an extremist group or movement that supports or engages in terrorist violence. The terrorist organisation is regarded as a legitimate expression of a political viewpoint. This model is criticised for being a linear, stepwise one. The argument here is that radicalisation is a much more multifaceted phenomenon. The steps or processes between the alienation of an individual or the attraction to radical politics and the willingness to commit a violent act are much more complicated than this reductive approach allows.

Kundnani (2012) notes that, since 2004, radicalisation has become a central concept in both terrorism studies and policy making. He terms it the 'master signifier of the late War on Terror'. The focus on psychological explanations and the identification of vulnerable individuals or groups means that the terrorist acts are presented as irrational and without any connection with the wider politics of the world. In addition, radicalisation has come to be associated with Islamic terrorism. This has meant that the focus for policies aimed at preventing radicalisation has been on Muslim communities, at the expense of attention to far Right and neo-Nazi groups. The politics of race in the UK mean that the populist parties of the Right have exploited terrorist attacks to pursue an anti-immigration agenda. In tracing the development of the concept of radicalisation Kundnani (2012) notes that there is a clear distinction made between the 'new terrorism', which is seen to originate or have its roots in Islamist theology, and the 'old terrorism' of Irish nationalism or Leftist politics. There are some important organisational differences. The 'old terrorism' was based on cells or an organisational structure – the IRA had a brigade structure with clear lines of command and control. The 'new terrorism' is characterised by much looser networks. This has very important implications for the policy response. One is in the area of civil liberties, because part of the focus of the policy response is to restrict the circulation of extremists' ideas. As with the political violence of the 1970s, the restriction on liberties means that not only are communities subject to potential harassment and surveillance but also these processes serve to confirm that the state discriminates against minority communities (Stanley and Guru, 2015).

The model of radicalisation that is adopted has important ramifications because it underpins the policy responses. There are a number of variants of the models that have been discussed here. The focus on radicalisation and terrorism motivated by a particular reading of Islamic theology means that religious conversion – particularly in the prison context – is regarded as a key point and as a gateway to radicalisation. These models of radicalisation become policing tools that are used to justify interventions in communities, and also the wider surveillance of whole communities.

Policy responses

The Prevent Strategy, an attempt to win over 'hearts and minds', is the key UK government programme aimed at tackling radicalisation. It was originally introduced in 2003 and formed part of an overall post 9/11 counter-terrorism approach (CONTEST) to identify and divert individuals from radicalisation and involvement in terrorism. Following the attacks in London on 7 July 2005 (7/7 attacks), which were carried out by 'home-grown' terrorists, the importance of the Prevent Strategy increased. It seeks to prevent radicalisation and the subsequent commission of terrorist acts and has three core aims:

- to respond to the ideological challenge of terrorism;
- to prevent people from being drawn into terrorism and to ensure that they are given appropriate advice and support;
- to work with sectors and institutions where there are risks of radicalisation (HM Government, 2011).

Section 26 of the Counter-Terrorism and Security Act 2015 established that specified authorities, for example, higher education institutions, need to have 'due regard to the need to prevent people from being drawn into terrorism'. This means that a whole range of public sector organisations have to work together to ensure that there are policies and procedures in place to identify those at risk of radicalisation, to divert them from a path to terrorist acts and to engage with communities. The 2015 Act made Channel – the programme of deradicalisation – a legal requirement for public bodies. These bodies are required to identify vulnerable or at-risk individuals.

One of the major concerns for social work is that Prevent and other approaches involve social workers in a policing role. Social work is, in the broadest sense, involved in the management of marginalised groups. However, whether it be in child protection or mental health, this is usually in a complex role that requires the balancing of the rights of individuals against those of the wider society. The role in the context of Prevent and other approaches to radicalisation seems very different. One of the major concerns is that such approaches pathologise Muslim communities (Guru, 2010; 2012) and that the narrative of the 'war on terror' implies that all Muslims have some responsibility for terrorist attacks. This discourse also overlooks the many factors lie at the root of causes of radicalisation. These include key issues that social workers have traditionally sought to work with individuals and communities to tackle – inequality, and discrimination across a range of areas such as high rates of unemployment, low wages, lower rates of educational achievement, increasing rates of imprisonment. In addition, Islam is subject to vilification. The 'war on terror' has been increasingly presented as part of Huntington's 'clash of civilisations' (Huntington, 1996). In 2011 David Cameron made a speech in which he argued that 'state multiculturalism' had failed and that the UK needed a stronger national identity to prevent people turning to all kinds of extremism.

Guru (2010) argues that social work as a profession largely absented itself from debates about the impact of the 'war on terror' and that this is a modern manifestation of a core dilemma for social work practice. Stanley and Guru (2015) highlight the possible implications for social work practice of the Prevent agenda. There are a number of concerns here. As noted above, the strategy is based on the identification of those who may be at risk. Stanley (2018) argues that there is a need to deconstruct the discourse of risk. It is clear from a wide range of social work settings (Webb, 2006) that the discourse of risk can and usually does lead to a much more managerialist and interventionist form of social work practice. In this context, it is always complex and difficult for social workers to intervene in areas that can be seen as matters of family choice and faith. In addition, there is a danger of a moral panic creating an atmosphere where all Muslim families are seen as posing a risk. This is clearly nonsense, but also adds to an environment which is hostile to minority communities. There is a danger that such policies add to the marginalisation of certain groups, thus adding to wider resentments. It is also not really clear what social workers are being asked to do in response to some of the concerns that are being raised. The discourse and processes of risk have within them the potential for false positives. The implications of these for the families and individuals involved need to be examined. Finally, there is a danger of overreaction. In August 2018 a nursery in Brighton had its Ofsted rating downgraded because inspectors felt that staff did not know how to protect children from potentially being radicalised.[1]

Conclusion

Political violence and terrorism are not a new political phenomenon. It should be emphasised that radical political views do not necessarily involve a commitment to carry out violent acts in a political cause. The civil rights movement in the US in the 1950s and 1960s showed that it is possible to be committed to nonviolent means to achieve radical political goals. Since 9/11 radicalisation has been a term largely associated with acts of terrorism committed by those inspired by a particular interpretation of Islamic texts. This focus on radical Islamic groups ignores or minimises fascist and neo-Nazi groups. A commitment to the use of violence in the furtherance of political aims cuts across the political spectrum. Current approaches to radicalisation focus on the psychological and sociological processes whereby vulnerable individuals become attracted to a political cause. Such an approach has been criticised for depoliticising the protest and for ignoring the geopolitical contexts which give rise to the protest. The Prevent Strategy requires public authorities to work together to identify at-risk individuals, and has been criticised for limiting legitimate political debate.

Critical questions

1 Can acts of political violence and terrorism ever be justified?

2 Are restrictions on civil liberties introduced in response to terrorism necessary or a loss of freedom?

3 Are there circumstances in which liberal democratic governments should negotiate with terrorist organisations?

4 To what extent are the criticisms of the current Prevent Strategy justified?

Further reading

- Guru, S. (2010) 'Social work and the "war on terror"', *The British Journal of Social Work*, vol 40, no 1, pp 272–89.
- Guru, S. (2012) 'Under siege: families of counter-terrorism', *The British Journal of Social Work*, vol 42, no 6, pp 1151–73.
  These two articles examine the impact of the war on terror on communities and families. They examine the involvement of social work in these processes.

- Kundnani, A. (2012) 'Radicalisation: the journey of a concept', *Race and Class*, vol 54, no 2, pp 3–25.
  This article outlines the development of the concept of radicalisation as a process post 9/11.

- Moghaddam, F.M. (2005) 'The staircase to terrorism: a psychological exploration', *American Psychologist*, vol 60, pp 161–9.
  This paper outlines radicalisation as a psychological rather than a political process.

- Stanley, T. (2018) 'The relevance of risk work theory to practice: the case of statutory social work and the risk of radicalisation in the UK', *Health, Risk and Society*, vol 20, no 1–2, pp 104–12.
- Stanley, T. and Guru, S. (2015) 'Childhood radicalisation risk: an emerging practice issue', *Practice: Social Work in Action*, vol 1, pp 1–14.
  These two papers examine the impact of the Prevent Strategy in the context of children and family social work. They discuss the ethical challenges that such work presents.

References

Amnesty International (2012) *USA: Guantanamo: A Decade of Damage to Human Rights and the 10 Anti-Human Rights Messages Guantanamo Still Sends*, www.amnesty.org/en/documents/AMR51/103/2011/en/ [accessed 19 July 2018].

Becker, J. (2014) *Hitler's Children: The Story of the Baader-Meinhof Terrorist Gang*, Bloomington: Author House.

Borum, R. (2011) 'Radicalization into violent extremism I: a review of conceptual social science theories', *Journal of Strategic Security*, vol 4, no 4, pp 7–36.

Bull, A. (2015) 'The red brigades and the discourse of violence. revolution and restoration', *Journal of Modern Italian Studies*, vol 20, no 3, pp 410–12.

Burke, J. (2007) *Al-Qaeda: The True Story of Radical Islam*, London: I. B. Tauris.

Chakraborti, N. (2017) 'Future developments for hate crime thinking: who, what and why?', in *Hate Crime*, Cullompton: Willan Publishing, pp 21–34.

Dwyer, J. and Flynn, K. (2005) *102 Minutes*, New York: Times Books.

Guru, S. (2010) 'Social work and the "war on terror"', *The British Journal of Social Work,* vol 40, no 1, pp 272–89.

Guru, S. (2012) 'Under siege: families of counter-terrorism', *The British Journal of Social Work*, vol 42, no 6, pp 1151–73.

HM Government (2011) *CONTEST: The United Kingdom's Strategy for Countering Terrorism*, www.gov.uk/government/uploads/system/uploads/attachment_data/file/97994/contestsummary.pdf [accessed 8 February 2015].

Huntington, S.P. (1996) *The Clash of Civilizations and the Remaking of World Order*, New York: Simon and Shuster.

Joffe, J. (2013) *The State vs. Nelson Mandela: The Trial that Changed South Africa*, Oxford: Oneworld Publications.

Kundnani, A. (2012) 'Radicalisation: the journey of a concept', *Race and Class*, vol 54, no 2, pp 3–25.

Laqueur, W. (2017) *A History of Terrorism*, Abingdon: Routledge.

Michel, L. and Herbeck, D. (2015) *American Terrorist: Timothy McVeigh and the Oklahoma City Bombing*, London: BookBaby.

Moghaddam, F.M. (2005) 'The staircase to terrorism: a psychological exploration', *American Psychologist*, vol 60, pp 161–9.

Pilkington, E. (2015) '9/11 "Dust Lady" Marcy Borders: depression, rehab, back from the brink – then a final bombshell', www.theguardian.com/us-news/2015/sep/21/911-dust-lady-marcy-borders-depression-rehab-back-from-the-brink-then-a-final-bombshell

Purvis, J. (1995) 'The prison experiences of the suffragettes in Edwardian Britain', *Women's History Review*, vol 4, no 1, pp 103–33.

Stanley, T. (2018) 'The relevance of risk work theory to practice: the case of statutory social work and the risk of radicalisation in the UK', *Health, Risk and Society*, vol 20, no 1–2, pp 104–12.

Stanley, T. and Guru, S. (2015) 'Childhood radicalisation risk: an emerging practice issue', *Practice: Social Work in Action*, vol 1, pp 1–14.

Webb, S. (2006) *Social Work in a Risk Society: Social and Political Perspectives*, Basingstoke: Palgrave Macmillan.

Winter, A. (2016) *Island Retreat: 'On Hate, Violence and the Murder of Jo Cox'*, www.opendemocracy.net/en/opendemocracyuk/island-retreat-on-hate-violence-and-murder-of-jo-cox/ [accessed 18 February 2018].

Conclusion

Kate Parkinson

This book has provided a comprehensive introduction to the impact of political ideology and party politics on social work practice and its context.

Part I provided an overview of contrasting political ideologies and how each has played a role in shaping both historical and contemporary social work practice. Part II linked political ideology to traditional areas of social work practice: children and families, adult social care, mental health and criminal justice. It is hoped that readers will have gained an understanding of how political ideology has shaped legislation, policy and practice in these areas. Part III discussed contemporary and emerging areas of social work practice and identified the rapidly changing environment for social workers and service users alike, influenced by globalisation, austerity and neoliberal ideology.

Social work is political. This book has aimed to make clear the links between party politics, political ideology, social and economic factors and social work practice. It is hoped that readers will have gained an understanding that social work is inevitably shaped by the politics of the day and that social workers need to be cognisant of the impact of government policy on their working environments and on the lives of people whom they support. Such an understanding enables social workers to support people more effectively and, in recognising the impact of poverty, inequality and discrimination, to undertake more accurate and robust assessments of need and risk. It also enables social workers to protect the ethics and values of their profession and to challenge policy and practice which is not congruent with these values and with the Global Definition of Social Work (2014). This definition will become increasingly pertinent as the world continues to face global challenges such as the mass migration of people in response to natural disasters, war and conflict and the growing impact of climate change.

The editors and authors make no apologies for the overall left-leaning nature of this book. Many of them are social work academics with significant practice experience in social work and they inevitably embody the values of social work, which are essentially based upon socialist and social democratic principles. The Global Definition of Social Work (IFSW, 2014) is clear that social work is a profession underpinned by the principles of social justice, empowerment and equality. However, it is becoming increasingly difficult, in the current neoliberal environment, for social workers to practise in a manner which is congruent with these values.

In adopting this position, the authors are not suggesting that other political ideologies have not influenced social work practice in a positive manner. Indeed, liberal ideologies of freedom, the right to choose and self-determination are clearly embedded in social work legislation, policy and practice. Furthermore, they embody principles of empowerment. In addition to this, the origins of social work practice lie in conservative ideology and a need to support the 'morally feckless' working classes and maintain social order. What the authors are clear about, however, is that a neoliberal approach to welfare is not congruent with the values and principles of social work practice and the Global Definition of Social Work (2014).

Part III has made reference to the emergence of radical social work practice, which is in response to the changing context of social work. Social workers are struggling to hold on to their professional values and practice in a compassionate manner underpinned by the principles of social justice, equality and empowerment. This has prompted radical social work movements such as SWAN and Social Work without Borders to challenge legislation and government policy which promotes poverty and inequality, oppresses individuals and undermines the values of social work.

In this changing political and economic climate, just as the practice of social work is adapting, so too is the training and education of future social workers. The introduction of fast-track routes to social work for graduates with good first degrees, such as Frontline and Step Up, where students are paid to train as social workers, has the underlying aim of improving the quality of social work practice. In addition to this, the new social work apprenticeship is aimed at students training 'on the job', the aim again being to improve standards. The benefits of these routes are that people are being paid to train as social workers, whereas if students train through the traditional university route they have to fund their own education. However, there is a danger that a fast-track approach and 'on the job' training will omit a focus on the critical and theoretical basis of social work practice. There is a further danger that key social work values will become overlooked if the focus is solely on the mechanics and processes of the job.

The suggestion that social work education needs to improve so as to boost practice standards implies that social work education was not of a high standard in the first place. The suggestion undermines the status of academic institutions that have been leading on social work practice for decades and begs questions about their future role in the training of social workers. Furthermore, it ignores the bigger picture, failing to acknowledge that shortcomings in social work practice are likely to be caused, or at the very least exacerbated, by the difficult working environments that social workers face: increased caseloads, reduced resources and a risk-averse practice approach.

A likely additional challenge that social workers will encounter in the coming months and years is the impact of Brexit. This is an uncertain time and economists have already predicted that Brexit will be potentially disastrous for the UK's economy. Levels of unemployment, poverty and inequality are likely to rise, which will inevitably lead to an increase in the numbers of people being supported by social workers. Furthermore, if the post-Brexit 'fall-out' mirrors the impact of austerity, there will be a reduction in social work services and support, creating an increasingly difficult practice environment for social workers.

In view of the above discussion it is clear that the challenge for contemporary social workers is to maintain their compassion- and values-driven approach to practice in an increasingly neoliberal context. It is crucial that social workers stay true to these values and continue to challenge social injustice and inequality and to ensure the rights and dignity of those whom they are supporting. The authors hope that this book will have inspired its readers to do just that. Furthermore, it is hoped that readers now have an understanding of why politics in social work matter and how politics and social work are inextricably linked.

Reference

IFSW (International Federation of Social Workers) (2014) *Global Definition of Social Work*. Available at: www.ifsw.org/global-definition-of-social-work/

Notes

Chapter 1

[1] Though this was not the case at the time when he developed his theory, Marx foresaw the enormous growth of the working class, which, by the mid-20th century, was the most numerous class globally (Callinicos, 2010).

[2] For discussion of these strands see Molyneux (2012) and Vickers (2015).

[3] For a critical analysis of this perspective see Molyneux (2003).

[4] Other terms for this approach include social democracy and democratic socialism.

[5] In this approach the working class is defined not in terms of subjective individual perceptions of class identity and affiliations, but instead is understood as an objective feature of the exploitative economic relationships within which workers are situated. The working class should therefore be understood as all those who need to sell their labour power in order to live under capitalism (Callinicos, 2010). There is further discussion below of contemporary changes in class structure.

[6] This paradigmatic event was led by the revolutionary socialists of the Bolshevik party and initially established a democratic workers' state. However, this already economically under-developed state was rendered even more vulnerable by its isolation after the failure of a wave of revolutions across Europe. The interconnectedness and dominance of the global capitalist system meant that the possibility of the survival of socialism in a single country was always tenuous, and by the late 1920s the Bolshevik regime had degenerated into a Stalinist bureaucratic state capitalism (Callinicos, 2010).

[7] Other influences on radical social work included feminism, Freirean consciousness-raising and libertarian and counter-cultural politics (Langan and Lee, 1989).

[8] Conscientisation is a strategy that can be employed by social workers in their practice both to support communities in recognising oppressive social structures and as a participatory method for challenging and mobilising against such structures. This concept was initially developed by radical theorist Paulo Freire, and utilised by practitioners within the reconceptualisation (radical social work) movement that emerged in Latin America from the 1960s onwards (Ferguson et al, 2018).

[9] The name of this initiative highlights its close links with the wider Occupy movement against inequality noted in the first part of the chapter.

Chapter 6

[1] See: The Implications of Luke Davey vs Oxfordshire County Council case 29 September 2017, https://dpac.uk.net/2017/09/the-implications-of-luke-davey-vs-oxfordshire-county-council-case

[2] 'Wednesbury unreasonable' refers to a decision or reasoning that is so unreasonable that no reasonable person acting reasonably could have made it, a precedent set by the case *Associated Provincial Picture Houses Ltd v Wednesbury Corporation* (1948) 1 KB 223.

Chapter 8

[1] These included paraldehyde, laxatives, chloral hydrate and, later, insulin coma, psychosurgery and electroconvulsive therapy.

[2] This term refers to survival of the psychiatric system, rather than of mental distress (Beresford, 2012).

[3] Christopher Clunis was a former service user. Other cases include those of Benjamin Silcock and Michael Stone (Trueman, 2013).

[4] The Mental Health Alliance was a broad-based campaign involving over 70 groups representing practitioners, users, human rights activists and lawyers.

[5] The Mental Capacity Act 2005 covers England and Wales, with Northern Ireland adopting an almost mirror statute in 2016, and Scotland enacting the Adults with Incapacity Act (Scotland) Act 2000.

[6] As well as practitioners from other mental health professions.

[7] This adapts a framework developed in Ferguson and Woodward (2009).

[8] We recognise that, like the recovery approach, there is a potential for such approaches to be co-opted within the managerialist environment of statutory NHS services.

[9] Similar initiatives include the Paranoia Network and Unusual Beliefs groups, among others.

[10] Also, BASW led on the Boot Out Austerity campaign and march, which was supported by SWAN (Shennan and Unwin, 2017).

[11] This adapts a slogan from the Global Justice or anticapitalist movement of the early 2000s: 'another world is possible'.

Chapter 10

[1] http://england.shelter.org.uk/campaigns_/why_we_campaign/housing_facts_and_figures/subsection?section=homeless_households

Chapter 11

[1] Although designed initially for the protection of refugees displaced throughout Europe by the events of the Second World War, it became increasingly necessary, in light of a perceived global need, for the Convention's scope to be expanded to encompass the problem of displacement around the world. In 1967 a protocol that removed the geographical and time limitations written into the original Convention was also introduced. A total of 140 states have since acceded to one or both of these instruments.

[2] For a detailed explanation of the NASS system see Robinson et al (2003).

Chapter 12

[1] To read further exchanges during this hearing, access the transcript via this link: https://publications.parliament.uk/pa/cm201415/cmpublic/seriouscrime/150115/pm/150115s01.htm

Chapter 14

[1] https://www.theguardian.com/education/2018/aug/02/anger-ofsted-claims-nursery-failing-guard-against-radicalisation-brighton

Index